THE GREAT DIAMOND ROBBERY
& OTHER RECENT MELODRAMAS

A series in twenty volumes of hitherto unpublished plays collected with the aid of the Rockefeller Foundation, under the auspices of the Dramatists' Guild of the Authors' League of America, edited with historical and bibliographical notes.

BARRETT H. CLARK
GENERAL EDITOR

Advisory Board

ROBERT HAMILTON BALL, QUEENS COLLEGE
HOYT H. HUDSON, PRINCETON UNIVERSITY
GLENN HUGHES, UNIVERSITY OF WASHINGTON
GARRETT H. LEVERTON, FORMERLY OF NORTHWEST-
ERN UNIVERSITY
E. C. MABIE, UNIVERSITY OF IOWA
ALLARDYCE NICOLL, YALE UNIVERSITY
ARTHUR HOBSON QUINN, UNIVERSITY OF
PENNSYLVANIA
NAPIER WILT, UNIVERSITY OF CHICAGO

A complete list of volumes, with the names of plays contained in each, will be found on pages 256-7 of this volume.

THE GREAT DIAMOND ROBBERY

& Other Recent Melodramas

BY

EDWARD M. ALFRIEND & A. C. WHEELER
CLARENCE BENNETT · CHARLES A. TAYLOR
LILLIAN MORTIMER · WALTER WOODS

EDITED BY GARRETT H. LEVERTON

WILDSIDE PRESS

CONTENTS

INTRODUCTION

LIKE the plays of the theatrical period it represents, *Recent Melodramas,* as part of the title of this volume, needs a sub-title. Recency of the plays will have to be sufficiently elastic, as part of the title, to cover a form of drama that began to make its appearance as early as the middle of the eighteenth century, reached the peak of its popularity at the turn of the present century, and may even today be seen in the repertoire of a few travelling dramatic tent shows which still perform in the more remote sections of the country.

Melodrama—drama with melody, or music—developed in France in the early years of the nineteenth century and was a reputable dramatic form until the playwrights of the Ten-Twenty-Thirty theater carried emotion, characterization, sentiment and dialogue to such lush extremes that violent revolt arose to demand theater entertainment which had some slight respect for the playgoer's intelligence and his sense of the probable. This revolt against artificiality and sentimentality has been so thorough that even today the adjective, melodramatic, is in popular usage a term of ridicule and contempt. Only in academic circles does the term remain as a definition of a valid dramatic form, and this definition is a far cry from the popular connotation of the word. It would therefore seem more accurate to identify the plays of this volume by a term other than the unqualified word, melodrama. Perhaps the best classification would be one which relates them to the type of theater wherein they found their greatest popularity—the Ten-Twenty-Thirty theater.

Subtlety was not a virtue of the Ten-Twenty-Thirty plays. It was whole hog or none. In dialogue, the soul-thrilling mock heroics and rhetorical contrast are still remembered for lines such as:

"Thank Heaven I arrived in time."

"You spurn my love, but the day will come when I can rend your heart as you are rending mine."

"I am coming back and it will be when I am least expected."

"Not without one kiss from those voluptuous lips."

Read any play of the period and you will find it plentifully filled with this heroic rhetoric which was calculated to (and did) throw the audience into a frenzy of emotion and pile up dollars at the box office.

The plots of the plays were very much alike. Audience interest was not so much in the nature of the story as in the physical heroics or mechanical sensations which might be introduced. Everyone knew what the outcome of the plot would be, but the thrill lay in watching the huge whirr of a circular saw as it approached the log to which the heroine had been tied by the villain. Not until the saw had touched the heroine's dress would the hero arrive, just in the nick of time to throw the lever and save his sweetheart from permanent bisection. Never in the history of these plays had the hero failed to arrive either a second too late—or too early. The audience revelled in this use of theatrical trickery and gave little heed to any cause and effect relationship of dramatic incident. The plays had a very simple code of morality. Villainy must always be punished and virtue always receive its just reward.

The characters of the plays were types rather than individuals. Characters had names but that mattered little. Actually they were the hero, the heroine, the villain or "heavy," the adventuress, the toby, the rube, a foreigner, etc. Characters were always one hundred per cent true to type. Never a villain with even one tiny redeeming quality nor a hero with even a suggestion of a fault. Make-up and costuming were also according to type. Blond curls and white dress for the heroine, and boots, rawhide whip and long black mustachios for the villains. Red wig and blacked-out teeth for the rube and red dresses and large jewels for the adventuress. Foreigners also were always acted according to type. Although it is doubtful if many of us ever saw foreigners behave in the way these plays represent them, it is fairly safe to say that many Americans, because of early contact with these plays, still believe all Frenchmen to be debonair, well dressed and passionate; all Englishmen to be monocled and completely lacking in a sense of humor and all Irishmen to be red-nosed, happy, and hunting a fight. Likewise the Chinaman, the Jew, the German, the Italian and others have all been typed and the impression provided by the plays of this Ten-Twenty-Thirty theater remains basic in the average American's concept of a foreigner.

There is little need for lengthy comment on the plays of this type. They are widely known and little respected. Amateurs (and professionals) produce them so that the audience may laugh at them. Critics and scholars regard them as the epitome of all that is bad in playwriting and acting. Text-books in American literature do not even mention the existence of this large field of dramatic writing. But in spite of all the indictments which can be piled up against the plays of the Ten-Twenty-Thirty theater, one rather challenging fact remains to disturb the scoffer. In spite of volumes of vitriol, these plays still remain the show pieces of a theater which came closer to reaching a universal audience than any other theater in all of history. Every village and town throughout the country had its Opera House or its Academy of Music. Each theater had four of five stock sets of scenery—the cottage interior, the palace set, the prison, the center-door-fancy, and an exterior. Travelling companies fitted their entire repertoire into these stock sets and the theater was packed nightly at admission prices of ten cents for the gallery, twenty cents for the balcony, and thirty cents for seats on the main floor. Actors did vaudeville acts in front of the curtain while between-the-act scene changes were made, and a set of dishes was given away on Saturday night to the holder of the lucky number. Throughout the country this theater flourished. Today's critics and historians speak of the American theater as having "grown up" and "matured." Perhaps so, but today's managers would give much for even the tiniest fraction of the popular support and universal enthusiasm accorded the plays and actors of the Ten-Twenty-Thirty theater.

It is unfortunate that what would have been the sixth play of this volume had to be omitted. In many respects, *The Fatal Wedding*, by Theodore Kremer, is one of the most characteristic plays of the period. Upon the author's death, rights to the play were inherited by relatives living near Cologne, Germany. The present war has made it impossible to locate these heirs and obtain the necessary permission to publish the play. However, in action, story and dialogue, *The Fatal Wedding* follows the same formula as the other plays of the volume. Its omission is regrettable primarily because of the play's importance as a leading box-office success throughout most of this period.

Theodore Kremer was a graduate, in music, of the University of Leipsig. He is the author of seventy-five successful melodramas. A. H. Woods produced approximately fifty of them and states that all were successes. *The Fatal Wedding* was the most spectacularly successful of all of Kremer's plays and it not only made a fortune for the author but it laid the foundation for the theatrical dynasties of Sam Harris and A. H. Woods.

Kremer began his career as an actor in Australia and came later to San Francisco where he began to write. His better known melodramas include such successes as *The Bowery After Dark, Wedded and Parted, Fast Life in New York, A Race for Life, Queen of the Convicts, Fallen by the Wayside, The King of the Bigamists,* and *Secret Service Sam. The Fatal Wedding* opened in Brooklyn in October 1901. Three weeks later it was presented at the Grand Opera House in Manhattan under the management of Sullivan, Harris, and Woods. For several seasons the play toured all over the country, breaking records for house receipts. In 1910 it was still one of the most successful of the stock-company offerings. Much of the play's success was due to the long series of intense situations which reached a climax in the escape of the hero across a rope over a yawning chasm.

Kremer made several attempts to write for the higher-priced houses but all of them met with failure. He retired with his fortune to a home in Cologne, Germany, where he died in 1923.

A ROYAL SLAVE

Clarence Bennett, author of twenty-eight plays which were performed during the many years he was associated with popular melodrama, is one of the most versatile personalities of the period. He began as an actor at McVickers Theatre in Chicago. There he was seen by Edwin Booth and taken on tour as a member of the Booths' company. Later, he established himself in such rôles as Hamlet, Svengali, Monte Cristo, and as a comedy Mephistopheles in his own adaptation of *Faust*. For forty-five years he was associated with a number of managers in the operation of his own companies, and during that time toured the United States, several provinces of Canada, and as far south as Mexico City.

Bennett was known not only as a highly successful actor, but also as a water-colorist and scene designer. He designed many of his own spectacular lithographs, and invented a process for painting scenery known as "diamond-dye scenery." He was among the first to paint many of his drops on scrim, thus making it possible to transport some of his most elaborate scenic efforts in trunks. He was also an early experimenter with salt-water dimmers. The Reading (Pa.) *Herald*, reviewing his production of *A Royal Slave*, comments on Mr. Bennett's skill in stage effects: "To add to the realism of the play, he has provided the finest scenic effects ever displayed on our stage, the whole forming a most exceptional entertainment. The beautiful scenery alone is well worth the price of admission."

The history of the Bennett companies is the history of a trouping family. Clarence Bennett, Mrs. Bennett, and two daughters, Edna Marshall and Lydia Marshall, were in the early companies of *A Royal Slave*. Through all of her husband's long career, Mrs. Bennett was associated in the business management of their many ventures. As part of their varied theatrical activities, the Bennetts even got out a house organ known as *The Bennett Journal*. It was circulated among the various companies simultaneously playing the Bennett successes in various parts of the country. It contained four pages of news of their repertoire and its success, and included special articles and poetry by Mr. Bennett himself.

Mr. Bennett's daughter believes *A Royal Slave* to have been written by Mr. Bennett in the '80's, but not immediately included in the Bennett repertoire. It was Mrs. Bennett who first realized its box-office possibilities. In the play's first year Mrs. Bennett booked a short tour and then "wildcatted" the rest of the season, doing such phenomenal business that the play was permanently installed in the repertoire as the backbone of the business.

By 1900 the play was protected by copyright, but the exact date of the first try-out performance is not known, nor is the program available. The first available review comes from the St. John, New Brunswick, *Daily Telegraph,* of Tuesday, April 12, 1898:

"The splendid production of Clarence Bennett's great romantic play, *A Royal Slave,* proved the greatest triumph ever scored by any repertoire company that has played in St. John. The play is remarkably picturesque in costume, scenery and situation. It offers the finest opportunities for artistic work from the brightest comedy to the most intense acting, and the entire company proved themselves equal to its most trying requirement. Mr. Bennett, the actor-manager, appears in the title rôle, and proved himself master of his art in its most noble phases, the romantic and tragic.

"The scenery was the finest ever seen here in any repertoire production. A fine orchestra and a splendid line of specialties form a most pleasing innovation in relieving the monotony between acts. Miss Maude Malton in her wonderful fire, electric, and stereopticon dances; Miss Malton in her beautiful ballads, and Miss Clayton in her fine illustrated songs, were among the most striking and their work was of the highest order. No company has won such hearty applause or created such enthusiasm as this one. The house was filled to the doors and the standing room in the balcony was at a premium."

A Royal Slave played continuously in the seasons between 1898 and 1915. Theatrical notes of the times are constantly reporting that some actor had just left to join the eastern, western or southern, *Royal Slave* companies. In 1902 they were heading for Wallace, Idaho; in 1903, for Rhinelander, Wis.; in 1904, for some one of the companies in Georgia, Alabama or Tennessee; in 1905, for Glens Falls, N.Y.; in 1906, for Ashland, Neb.—and so on for the surprising number of years during which it proved to be the *pièce de résistance* in the melodrama houses.

During its long life, the play had many casts. Clarence Bennett was the well known Aguila, and Walter Hubbell was one of the last to play the part. Bernice Belnap was one of the first Countesses, and Lulu McConnell one of the first Isadoras. James Kirkwood and Willard Mack were members of *Royal Slave* companies, and with the Gordon-Bennett company, Margaret Neville was, for a time, the feminine lead.

The script as here printed, comes directly from one of Mr. Bennett's prompt books, noted with longhand directions, and containing the author's watercolor designs for the sets. The scene plots are of particular interest in indicating the extent of the scenery which the Bennett companies carried.

Among the many other successes written by Clarence Bennett are: *Ivan's Oath, Cape Cod Folk, In Pennsylvania, The Shadow of a Crime, A Noble Revenge, Thy Neighbor's Wife,* and *Uncle Sam in Cuba.*

THE GREAT DIAMOND ROBBERY

When Colonel Edward M. Alfriend and A. C. Wheeler collaborated in writing *The Great Diamond Robbery,* they combined a varied experience in the theater. Colonel Alfriend had come to New York from Richmond, Va. He had served in the War between the States, commanding a company which he organized. In 1865 he returned to Richmond and the insurance business, but the theater always held a great fascination for him. In 1889 he left Richmond permanently and went to New York with the intention of becoming a dramatist. Among Mr. Alfriend's plays were: *A Foregone Conclusion,* produced by the Madison Square Company; *Across the Potomac,* a Civil War play in which he collaborated with August Pitou; *The Louisianians,* a romantic drama produced in repertoire by Robert B. Mantell; *New York;* and *The Great Diamond Robbery.*

A. C. Wheeler, born in New York, was a critic, essayist and novelist with a wide newspaper experience. While he was a member of the editorial staff of the *Milwaukee Daily Sentinel,* he first began to write under the pseudonym of "Nym Crinkle." He also served as a reporter on the *New York Times* and as dramatic critic for the *New York World, The Sun, The Star,* and for a number of years was the writer of the famous "Nym Crinkle" column in the *Dramatic Mirror.*

The Great Diamond Robbery had its first performance at The American Theatre in New York City on September 4, 1895, with the following cast:

"Dick Brummage," W. H. Thompson; "Frank Kennet," Orrin Johnson; "Senator McSorker," Odell Williams; "Dr. Livingstone," Joseph E. Whiting; "Clinton Bulford," George C. Boniface; "Mario Marino," Byron Douglas; "Grandfather Lavelot," Joseph Wilkes; "Sheeney Ike," B. R. Graham; "Count Garbiadorff," George Middleton; "Jane Clancy," C. B. Hawkins; "Mickey Brannigan," James Bevins; "Jimmy McClune," Gustave Frankel; "Philip," Prince Lloyd; "Frau Rosenbaum," Madame Janauschek; "Mrs. Bulford," Blanche Walsh; "Mary Lavelot," Katherine Grey; "Mrs. O'Geogan," Annie Yeamans; "Peggy Daly," Fanny Cohen; "Madame Mervane," Florence Robinson; "Mary Watson," Ray Rockwell.

Although the play received both praise and blame from the critics, there was no doubt as to its success with audiences. In 1905—ten years after the New York opening—the play was still listed by theatrical journals as one of the most popular plays from coast to coast.

FROM RAGS TO RICHES

From Rags to Riches, a classic of the Ten-Twenty-Thirty theater, is one of a long list of melodramas written and successfully produced by Charles A. Taylor. The play had its initial performance at the Metropolis Theatre in New York City on August 31, 1903, and was immediately launched on a long and successful career which took it all the way across the country. In this play, Laurette Taylor (known at that time as Laurette Cooney), made her first New York appearance, and the rôle of "Ned" was played by young Joseph Santley.

The play was presented in several New York theaters. In November of its first season it was playing at the New Star Theatre on Lexington Avenue with the following cast:

"Edward Montgomery," Theodore Kehrwald; "Robert Brown," J. O. Cantor; "Herbert Bostwick," Frank Norton; "Charles Montgomery," Biglow Cooper; "Bella," Laurene Santley; "Mike Dooley," Sidney Olcott; "Chinese Sam," William Cummings; "Louis," John O. Cantor; "Antonio Succo," Albert Livinston; "Handsome Jack," William Gane; "Fritz," Fred Snyder; "Mother," Lillian Marlin; "Albert Cooper," William Morris; "Gertrude," Anna V. Risher; "Flossie," Laurette Cooney; "Ned," Joseph Santley.

Other popular and successful melodramas written by Mr. Taylor include: *Belle of the Rio Grande, College Boy and Widow, The Child Wife, The Cradle Robber, Daughter of the Diamond King, The Derby Mascott, The Fortune Hunter, The Girl Engineer, The Girl Waif, Held for Ransom, The King of the Opium Ring, The Queen of the Highway, Rich for a Day,* and *The Scarlet Throne.*

NO MOTHER TO GUIDE HER

Lillian Mortimer, author of *No Mother to Guide Her,* was one of the best-known leading women of the country in the popular- priced theater. She was not only an author and actress but she also produced the plays in which she starred. Although she was acting in her own plays as early as 1895, her greatest success did not come until 1905 when she first produced *No Mother to Guide Her.* During the first week of August 1905 this play drew high praise from the Detroit press. On December 4, 1905, the play opened at the Star Theatre in New York City with the following cast:

"Ralph Carlton," John Lane Connor; "John Livingstone," John T. Nicholson; "Silas Waterbury," Irvin R. Walton; "Jake Jordan," Frank B. Russell; "Farmer Day," Allen Elmore; "Tommy Fisher," Ray Carpenter; "Walter Perkins," H. A. Conels; "Frank Caldwell," Rau W. Gordon; "Parson Thomas," Charles C. Connor; "Officer Keough," Eddie Sargeant; "Policeman Toad," Jake Liebermann; "Captain Hennessey," Kirt Easfeldt; "Rose Day," Alice Morlock; "Lindy Jane Smithers," May Manning; "Mother Tagger," Eva Benton; "Bess Sinclair," Grace De Foy; "The Baby," by herself; "Bunco," Lillian Mortimer.

The play was highly successful in New York and in succeeding seasons duplicated this success all over the country. For a time Miss Mortimer left the melodrama theater to become a headliner in vaudeville, but in 1911 she returned to continue her success in *No Mother to Guide Her*. The play was still being performed by her in 1913. Among Miss Mortimer's other plays were: *The Shadow of the Gallows, The Girl of the Streets, Bunco in Arizona, A Man's Broken Promise, Kate Barton's Temptation, The Heart of the Plains,* and *A Girl's Best Friend.*

BILLY THE KID

Shot well, he did,
And out of many
A tight place slid
$5,000 on his head
Catch him
Either alive or dead.

* * *

Six million people have seen Billy the Kid. Have You?

* * *

To Managers of Theatres, Opera Houses or Town Halls in Connecticut, Massachusetts, Rhode Island, Vermont, New Hampshire, Maine, New Brunswick, Nova Scotia and Prince Edward Island:

Get Ready for Big Business!
Billy the Kid is headed your way.
Has Been Witnessed by over Six Million People.
Has played every important city in every State in the U.S
Is the Champion Melodrama of the World.
Is Seven Years Old and Still Breaking Records.

SEE:

The Famous Bandit Horse, "Silver Heels."
The Battle in the Dark.
The Hairbreadth Escape of Billy the Kid.
The Kiss Auction.
The Soul Stirring Bravery of the Boy Bandit.
The Famous Broken Heart Saloon.

The above is taken from the announcement sent out by the management of *Billy the Kid* at the opening of its seventh consecutive season of touring. Five additional seasons of continuous success were still to come.

Billy the Kid, written by Walter Woods, opened its career of twelve solid seasons at the New Star Theatre in New York City on August 13, 1906. *The Dramatic News* proclaimed it "better than The Girl of the Golden West and the best melodrama I expect to see this season." The New York cast was as follows:

"Stephen Wright," Thos. J. MacMahon; "Mary Wright," Lorena Ferguson; "Billy," Joseph Santley; "Colonel Wayne Bradley," John C. Fenton; "Nellie Bradley," Marion Leonard; "Boyd Denver," Paul Barnett; "Con Hanley," Geo. M. DeVere; "Jim Storm," Frank Gordon; "Bill White," James Liet (later listed "Light"); " 'Peanut' Givanni," Robt. G. Vinola; "Bud Monroe," Thos. J. MacMahon; "Hank Burke," T. Jerome Morley; "Arizona Jake," James Early; "Molly," Jessie Lansing; "Jennie," Adele Lyndon.

Among the other plays of Walter Woods are: *Between Trains, The Chicago Boy Bandit, The Girl of Eagle Ranch, Manuella, The Reformer, The Sweetest Sin, Way of the West, Within four Walls,* and *Woman's Place.*

GARRETT H. LEVERTON

New York City
August, 1940.

A ROYAL SLAVE

By Clarence Bennett

SCENE PLOT

ACT I.

Our leg drops in 1, 2, and 3. Our tree on 3rd leg drop. Our back drop in 4. Your wood wings to mask.

ACT II.

SCENE 1: *Same as Act I, except tree.* SCENE 2: *Our rocky pass drop in 1.* SCENE 3: *Your kitchen with jog and window set, as below. Our first act back drop.*

ACT III.

Our first act drop to back. Our third act drop in 4. Our tabs, right and left. Interior backings, right and left. Our fancy borders. Have short and long lines in 1 and 3 ready for tabs.

ACT IV.

SCENE 1: *Our cave drop must be above tormentor. Use prison wings or wood wings at tormentor.* SCENE 2: *Our fourth act drop in 5. Our horizon wings left. Use sea cloth, our set winter and ground roll. Our platform, upright against drop, our cloth to cover same.*

ACT V.

Our back drop in 5. Our drop with center opening just below this. Our cut drop in 4, between cut drop and with opening. Our platform. Our steps for platform. Our table with lines, use in Act III. Our borders. Interior backings, right and left.

PROP LIST

ACT I.

Fountain, with water connections and waste pipe complete up C. Rustic seat L.C. Tropic plants to dress stage. Cigarettes for Pedro, Jones, Countess. Knife for Aguila. Knife for Alacran. Dagger for Pedro. Bicycle for Jones. Note book and pencil for Jones. Heavy riding whip for Pedro. Purse for Carlos. Guitar L. by house tuned to play accompaniment.

ACT II.

Chimes in distance. Fencing swords and daggers for Pedro and Carlos. Locket for Pedro. Blood-stained handkerchief for Countess.

SCENE 3: Curtains, strung on rope, to draw, from stage screw C. C. 8 ft. high, to wing R. 8 ft. high. Cot bed in alcove R.C. Two chairs. Small table R. with crucifix and tumbler. Books on table. Lace scarf for Isadora. Dagger for Countess.

ACT III.

Small sofa R. of C.D. Two ordinary (light) parlor chairs R. and L. in 2. Table with handsome spread, crucifix, two handsome brass or silver candlesticks with candles, small dagger, L.2. Heavy curtains, on bar, on C.D. to close. Handsome furniture to dress stage. Swords for robbers. Knife for Alacran.

ACT IV.

SCENE 1: Chains and manacles for Juan L.1. Ditto for Aguila, C., fastened to floor, long enough for him to raise his hands as high as his breast. Whip (heavy), black bottle and combat knife for Matador. Old blankets, 1.R.1.E., one L.1.E. Riding whip for Pedro. Bunch of keys for Matador. Binding and rope for Aguila. Dagger for Pedro. Revolver for Jones.

SCENE 2: Shark ready L. Boat and oar ready and roped to draw on, L.4. Moon box lighted and ladder behind scene. Stump in island. Men to work sea cloth. Sash for Alacran. Mattress R.C. front of island. Plenty of salt and boy to throw it as directed.

ACT V.

Set same as Act III. Candles on table lighted, and matches for Padre to relight them. Dagger for Pedro. Swords for Carlos and Aguila. Trick candles for Padre. Locket for Carlos. Letter for Padre. Two soldiers, with guns ready, L.3.D. Blood-stained handkerchief for Countess.

CAST OF CHARACTERS

EL AGUILA, *an Aztec, "Child of the Sun"*

COUNT PEDRO MARTINEZ, *"El Capitan"*

HUMBOLT AGASSIS JONES, *American newspaper correspondent*

LIEUTENANT CARLOS CASTILLO, *officer in Mexican service*

PADRE DOMINGUS, *priest and physician*

JUAN ALVAREZ, *an insane captive*

BERNAL, *robber lieutenant, known as "El Alacran"*

PHILLIPPE, *robber guard, "El Matador"*

COUNTESS INEZ DE ORO

ISADORA DE ORO

BANDITS AND SOLDIERS

ANNETTA, *maid*

SYNOPSIS OF SCENES

ACT I: *Casa, or country seat of Countess de Oro, overlooking Valley of Mexico.*

ACT II, SCENE 1: *Wood in neighborhood of Casa de Oro.*
  SCENE 2: *Interior of Padre Domingus' house.*

ACT III: *Countess' house or hacienda near Puebla, near east coast of Mexico.*

ACT IV, SCENE 1: *Interior of cave of "El Capitan," near Puebla.*
  SCENE 2: *The islet of "El Toro," near Puebla.*

ACT V: *Same as* ACT III. *Night.*

NOTE: *The Padre can double Bernal; Carlos double Phillippe.*

ACT I.

Drop in 5. View of valley and distant city of Mexico at sunset. Popocatepetl in background. Scene to change with gauzes to moonlight. Mexican house with verandah set L.2. and 3. Low walls, gate C. Cross stage at back. Practical fountain with circular seat curb, C. Water plants in fountain, plants and flowers to dress stage. Tropical wings and borders. Countess R.C. on fountain seat. Pedro standing C.

INEZ. I hear, count, that the dreaded Capitan has surprised another silver train in the Sierra Madre, and robbed it of nearly half a million.

PED. Indeed? He is a brave fellow at all events. It seems strange that no one can capture him, or discover the secret of his identity.

INEZ. It does indeed, señor. He has carried on his depredations since I was a child, and yet no clue has been discovered that could lead to his arrest.

PED. He must be very wealthy by this time.

INEZ. It would seem so, señor. Do you know there is a slight romance in our family connected with him?

PED. Indeed, señora? I beg you will favor me with it. That is, of course, if the story is not a family secret.

INEZ. A secret? By no means! At least not from you, as you will shortly be one of the family. But I should not like the story to reach the ears of El Capitan, as it might attract his attention rather unpleasantly to us, and awaken in him a desire to investigate the mystery for himself.

PED. [*Smiling*] Have no fear, señora. I am good at keeping secrets.

INEZ. You must know, then—to begin my story, I once had a sister. I have never spoken of her to you. She fell in love with a young man named Juan Alvarez of Puebla, between whose family and ours there had existed for years a deadly feud. He was the last of his race, and on him my father centered all his enmity. When he learned of the attachment between Alvarez and my sister Mercedes, he of course opposed the union most bitterly. But in spite of his opposition, Mercedes eloped with and married her lover.

PED. What became of them?

INEZ. My father was a man of iron. He disowned Mercedes. But despite his curses, they lived happily together for about three years, when a child, a daughter, was born to them.

PED. Your story is interesting, señora. Pray go on!

INEZ. Señor Alvarez had a vast treasure in gold and jewels hidden. No one but himself knew where. Alarmed by the frequent depredations of El Capitan, he had determined to secrete it in a more secure place. And on the very day he purposed changing its hiding place, he was waylaid and murdered by El Captain.

PED. How do you know this?

INEZ. Our old peon, Aguila, who was very fond of my sister, was with Señor Alvarez at the time, and in defending him, was severely wounded and left on the ground for dead. Recovering, however, he brought back the dreadful news. My sister, nearly crazed by the death of her husband, not knowing where his treasure was hidden, exhausted her remaining resources in a fruitless search for him. And finally, driven to despair, she lost her reason and disappeared.

PED. But was the treasure never recovered?

INEZ. No, señor. Meanwhile I had married at my father's command, Señor Antonio de Oro, an old but wealthy banker of the capital. My father died, Isadora was born as the fruit of this loveless marriage. Then Señor Antonio died and I was free again! Free!

PED. But did you never try to find the treasure?

INEZ. Yes, señor. At my sister's death, Señor Alvarez' hacienda and estates at Puebla, remaining unsold, reverted to our family. I have searched there for it again and again, but always in vain. I could gain no clue to its hiding place.

PED. Do you not suppose, señora, that your old peon, Aguila, may know. You say he was with Señor Alvarez when he was murdered. Might he not have made this Indian the repository of the secret of the hidden treasure?

INEZ. No, señor. He is true to our family, and thoroughly honest. He was so fond of my sister he would certainly have revealed it to her.

PED. This old peon seems to hold a strange position in your family. He has been the nurse and confidant of three generations. He seems devoted to your race.

INEZ. He was the playfellow and friend of my father in his boyhood, my sister's guarding spirit and mine, and now Isadora's constant companion and protector. He is as devoted to her as a faithful dog. I never had any love for him, but still I keep him for his profound judgment and wisdom. His counsels have been of great value at times.

PED. His race rarely turns gray, but though he is rugged as an oak, his hair is white.

INEZ. The fever from his wound and the exposure made his long hair fall out. And when it grew again, it was snowy white.

PED. He is a strange being—humble, courteous, faithful to your family, a peon, a slave. He still has the dignity and bearing of a king.

INEZ. Because he is a king. He is the lineal descendant of the Montezumas who once ruled Mexico. His kingly grace and bearing he owes to the royal blood in his veins.

PED. [*Looks off L.U.E.*] Señora, there is Señorita Isadora and that Señor Castillo. They seem very much absorbed in each other's society.

INEZ. [*Showing displeasure*] Yes, I see.

PED. You do not seem pleased at his constant attentions to your daughter.

INEZ. Not altogether. [*Crosses R.*]

PED. Nor am I. As you know, señora, I love the señorita, your daughter, and this fellow's interference is very annoying to me. Who is he anyway?

INEZ. [*Half severely*] He is my guest, señor. But there, curb your jealousy. I promise you that I will see that you are not annoyed further. She is your affianced wife. You have my promise. That is enough. I have your interests at heart, señor. Leave her to me! But come with me. I do not wish to meet them now. Come. [*Going R.2.*]

PED. Your wishes are commands to me, señora. [*Exeunt Inez and Pedro R.2. Enter Isadora and Carlos through gate from L.U.E.*]

ISA. [*Looking at bouquet in hand*] Señor Castillo, you have as good taste as a lady in the arrangement of flowers. I shall treasure this as a token of your skill.

CARL. Ah, señorita—I have been dallying here among the roses, forgetting that I was only a soldier. But the order came this afternoon that calls me from this scene of happiness to duty. I must leave tomorrow!

ISA. [*Looking up gravely*] Oh, señor! You surely are not going away so soon.

CARL. I must. You cannot dream how bright these days have seemed to me. Bright with the glory of your presence, the sunshine of your beautiful eyes, the music of your voice. They are a sweet spell that will haunt my heart while I live.

ISA. Señor, brave men should not be flatterers.

CARL. The words that spring to our lips when we kneel before the Holy Mother, are not flattery, but devotion. Isadora, you are the saint shrined in my heart! You say I flatter, I answer "I love you."

ISA. [*Shyly*] Oh, Señor Carlos!

CARL. Tell me, Isadora—may I hope?

ISA. [*Toying with bouquet*] It is cruel, señor, to deceive those who trust us!

CARL. Can't you believe me?

Isa. [*Gives him her hand*] Yes, Señor Carlos. For our good padre says—
"Out of the fullness of the heart the mouth speaketh"—and if your eyes are
mirrors of your heart, I am sure it is full of truth and goodness!

Carl. [*Joyously*] It is filled with both, for it is full of you! I was but a
plain honest soldier till I met you. And then the world seemed changed. The
sunshine seemed brighter—the flowers sweeter, the songs of the birds more
joyous that such a bright being as you was in the world.

Isa. [*Coquettishly*] How pleasant sounds the gurgle of the fountain!

Carl. Yes! It is singing to you. And that lends it music. [*Pause*] Little
señorita, can you love me?

Isa. Oh, if I but dared to believe you!

Carl. Why do you doubt me? I swear to you that you have grown into
my heart till, while that heart shall beat, it will enshrine your image! There
is no present joy, no future hope that does not mirror your sweet face. And
in my soul I would treasure and guard your love always as a holy thing!

Isa. [*Coyly*] Do you mean what you say?

Carl. Mean it! I have laid my heart at your feet. You may read its truth
in my eyes!

Isa. Hearts are false and eyes too sometimes.

Carl. Why do you doubt me, Isadora?

Isa. [*Seriously*] I do not doubt you, Carlos. I love you! If you thirst for
my love, the draught is yours. Take me! Our hearts shall throb in unison,
our lives entwine till death, my Carlos!

Carl. [*Clasping her*] Darling! If I were dying, your kiss upon my lips
would, like the wizard's fabled elixir, awake my drowsy heart to love and
life again! Are you happy now?

Isa. Yes, Carlos—always, with you!

Carl. And can you trust your future, your life, your happiness to me?

Isa. If not, to whom can I ever trust them? You are my future, my life,
my joy!

Carl. Bless your sweet lips for those words. [*Kisses her*]

Isa. But, Carlos, are not love and happiness like the sweet cerus bloom—
a thing of beauty born at eve to fade and die ere morn? A thing too sweet
to last?

Carl. Nay, trust me, dearest! Shrined in our souls, it will bloom on forever. In hearts of truth love is immortal!

Isa. Dear Carlos! How sweet it sounds to call you by that name!

Carl. Sweet indeed, breathed by your lips. [*Kisses her*] I must do as an
honorable man should. I must tell your mother of our love and ask her for
her little girl. May I go to her now?

Isa. Yes, Carlos.

Carl. I cannot rest till I can call you mine! Good-bye! Little sweetheart! When I come back, I hope to bring you good news. Good-bye! [*Exit R.U.E.*]

Isa. He loves me! Oh, I am so happy! Dear, dear Carlos! Sweet flowers [*Toying with them*], you were his gift! [*Kisses them*] My brave, strong, handsome lover! I am so proud of him, I love him so. [*Sings:*]

> "Will you love me always, darling,
> Fondly, tenderly as now?
> When my eyes have lost their brightness,
> When the silver's on my brow?
> Will your kiss be just as tender,
> Just as fond your strong arms fold,
> And your voice as kind and gentle?
> Will you love me when I'm old?"

[*She looks off L.U.E.*] Here comes dear old Aguila! I must tell him. [*Hides up L., amid flowers. Aguila enters C. from L.U., sets large pulque jar by fountain, and seats himself, wiping perspiration away*]

Ag. The day is as hot as a fiend's breath! None but the sun's children dare stand before him today! I wonder where my little señorita is? My little nightingale should come when the stars peep through the twilight's purple curtains. [*Isadora steals up behind him and takes his head in her hands, kisses him on the hair*]

Isa. Who is it?

Ag. An angel!

Isa. [*Laughing*] Oh, no, Papa Aguila! It's only me.

Ag. Well, I was right!

Isa. Oh, no, you weren't! You didn't know me!

Ag. Not know you, my beautiful! Does the bee know the flower whose heart is full of sweetness? Whose kiss but yours ever blesses my old white brow? And it touches it with a glory like the sunlight on the snowy head of yonder mountain. A crown more royal than the one my fathers wore. There, at its feet!

Isa. [*Kneeling L. of him*] You are a king to me, Aguila.

Ag. [*Sadly*] No, only a peon. A poor old slave! Your old Aguila!

Isa. No! You are a Montezuma! A royal child of the sun! And, more than all, my dear old papa! [*Pats his cheek playfully*]

Ag. [*Moved*] My darling child! [*Looking in her eyes*] What makes my little señorita's notes so glad and tender today? Is there some singing joy making its nest amid the white blossoms of her young heart?

Isa. [*Demurely, taking his hand between hers*] Papa Aguila, I have never had a secret from you, and I must tell you this. The dearest, sweetest secret of all! For I know that no one loves me as you do—no one shares my joys and sorrows like you. There is a joy at my heart tonight!

Ag. I know what it is. I have read the hope in your bright eyes long ago, before you dared to own it to yourself. The Señor Castillo is young, brave and tender, and my little mistress is fair, sweet and gentle—and so your hearts turned toward each other like the courses of the brooks that blend their pure tides in one channel. You love and you are loved, and in that thought as in an urn, blossom the flowers of joy!

Isa. [*With bashful joy, laying her cheek against his hand*] How good you are! How wise. You know my heart before I do myself!

Ag. Ah, my child! May you never learn the bitter lessons of sorrow that crush the hope out of young hearts! Would I might shield you from it all! All!

Isa. Sorrow seems so far away tonight! But should it ever come, you will help me, will you not, you will always love me, Papa Aguila?

Ag. [*Clasping her*] Ah, would I not, my child. As the palm loves the singing brook purling in its shadow, and bends lovingly and tenderly over its pure, deep heart, so do I love my little señorita. So would I shelter her from the fierce heat of the countess' anger, from the mad hurricane of misfortune, though it should rend my withered branches and lay my old trunk in ruin beside her.

Isa. Dear old Aguila!

Ag. [*Rising and going L. with her*] Fear not, little one! Should trouble come, leave all to old Aguila. He will win back to you the joy that shall live when he is dust! Come, my bright eyes, come! [*Exeunt in house*]

Jones. [*Appears at back, C. from L.*] Well, by Jove! This is the neatest I have seen in this country. A perfect earthly paradise! Paradise and the peri. Where's the peri, I wonder? I'll reconnoiter! [*Writes in notebook*] "Hacienda embowered in feathery palms, amid whose waving plumes fitful gleams of tropic sunlight steal, like bright fairies, laying their tresses in the murmuring fountains, chasing the roseate shadows in and out among the bloom-laden bowers, kissing the perfume, breathing lips of flowers as rarely beautiful and purely bright as a saint's dream of Heaven." There! That will read well in the *Herald.* [*Enter Annetta from house, stands watching Jones*]

Ann. Buenos dias, señor!

Jones. Ah! The peri, by Jove! Your servant, señorita! I hope I don't intrude. I was coming down the pass, and seeing this beautiful spot, could not help hiding from the heat in such a charming place for a moment.

ANN. [*Curtseying*] Oh, señor, I am sure you will be most welcome. The countess' house is always open to visitors. I am sure she will be pleased to entertain the nice American gentleman.

JONES. [*Fixing his collar and tie*] Ahem! And you, my pretty little flower of Mexico! Would it please you to have me stay?

ANN. I am sure the señor would be a much more charming guest than that cross old Count Pedro Martinez.

JONES. What a lovely picture of tropic female loveliness!

ANN. A picture? Why, señor, are you an artist?

JONES. Well, no, not exactly.

ANN. I'm glad of that, for I don't like artists!

JONES. [*Quickly*] Oh, well, I am no artist! I never could draw anything, not even two pair. In fact the only thing I can draw is my salary—and mosquitoes!

ANN. You see, señor, there was an artist from San Francisco who boarded with mother, just back of the cathedral, in the city yonder; and he went away without paying his board. Mother is very poor, and could not afford to lose the money. Señor, is San Francisco in America?

JONES. What charming ignorance of geography! [*Aloud*] No, my dear, it is in China. The wretch was a Chinaman in disguise!

ANN. [*Coyly*] I am glad he was not an American! But there was a señor from New York who made a great deal of money selling shares in some silver mine, and when he left Mexico suddenly, the people here began trying to find out what they had bought, and they are still trying when they don't stop to rest and swear.

JONES. Oh, he was an Indian.

ANN. Oh, no, señor! We have Indians here. He was not dark like them. I am sure he must have been a white man.

JONES. No, you see he was from the Manhattan Reservation. They look like white men till you know them; but they are Indian savages all the same. I hope you have never had any newspaper correspondents down here.

ANN. I think not, señor. What is it like?

JONES. Well, it's a sort of gentleman angel, if you can imagine such a thing.

ANN. I cannot.

JONES. Well, there are such things, but they are rare. He goes about seeking whom he may interview, trying to be pleasant and see all that he can and get acquainted with everybody and get them to talk to him—

ANN. Oh, I see! You are a correspondent!

JONES. [*Starting towards her*] You are an angel!

ANN. [*Running into house, laughing*] Adios, señor!

JONES. She's a charmer! The prettiest girl I ever saw! I must not lose sight of her. Hello! Here comes someone! These Mexicans are like their cactuses, they blossom with welcome and wait their chance to stick you. [*Enter Carlos R.1E.*] Señor, I beg your pardon for this intrusion, but I stumbled in here quite unexpectedly, upon this little Eden. You see, I am an American writing up Mexican society, scandal, science, stocks, soldiery, spondoolix, et cetera. My name is Humbolt Agassis Jones, at your service.

CARL. [*Recognizing him*] What! My old friend Jones?

JONES. Castillo? Shake! I'm delighted to see you.

CARL. And I to see you, señor. We have not met since that night a month ago, when your bravery saved me from El Capitan and his band.

JONES. Friend Carlos, I guess we saved each other. You fought like a lion. I guess I am more indebted to you than you are to me.

CARL. Indeed, no! Señor Jones.

JONES. [*Laughing*] Wasn't it lively fun though? If you hadn't been such a crack shot, El Capitan and his cutthroats would have fallen heirs to our petty belongings—watches, wallets, wash-bills, toothbrushes and all. To say nothing of that little indispensable to travellers called life.

CARL. It was a narrow escape, señor. And we owe it to your reckless brav-'ery. You Americans never know when you are beaten. Well, I'm heartily glad to see you. [*Shakes hands again*]

JONES. What are you doing here? You sly rogue! Daphnis and Chloe, I'll warrant! Some fair señorita? Come! Confess!

CARL. Well, I will be frank with you. That is the reason of my prolonged stay here. But "The course of true love—" you know the adage.

JONES. What's the matter, old fellow? Is the fair divinity deaf to her worshiper, or is the Duenna lynx-eyed, or, worse than all, is her mama obdurate?

CARL. Neither. On the contrary, I am certain I am not an unwelcome guest, for the Countess Inez, my hostess, treats me with the most marked kindness. But when I try to have a word alone with the fair señorita, Isadora, I am always thwarted, I don't know how.

JONES. Castillo, we are sworn friends. Let me help you. Introduce me here, and rely on my aid.

CARL. Thanks, señor! I'll do it. It seems I must be doubly indebted to you. Both for life and happiness. You are indeed a friend.

JONES. There, there! You owe me nothing! It will serve my purpose as well. It will give me an insight into Mexican high life and society.

CARL. [*Looking off R.*] Ah, here comes our hostess. And with her, that old Count Pedro. He is always in my way!

JONES. Who is he?

CARL. I fear he is a suitor for the hand of Isadora.

JONES. So! He's the stumbling block is he? Well, I'll roll him out of your way. I'll keep him so busy he'll have no time to interfere. [*Enter countess and Pedro R.1.E.*]

CARL. Señora, pardon the liberty I take! A friend of mine was passing when we met quite accidentally. I presumed on your hospitality by detaining him. Allow me to present him to you.

INEZ. Your friends are mine, señor.

CARL. Thanks, señora! Permit me to introduce my dear friend, Señor Jones, from the United States. Señor Jones, the Countess Inez de Oro.

INEZ. You are most welcome, señor. I can only thank Señor Castillo for bringing us such a pleasant guest.

JONES. [*Kissing her hand*] Thanks, señora. So royal a welcome could only come from such queenly lips.

INEZ. [*Smiling*] I did not know you Americans were such adroit flatterers. Our gallants had best look to their laurels in the fine art of compliment. But pardon me! My guest and friend Count Pedro Martinez, Señor Jones.

JONES. [*Offers hand*] I'm glad to meet you, count.

PED. [*A dead shake*] Your servant, señor. [*Folds arms. Jones does sizing up business*]

CARL. Señor Jones and I have been sworn friends since a month ago, when being fellow travellers, we one night encountered El Capitan and his band in the Passo del Rey. I owe my life to his bravery that night.

JONES. Señora, don't believe him! He is as modest as he is brave. He fought like a tiger, and is the best shot I ever saw. But for him I should have been in paradise—or—perdition—tonight and a month's rent due.

PED. Señors, you were fortunate—few men have met El Capitan and lived to boast of it.

INEZ. Which proves how brave they both were.

PED. Still, señora, their escape was little short of a miracle.

JONES. [*Aside*] Where have I seen him before?

CARL. [*Aside to countess*] Señora, may I have the honor of a word with you, alone, when convenient?

INEZ. [*Up L.*] Certainly. Count, will you kindly play the host for me for a little while, and show Señor Jones around the grounds? I wish to speak to Señor Castillo a moment, and then we'll join you.

PED. [*Down R.C.*] Your wishes are pleasures to me, señora.

INEZ. [*To Jones who goes up L.*] Señor, make yourself perfectly at home here. I am only too happy to have the pleasure of numbering you among my guests.

JONES. I shall need no coaxing, señora. An angel's invitation to a paradise is sure to be accepted. [*They talk together, Jones points off to vista at back*]

BERNAL. [*Peers from trees, R.2.*] Hist, señor! I am here. [*Aguila enters L.U., sees Bernal, stops*]

PED. Caution! Watch your chance. He, Castillo, is in my way. A quick blow and be off. You can steal my horse.

BERN. My own is near by.

PED. Good! [*Exit Bernal, R.W. Exit Aguila R.U.E. Annetta enters from house*]

JONES. [*Aside*] The angel again, by Saint Thomas Jefferson!

INEZ. Annetta, tell Parquita to prepare the west room for a guest and tell Manuel to be ready to start down to the city.

ANN. Yes, señora. May I go with him?

INEZ. Yes.

JONES. [*Crossing R. behind Inez, aside to Annetta*] I am going to stay here!

ANN. I am glad, señor.

JONES. Are you, little sweetheart? [*Inez looks around, Annetta slips into house, Jones goes up C. expatiating in pantomime on the beauties of the scene*]

INEZ [*To Pedro*] Pardon my breach of etiquette, señor. I thought you had joined us.

PED. It is nothing, señora. [*To Jones*] Come, señor—I will be your guide. [*Jones and Pedro bow to Inez and exit R.3.E. Tremolo, pianissimo, passionate, till countess off*]

JONES. [*Aside, as he goes*] It isn't the first time he has been "guyed."

INEZ. [*Coming down with Carlos*] Now, Señor Carlos, we are alone. What is it?

CARL. Señora, you have been so kind, so good, but I have the greatest of all favors to ask of you.

INEZ. Señor Carlos, what would I not do for you?

CARL. You give me courage, señora. I love your daughter. Will you give her to me for my wife?

INEZ. [*Sits on fountain seat C.*] Sit down by me, Carlos. I want to talk to you. You are a strong, brave, noble man. You do not want this child. She is not your equal in any way. She is not mate for such a man as you. This is a mere passing fancy!

CARL. A passing fancy, señora? I love her, I adore her! Won't you give her to me?

INEZ. [*Breaking forth passionately*] Oh, Carlos! I cannot! I cannot!

CARL. [*Surprised*] Cannot? Why, señora, why?

INEZ. Listen, señor, and then condemn me if you will. My father was a man of iron. His will was law. He forced me, a motherless girl of fourteen into a hated marriage with Señor de Oro, a man older than himself. His only merit was his hoarded gold. I was sold to him, body and spirit. I cannot call that hated union a marriage! I loathed him!

CARL. Poor señora! What misery, what despair!

INEZ. Do you pity me, Carlos? Nay, listen. Isadora was born as the child of that loveless marriage. I almost hated the child for her father's sake. Then he, my master, my owner—I will not call him husband!—died, and I was free at last. My heart, chilled in its budding hope, lay frozen in my breast till I met you. Turn away your face, Carlos! Do you not see all? I cannot give you to her because I love you!

CARL. [*Amazed*] You—love—me!

INEZ. Yes! Don't speak, Carlos! I love you! Your touch thrills me and makes my heart leap, my blood run riot in my veins! I never knew I had a heart till it wakened at the music of your voice! Now it is a tide of passionate love that sets toward you as the river toward the sea! She is but a child, cold and weak as her father before her.

CARL. I love her, señora! I will be a good son to you and love you as a mother.

INEZ. [*Wildly*] Mother! I am not an old woman, Carlos! As a son? Never! As my own, my lover, my husband, my life? Yes, always! With a love that defies death itself! You are the only being I have loved since my childhood. I cannot lose you thus! Oh, Carlos, forgive me. I cannot crush my love, my hope! Your words stung me till they wrung this cry of despair from my lips and tore the hidden secret from my heart! Oh, Carlos, I love you so!

CARL. Oh, I am so sorry for this, countess! Sorry for your sake, for all our sakes!

INEZ. Beware! Love passionate as mine makes us angels or fiends. If returned, its warmth and light are poured out like the sunshine on the flowers. If pent and curbed, its fierce heat blasts what it would have cheered and blessed.

CARL. Pardon me, señora! I cannot control my heart! Will you not let me be your friend, your son, giving you that pure love a son may give a mother?

INEZ. [*Starting up*] No! If you cannot be mine, I will not place before me the torturing sight of your affection for another, the caresses that might have been mine but for her. [*Pedro appears R. at back, listening*]

CARL. Think of your child's happiness.

INEZ. [*Laughs bitterly*] I have wasted my life in sacrificing my heart to the happiness of others; you have said it, "I cannot control my heart!" Listen! To watch her love for you, your tenderness to her, would drive me mad, and I should kill you both! [*Pedro exits R.3. Countess falls on knees, arms around him*] Oh, hear me, Carlos! At your feet, forgetting all my pride, I plead for your love! Strong natures such as yours crave more than the weak return of cold hearts like hers. Think of the wealth of my love for you, and contrast it with the poverty of hers! Renounce her, Carlos, and take my heart, my soul, my life if you will!

CARL. [*Freeing himself*] Woman! Are you mad?

INEZ. [*Starts up, laughing wildly*] Perhaps I am. I hope so! To breaking hearts madness is a sweet oblivion, a blest lethe of forgetfulness. [*Falls onto bench*]

CARL. Are you a mother? Can you stand in the way of your child's happiness, and let your selfishness cast its shadow over her young life? Would you doom her to suffer the misery of seeing her blighted hopes realized by the cruel mother who could have saved, and has betrayed her? Woman! The very tigress is more tender of its young!

INEZ. You spurn my love! The day may come when I can rend your heart as you are rending mine! Will I spare you then, will I show mercy? Aye! The same mercy you show me now! I have laid all on the altar of my love! You scorn the offering. Tremble lest the angry flame leap up consuming the idol at whose feet it burned! Mark me! I would kill her with my own hands before you should have her! You have your answer! Farewell, señor—Ha! Ha! Ha! [*Exits in house, laughing bitterly. Pedro comes down L. slowly, from R.3.E.*]

CARL. [*Sinks in despair on fountain*] Name of Heaven! This is terrible! Is it love or madness? Does all hope end here? [*Starts up*] No! By the angels! I will win her yet! I [*Turns R. facing Pedro*] Your pardon, señor! I did not see you. [*Crosses Pedro to R.*]

PED. [*Detaining him*] Stay a moment, señor. I am here with the countess' consent, as a suitor for her daughter's hand, and I want no interference.

CARL. [*Defiantly*] Should she ever become your wife, you would then have some right to dictate who her friends may be, certainly not now.

PED. [*Hotly*] My rights and my actions are my own, and not subject to the approval of a fortune-hunting adventurer.

CARL. [*Quickly*] Señor—[*Restrains himself*] My blood is as pure as yours, a noble! If my purse is lighter, so is my greed.

PED. [*In rage*] Greed, fellow!

CARL. It has never been necessary for my family to hide the sources of its wealth!

PED. [*Attempts to speak*] Ah—

CARL. [*Interrupts him*] Nor have I grown old in low cunning, craft and wickedness!

PED. [*Starts to strike him with glove*] Fool! Your life shall pay for this!

CARL. [*Grasps wrist*] You forget that you are playing the gentleman! We are guests here, and have no right to settle our differences before the doors of our hostess.

PED. Enough, señor! You shan't have that excuse! Words are useless between us! If your heart is as brave as your tongue, meet me tomorrow morning at sunrise, at yonder bridge. Our meeting without witnesses, and our cause to the tribunal of brave men. [*Touches sword*] These!

CARL. [*Bows*] I will be there, señor. Till then farewell! [*Exit C. and L.*]

PED. [*Countess enters from house*] Dog—I'll cut his heart out! [*Sees countess*] Ah, señora.

INEZ. You seem annoyed, count, what is it?

PED. I am annoyed, señora. I cannot brook that Castillo's attentions to Isadora. Give her to me at once!

INEZ. I will, señor. You shall be wedded tomorrow if you will.

PED. [*Kissing her hand*] Señora, you are too good! Tomorrow let it be then! And now, good-night!

INEZ. Good-night, count. Tomorrow, at noon. Good-bye till then! [*Exit Pedro, C. and R.*] Ha, ha! Carlos Castillo! The game is mine. [*Exit R.1.E. Enter Carlos C. from L.*]

CARL. My darling! I may never see her again! But if I live she shall be mine, I swear it! My dear one, my beautiful, good-bye, good-bye! [*Sees guitar by hammock on porch*] Ah, Isadora's guitar! It shall be my messenger, and bear her my adios. [*Sings. Music tremolo, hurry, pianissimo*]

> Dark night o'er the sad earth fell,
> Sad to bid the day "Farewell"!
> Sad and dark my spirit true,
> As it bids farewell to you—
> Soft the night wind's gentle sigh,
> In the rose-heart dew-tears lie.
> Thus my heart, with sigh and tear,
> Bids farewell to thee most dear!

Though the happy day is done,
There will come another sun—
Though we part in grief and pain,
Darling I'll come back again!
Love, I leave my heart with you!
Keep your heart to Carlos true!
Sad the word as tolling knell!
Oh, my life! Farewell! Farewell! [*Lays down guitar and turns to go. Up C.*]

Isa. [*Cautiously at door*] Hist! Carlos!

Carl. [*Turns quickly*] Isadora! [*Clasps her. Bernal creeps out R.2. with knife. Draws back to stab Carlos. Aguila springs on after him, wrenches knife from him and knocks him down. Chord fortissimo*]

Ag. Coward!

Bern. [*Skulking off R.*] You red devil! We shall meet again!

Ag. [*Picking up knife*] Never but once, and then I'll leave you for a buzzard's feast.

Isa. [*Going to him*] Are you hurt?

Ag. No, estrella de mia alma!

Carl. Aguila, you have saved my life! I shall not forget this, my friend. [*Offers purse; Aguila refuses*]

Ag. All for her, señor! Be kind to her and make her happy, and old Aguila will be repaid a thousandfold! [*Puts her in Carlos' arms. Going up C.*]

Carl. I will! I swear it! [*Calls*] Aguila!

Ag. [*Turns*] Señor?

Carl. You are my friend. Meet me tomorrow morning, half an hour after sunrise, at yonder bridge. I may need your aid to care for a wounded man.

Ag. I will be there, señor. Say nothing of that murderous dog! Leave him to me. I will guard you as though you were my own son, for you are her happiness! Good-night!

Isa. [*Rushing to his arms*] Dear old Papa Aguila! Bless you! Bless you!

Ag. Flor di cielo! My darling child! [*Kisses her and exits C. and L.*]

Carl. [*Hurriedly*] My life, my hope! I must leave you. Your mother will not yield. But fear not! I will win you yet! Good-bye, my dear one!

Isa. [*Clinging to him*] Oh, Carlos! My heart will break! Must you leave me?

Carl. Yes, dearest, for your sake. But the countess must not see us together here! Aguila shall tell you our plans. If I am seen here, you will suffer for my rashness. Be brave, little woman! [*Kisses her*] I'll soon come back. [*Chord segue as before*]

AG. [*Rising at back*] Hist! Señor Carlos! Away! [*Exit Carlos C. and L.*]

INEZ. [*Coming on R.2.E., seizing Isadora's wrist*] You wretch! I saw your clandestine meeting with your lover! Girl, mark me! You shall renounce him! Tomorrow, at noon, you wed Count Pedro Martinez!

ISA. [*Starting up*] Never!

INEZ. [*Enraged*] I swear it, girl! Tomorrow you shall be his bride or death's. Choose then! Your answer! [*Chord, hurry, pianissimo, suit action*]

AG. [*Springs up, Isadora in arms*] No! [*Pedro appears at back with riding-whip. Comes down back*]

INEZ. Dare you defy me?

AG. Yes! I have been the slave of your family for sixty years! I have obeyed your slightest wish, not through fear, but love and duty to your race. That love makes me defy you now.

PED. [*R.C. Threatens with whip*] Dog! [*Aguila raises hand commandingly*]

AG. Hold! I am a peon, a slave—the Spaniard's faithful dog, as you will, but not a cur to—One cut of that whip, and I am a sleuth-hound at your throat—the blood of kings is in my veins and cannot brook a blow!

PED. [*Strikes at him with whip*] Dog! Take that!

AG. [*Wresting whip from him, throws Pedro C. on his face*] And with it, your life! [*Draws machete*]

ISA. [*Kneeling R. of Aguila*] Stay, Aguila, spare him for my sake!

AG. I can wait! [*Inez, R. opposite 2. Pedro, Aguila, C. Isadora, kneeling R.C.*]

PICTURE

ACT II.

SCENE 1: *Eight bars lively at rise. Handsome tropic landscape, 2. Bridge to run on R.2. with connected groundpieces, to draw off. Scene fixed for boxings to revolve up from tormentors for Scene 2. Early dawn. Distant chimes ringing at rise. Valley of Mexico.*

JONES. [*Discovered sitting on bridge, writes*] "Beautiful view, snow-capped mountains, faint cathedral chimes, purple leagues, tropical sunrise, distant city, lovely valley, seen through lace-like llanos and plumy palms, fern embowered limpid brooks." Limped brooks? No! It runs crooked but it don't limp! "Staggering brooks" is better. [*Corrects*] There, that will do for the sketch. I'll put in the coloring later. [*Sings*] Hello, who's that? [*Looks back of him*] Carlos, as I live. Buenos dias, caballero!

CARL. [*Smiling, enter R.2.*] Buenos dias, Señor Humbolt. You are out early.

JONES. Yes, and you too. You see I am up to catch the tropic sunrise and dish up a little journalistic mess for that gossip gormand, the American Public. But what gets you up at this hour?

CARL. [*Evasively*] I could not sleep. Besides, I had an appointment at daylight.

JONES. Isn't the view fine from this point? I could linger here for hours admiring it.

CARL. My friend, will you do me a favor?

JONES. Certainly, Carlos. What is it?

CARL. [*Sun gradually up*] Go and find Aguila, the old Indian—

JONES. I say, Carlos, why are you so anxious to get rid of me? Oh, I see! The appointment at sunrise. I beg pardon! Oh, you sly fox! A love tryst, and this the trysting place! And I am in the way! "Two's company, three's a crowd!" Ha, Ha, Ha, Ha!

CARL. [*Gravely. Takes Jones' hand*] My friend, it is a tryst of death! I have an appointment to fight Count Pedro Martinez here, at sunrise.

JONES. I'll be your best man. No, that is, I mean, your second.

CARL. The duel was to be without seconds. That was the agreement, and I must hold to it. But I thank you. There! Leave me now and return with Aguila in half an hour. One or the other of us will need your good offices. Should I fall, tell Isadora.

JONES. [*Grasping his hand*] I will do as you wish, Carlos. But I don't trust that Señor Count. I dread foul play from him.

CARL. I have no fear. He is at least a gentleman.

JONES..[*Aside*] I doubt it! [*Aloud. Shaking Carlos' hand warmly*] Goodbye old fellow, and good luck! If Mr. Count harms you, he will owe me the next dance! It will be "Pistols for Two! Balance all, Second Couple Lead Out!" I'll fill him as full of windows as a Long Branch cottage! [*Exit R.2., over bridge*]

CARL. This is an unpleasant affair, and the sooner it is over, the better. What detains Martinez? [*Looks off R.*] Here he comes now. [*Enter Pedro, R.1.E.*] Good morning, señor!

PED. Good morning! You are prompt. [*Music through fight till Carlos falls*]

CARL. [*Preparing*] Yes. [*They drop jackets and serapes and sombreros. Serape round L. arm. Pedro drops locket. They fight. Count crowds in and hits Carlos on head with knife and stabs him. Carlos falls. Pedro rises, laughs*] *cruelly, throws off serape. Chord fortissimo. Inez enters R.2. as Pedro kneels to finish Carlos. Inez throws him R.]*

INEZ. Hold! Murderer! You have killed him! [*Kneels, takes Carlos' head on knee, staunching blood with her handkerchief*]

PED. [*Smiling*]   Yes, señora, according to the code! Dead, but all fairly.

INEZ.   Fiend! You murdered him!

PED.   He was your lover.

INEZ.   It is false!

PED.   Señora, I heard your burning words of love to him last night, by the fountain. I heard him spurn your heart! I have avenged you!

INEZ. [*Furious*]   Are you my bloodhound to track to death all that offend me? Assassin! Did I bid you drive your cruel steel through that heart around which my own heart-strings had twined?

PED.   No, señora. But as I am to be your son, I killed the man who insulted your love and crossed mine!

INEZ.   What! You my son, and your hands red with his blood? Never! Tomorrow's dawn sees her in the convent of Santa Madre. Begone, monster! Never let me look upon your face again!

PED. [*Bowing*]   As you will, señora. Farewell! You will repent your anger, and give her to me yet!

INEZ. [*Fiercely*]   Never! Go!

PED. [*Smiling*]   We shall see! [*Exits R.1.E.*]

INEZ. [*Passionately*]   Oh, Carlos! Forgive me! Speak to me! Did I bring you to this? Look up, Carlos! I forget your words of scorn, forget all save that I loved you! [*Kisses him*] Oh, that my kisses might breathe their passionate life into your lips! Were my heart cold in death, your clasp would make it leap to life again, though my soul stood at the gates of paradise! Your kiss would lure my spirit back from Heaven to you! Oh, are you dead? [*Feels heart*] No, no! He lives! His heart beats faintly yet! Perhaps I may save him! [*Enter Jones over bridge*] Oh, Carlos! You shall not die! You shall not!

JONES.   What! Carlos wounded? Ah, señora! Let me lead you away. This is no place for you. This is no sight for woman's eyes.

INEZ.   But to leave him thus!

JONES. [*Kneels, feels heart*]   Leave him to me. You can dispatch for a doctor, and send me aid to bear him where he can have careful nursing. Thank Heaven, he lives!

INEZ.   Ah, señor, you are too kind! Save him for Heaven's sake!

JONES.   Fear nothing, lady! He is my friend. I shall do all in my power for him. [*She staggers*] But you are faint! Let me help you across the bridge. [*Exit with her over bridge. Aguila and Padre enter L.1.E.*]

AG. There, padre, I have told you all. You are her friend! The Church, your sacred office, your wisdom can protect her, poor child! I can do nothing! I am only a slave!

JONES. [*Running on R.2.E.*] Aguila! Padre! Quick, Carlos has been wounded! See! [*All to body. Aguila lifts him tenderly and, after, puts him on Padre's knee for examination*]

PADRE. Wounded? Nomen coeli! Let me look! [*Takes him on knee. Aguila rises at back*] The Saints be praised! He lives! [*Pause for business*] I do not think the wound is deep. And this handkerchief has stopped the flow of blood. I can save him.

AG. [*Seeing locket. R.C.*] Ah, what is this? [*Picks it up*] Saints in Heaven! My dear lady—my Mercedes' picture!

PADRE. [*Surprised*] Mercedes!

AG. Yes! How came it here? Master Juan wore this locket the day he was captured by El Capitan! I was with him, and was left in the pass for dead.

PADRE. Then the man who lost it must have been El Capitan!

JONES. Yes, that is certain! We have got him then!

PADRE. [*Surprised*] What do you mean? It cannot have been him, for he was a mere boy at the time.

JONES. No! I mean his antagonist. He must have lost it.

PADRE. Who was he?

JONES. Count Pedro Martinez. Carlos told me, not half an hour ago, that he had an appointment to fight the count, here, at sunrise.

AG. [*Aside*] Ah, the assassin last night! I see it all! El Capitan's hireling!

PADRE. Come! Bring him to my house at once! Not a word of this to a living soul, I charge you. Come! Follow me! [*They bear Carlos off L.1.E.*]

SCENE 2.

JONES. [*Entering R.1.E. looks R. and L.*] Nobody in sight along the pass. Aguila will take some short cut, I suppose. Indian like, he knows every by-path in the country. Hello! What is that, through the trees, yonder? The flutter of a petticoat! Oh, Annetta! Sweet Annetta! Would to goodness I could get her! I would not envy kings their thrones, if she'd be Mrs. Humbolt Jones! Short meter, please!

ANN. [*Entering L.1.E.*] Oh, señor! I am so glad I have found you!

JONES. So am I, my sweet Annetta! But you look frightened. What's the matter?

ANN. I *am* frightened, señor! But it's for you.

JONES. For me? Why, what have I done?

ANN. I have an awful secret to tell you!

JONES. A woman and a secret! All right, Annetta. I'll help you keep it.

ANN. Oh, señor! this is no jest. You are the friend of Señor Castillo; and you and he fought with El Capitan's band, in the Passo del Rey and escaped from them, did you not?

JONES. [*Surprised*] Yes. But how in thunder did you find that out?

ANN. Listen, señor! Last night I went down to the city, to visit my mother, who is poor; and to whom I take my wages as often as I can go to her. Well, she was sick; and I went for a doctor for her. As I was coming home, I saw two men near the back of the cathedral. They were rough-looking men, and I was afraid; so I crept into one of the dark corners and waited for them to pass. They were talking earnestly and did not see me. I heard one of them tell the other that El Capitan wanted him to skulk around the Hacienda de Oro and kill Señor Castillo; but that the Indian had balked him; but that he would finish his work, and would not forget to put that red watch-dog to sleep, and that American too! For, said he, he finished six of the best men in the band, in the Passo del Rey; and that one of them was his brother.

JONES. Oh! He will, will he? Well, if he "monkeys" with me, he'll join his brother in the Happy Hunting Grounds quicker than a "jay" will bite a three card monte!

ANN. I was so frightened, señor! It seemed that I could not get back here quick enough to tell you.

JONES. So, you little dear, you didn't want me to be killed, eh?

ANN. Oh, no, señor!

JONES. Well, my Guardian Angel, it was very kind of you to take so much pains on my account; and I am very grateful to you. I shall be on my guard, you may be sure. But I am not afraid of them.

ANN. Oh, señor! You do not know that terrible El Capitan.

JONES. Oh, yes I do! I had a short call from him and his whole family in the Passo del Rey. It was a very lively visit, too!

ANN. They glide like snakes and bite you from the thicket, when you least expect it!

JONES. Yes, but sometimes the snake gets "snaked" out of his nest! Why don't they catch the scoundrel?

ANN. Oh, I forgot to tell you the rest. The man who threatened to kill you, told the other one the shortest way for him to go home with his goods to the cave, was by the Passo del Ferdinand, to the mouth of the Toreador's Cañon; and then to follow up the stream for a mile, where, by the large fallen pine tree across the stream, he would see the path that led to the cave.

JONES. [*Dancing for joy*] We've got him, Annetta! [*Seizing her and waltzing her around*] We've got him! Tol-de-rol-de-rol, -de-rol! Tol-de-roodle-de-ray!

ANN. Got whom, señor?

JONES. El Capitan and his whole nest full of snakes! Listen, my darling Annetta. Don't say a word of this to anyone! The Government of Mexico offers a reward of ten thousand dollars for the capture of El Capitan. Now, you say your mother is poor. You have discovered his hiding-place, and that money is yours!

ANN. Mine! Why, I cannot capture him, señor! I am only a weak woman.

JONES. See here, Annetta! Don't you breathe a word of this to a soul! You have trapped him, and I'll capture him for you. You get the money and I'll get lots of fun and a "crackerjack" of a newspaper article! Your mother will be comfortable for the rest of her life, and you can be a lady of fashion.

ANN. I don't care about myself, if mother could have a nice home in her old age and not be poor.

JONES. You are a good little daughter, and would make an angel of a wife; and that is just what I need in my business.

ANN. But, señor, you had better not try it.

JONES. What? Getting married?

ANN. No. Capturing El Capitan. You might get killed.

JONES. Then you don't want me to get killed, eh?

ANN. Why, certainly not! I—I—

JONES. [*Eagerly*] Well, "You—you" —you love me a little bit, then?

ANN. Well, I'd like you much better alive, señor.

JONES. Yes! I wouldn't be an interesting corpse! See here, Annetta! Let's get down to business! I'll catch that blankety blank robber and get the reward for you. I don't want a penny of it; but want to put your mother on "Easy Street." I've never seen her; but I like the old lady for your sake. Now I am not a bad sort; but average up pretty well on a general invoice. I love you harder than a Mexican mosquito can bite; and I want you to marry me! There! What do you say?

ANN. [*Laughing*] Much obliged!

JONES. You're welcome.

ANN. But, señor! I hardly know you!

JONES. Not know me? Why, we're partners in business! Annetta, Jones and Co. Robber Catchers, Cave Finders, Etc., Etc. Look here! If you don't consent, I'll go and get killed by El Capitan and every one of his band that I come across! I am determined to get married or murdered.

ANN. Well, don't get killed, señor; and we'll try to get better acquainted. I must have time to make up my mind, you know.

JONES. Remember! I can't hope to live unless I live to hope!

ANN. You'd better live to hope, then, señor!

JONES. [*Trying to kiss her*] My angel!

ANN. [*Eluding him*] Wait till we're better acquainted! I haven't given you my promise yet, remember! [*Exits L.1., laughing*]

JONES. No; but you will! You shall! Like General Scott, I have set my heart on the conquest of Mexico! Well, I must be off for the padre's! We'll catch that cuss as sure as Lord made little apples! [*Exit L.1.*]

SCENE 3: *Interior of priest's house. Door with curtains R. flat, window in flat, C. Set door L.U.E. backed exterior. Couch in C. at back. Large robe or mat L.C. at back. Door L. flat backed interior. Chairs R. and L. opposite 2. Carlos insensible, on couch, Jones and padre over him. Aguila on watch at window.*

PADRE. Watch close, Aguila. Warn us of anyone's approach. I think he is regaining consciousness. The wound is not deep, and he is only weak from loss of blood. He has received a hard blow on his head that has done the most of this.

CARL. [*Opening his eyes*] Water! [*Jones gives it*] Where am I?

JONES. Among friends, Carlos. How do you feel?

CARL. Very weak. Am I wounded?

PADRE. Not very badly. I will have you on your feet again in a few days if you will obey me.

CARL. To whom am I indebted for this kindness?

JONES. To the good padre and faithful old Aguila.

CARL. [*Taking Jones' hand*] And you, my more than friend!

PADRE. Yes, señor.

JONES. Padre, you should know your patient. This is Colonel Carlos Castillo.

PADRE. [*Surprised*] Son of Antonio and Maria de Castillo?

CARL. [*Surprised*] Yes, padre! How did you know that?

PADRE. Thank Heaven that I can serve you! I have not seen you since you were a child. Carlos, you are my sister's son!

CARL. [*Trying to rise*] What! My uncle, Padre Domingus?

PADRE. [*Taking his hand*] Yes. There! You must lie quiet now, my boy. The Holy Word says "Thou shalt not kill." My son, you have nearly lost your life by disobeying Heaven's command. I must heal you body and soul.

CARL. Uncle, there are some insults no man can bear. I am a soldier, and it is better to die like a man than live like a coward!

PADRE. [*Soothing him*] There, there, my son! I'll not be uncharitable to you! Young blood is hot, and who knows? Had I been a soldier instead of a priest of Heaven, I might have done as you did! Who was your antagonist?

CARL. Count Pedro Martinez.

PADRE. Did you see him drop anything where you fought?

CARL. Yes. I remember, when he threw off his serape, I saw something glitter and fall. It was about the size of a coin, and was gold.

JONES. We have the rat in the trap!

PADRE. [*Showing locket*] Might it not have been this?

CARL. I think likely. Did you find it there?

PADRE. Yes. Listen, my son! You may do the state a better service than risking your life in a duel. Fourteen years ago Juan Alvarez was waylaid and probably murdered by El Capitan. On that day he wore this locket. It contains the picture of his wife, Mercedes. It has never been seen till today. The man that lost it was probably the one who took it from the body of Alvarez.

CARL. [*Excited*] El Capitan?

PADRE. El Capitan!

CARL. [*Trying to rise*] I will go at once to the guards—

JONES. [*Restraining him*] No, Carlos! Remember your wound—

CARL. 'Tis nothing! A soldier's trade is to give and take hard knocks like a man. I will seize his servants. They shall confess.

PADRE. No! You must let your wound heal first.

CARL. [*Wildly*] And in the meantime he may win her? What! Spare my body and lose my soul's hope? What is the pain of this scratch to a broken heart?

JONES. Hear me, Carlos! Leave him to me. Aguila will guard the little señorita.

AG. Yes, with my life!

JONES. For her sake, you must remain here under the good padre's care. I'll track that wolf, and if he shows his teeth at the American eagle, there won't be enough of him left to write an epitaph over! Good-bye. I'll see you later! [*Exit door L.U.E.*]

AG. [*At window*] The little señorita is hastening up the walk. [*Tremolo pianissimo till Isadora on*]

PADRE. Quick! Help me in here with Carlos! [*They lift him off in cot D.R.F.*] My son, not a word till I bid you! The sudden shock might kill her or drive her mad. If you love her, keep silence.

CARL. I will, padre, I will! [*Padre closes curtains. Knock at D.L.3.*]

PADRE. [*Seated R.*] Enter! [*Isadora runs in, dropping shawl. Falls on her knees by padre*]

Isa. Oh, padre! Carlos, my Carlos! My love, my life, is dead.

Padre. [*Stroking her head*] There, there, calm yourself, my child. We are all mortal. Let us hope for the best.

Isa. Hope! What hope is there for me now? Speak of hope to the condemned wretch, to the castaway, struggling with the waves, for they have still a thread to cling to. But not to the woman whom death has robbed of all that life held dear to her! The word is but a cruel mockery! These are not childish tears that a caress can soothe. Mine is a loving woman's woe!

Ag. [*Wiping away his tears*] Poor child! It seems so cruel not to tell her! [*Turns to window*]

Padre. My child, remember you are a Christian! Have faith in Heaven! Through faith the dead have been called back to life! Remember the story of Lazarus. "Though dead, he yet lives."

Isa. [*Looking up*] Oh, good Padre Domingus! I see the joy in your eyes! He is not dead! You fear to tell me suddenly! See! I am strong! Tell me! If you have any mercy, tell me! Is there any hope?

Padre. Yes, my child!

Isa. Alive? Thank Heaven! Bless you for your kind words of comfort! [*Sobs on padre's breast*]

Padre. There, calm yourself, my daughter! He is alive, but it must be a close secret for a time. Can I trust you?

Isa. Trust me? For Carlos' sake? O father, yes! But why must it be a secret?

Padre. You shall know all in good time.

Isa. But where is he? May I not see him?

Ag. [*At window*] Oh, padre, the countess! [*Music, hurry, pianissimo, till countess on*]

Padre. Quick, my child! Not a word, not a breath or you are lost! Your lover is in there! In! In! [*Isadora flings open curtains*]

Isa. [*Falling on knees by couch*] Carlos!

Carl. [*Clasping her*] My darling! [*Padre closes curtains. Knock L.3.E. Aguila throws himself in L.U. corner, under rug*]

Padre. [*Killing time*] Coming! Coming! [*Opens door*] Ah, my daughter! You are welcome. Come in!

Inez. [*Enters and comes C.*] Padre Domingus, you are the skilled physician both of the body and the stricken spirit. You devote your life to healing the ills of all that come to you in sickness or affliction. I have come to claim your good offices for my poor, heartbroken child!

Padre. Your child? What do you mean, señora?

INEZ. Padre, my daughter's lover has been killed in a duel. The blow has broken her heart. I come to you to crave an asylum for her within the convent's holy cloisters. There she may end her sad days in thoughts of Heaven, and learn consolation from the sweet and solemn service of the Church!

PADRE. I understand you, countess, better than you think. The convent is a refuge for the world-weary spirit, not a prison in which malice or treachery locks its victims. You cannot use the Church of God to do the work of Hell!

INEZ. [*Astonished*] Padre! What do you mean?

PADRE. You look on your child, not with a mother's, but a rival's eye, and would make the Church the toil of your wicked plans. Thou monster!

INEZ. False priest! You have refused her the convent's refuge, then she shall wed Count Pedro Martinez!

PADRE. If you try to force her into such an unholy marriage, I know the secret of your cruelty to your dead sister, and will blast you with it.

INEZ. [*Startled*] What? Do your worst! I have wealth and power, and I will crush you!

PADRE. Though you were an empress, what were your puny power to me? I am the servant of the King of Kings! What is the little might of man matched against a holy faith, throned in the faithful hearts of millions?

INEZ. She is my child, and must obey me!

PADRE. We shall see! If you refuse your consent to her marriage with Carlos, I will crush you! [*Music, hurry, pianissimo, till curtain*]

INEZ. [*Catching at his words*] If I refuse? Ah, he lives, then! [*Sees shawl*] See! She, too, has been here! [*Tears open curtains*] So! I have found you? [*Drags her L.C.*]

ISA. [*Kneeling at her feet*] Mercy, mother, mercy! Do not tear me from him! My heart will break!

INEZ. [*Seizing her wrist*] I care not! Come!

CARL. [*Struggles up*] You human tigress! You shall not! Would you kill her? You have said it! You—ah! [*Sinks exhausted by bed. Padre springs to catch him*]

PADRE. Woman! Would you have his blood on your hands?

INEZ. I'll bend her to my will though she goes mad! [*Throws Isadora to her L., as Aguila, throwing off rug, springs and catches Isadora with his L. arm*]

AG. Not while I live! [*Countess with a cry of rage, draws stiletto from her hair, stabs at him. He catches her wrist in R. hand. She drops dagger*]

PICTURE

ACT III.

House near the coast, at Puebla. Handsome Mexican interior. Large window with wooden shutters to open in, in C. Backed by garden in 4. Large panel pictures R. and L. of C. window. R. picture to open. Black or stone backing to panel. Set door R.3.E. Scene boxed. Dressing table L.U.E. NOTE: *This can be set with three-door fancy, or with plain chamber by having drapery over C. window. Enter countess R.3.E. At rise, eight bars of stormy music.*

INEZ. I have her safe at last! It was a good thought of mine, to bring her here to Puebla. They will not follow us here! She shall not elude me this time! Locked in this room, she cannot escape! I will send for Count Pedro at once. He shall marry her immediately. Though she kills herself at the altar, I care not! I hate her for her father's sake! What is Antonio de Oro's brat to me? I was but the slave bought with his gold! She is the child of hate, not of love! I owe her nothing. Would I had strangled her in her cradle, then she would never have risen between me and my love! Oh, Carlos, Carlos! My darling! You shall be mine. I would sell my soul for you! As for that red traitor, Aguila, he shall die! Defiance to me! His mistress! Manuel has promised to silence him forever! Poor Manuel! Poor faithful fool! He would go to his death at my bidding! He shall stab him while he sleeps. No dog of a peon shall defy me and live! [*Laughs wildly. Grasps her head*] Oh, my brain! My brain! Am I going mad? No! No! I will not! It is only this sleepless fever of desperation. With her once out of my way and Aguila dead, I can rest! [*Jones passes window R. to L.*] Who is that? [*Runs to window*] The American señor! How could he have followed us here? I must be calm! [*Calls R.1.*] Annetta!

ANN. [*Entering R.1.*]   Yes, señora countess!

INEZ.   There is a gentleman coming: Señor Jones. Admit him and make my excuse. I will see him presently.

ANN.   Very well, señora countess. [*Exit Inez R.1.E. Jones knocks, L.U.E.*]

ANN. [*Opening door*]   Good morning, Señor Jones! Come in!

JONES. [*Entering*]   What? My sweet Annetta? And alone too? I'm in luck!

ANN.   The countess told me to say she would be in, presently.

JONES.   Then, to business! Will you marry me?

ANN.   Why, you have not captured El Capitan yet?

JONES.   Was that the condition? I am going today. I was only waiting for your answer. I wanted to know whether I was to get married or massacred.

ANN.   Oh, you mustn't get killed! It isn't a bit nice!

JONES. To die is bitter, but it is better than to love Annetta and then not get her!

ANN. Why, señor! I am only a poor girl, a servant! I am no wife for a gentleman like you.

JONES. Annetta, the accident of position cuts no ice with Jones! Poverty is no crime; and a servant may be more of a lady than the mistress she serves! Annetta, a poor girl who is a true, pure woman and a good daughter, is a queen among women if she is crowned with a servant's cap! I want a wife who is a wife. Put your head here, please, and say: "Yes!"

ANN. [*Putting head on his breast*] Well, then, yes!

JONES. America has taken Mexico!

ANN. No! Mexico has taken America!

JONES. Well, America and Mexico have signed an eternal treaty of love and union. Let's sign the treaty, thus! [*Kisses her*] Signed, sealed and delivered! Now El Capitan is a dead man!

ANN. Is he dead?

JONES. Well, no, not yet. He's just hanging round till I get there, but he will be!

ANN. Hist! The countess! [*Enter Inez R.1. Annetta bows and exits L.1.*]

INEZ. Ah, Señor Jones! I am glad to see you. Come in.

JONES. [*Entering*] Pardon my intrusion, countess. Do not think I wish to interfere in your affairs. I have come as the friend of Carlos—

INEZ. [*Graciously*] And you are welcome! It is no intrusion, señor. I am very glad that you have come, for I can say to you what I could not say to him. You think me cruel, heartless. I am not. When you know all, you will see I am just and right.

JONES. It is not my place to question the actions of a lady under her own roof, señora.

INEZ. Will you hear me, señor?

JONES. Certainly, señora.

INEZ. Do you think I could be cruel to my own child, señor?

JONES. [*Evasively*] Such things have been before now.

INEZ. I am a friend of Carlos. To justify myself and cure him of his foolish infatuation, I must unveil the skeleton in our family. Know, then, that Isadora is not my child!

JONES. [*Surprised*] Not your child?

INEZ. No. She is the child of Señor Antonio de Oro, my husband, by a slave! Carlos is of noble blood, one of the oldest Spanish families. I love him as though he were my own son. Now what sort of hostess would I be, señor, to let him wed this child of shame?

JONES. [*Incredulously*] If this be true, señora, how came you to rear her as your own child?

INEZ. My husband was so much my senior, that my love for him was more the love of a daughter. Hence I was free from those jealousies that would have tortured a wife. He loved the bright child, and as we had lost our own daughter in infancy, to please him I reared Isadora as my own child.

JONES. Pardon me, countess! But it seems hardly credible.

INEZ. It is true nevertheless. No matter what that scheming padre may say to the contrary. He knows nothing of the truth. In fact, I have hidden all evidence of the secret so carefully that I now have no proof to confirm my statements. But the fact remains. I feel that I have only done my duty by Carlos, although he may feel unkindly toward me.

JONES. Does Señorita Isadora know of her origin?

INEZ. No, señor. No one would ever have known of it, if I had not been driven to reveal it. I will be frank with you, señor, for I feel that I can trust you. I love Carlos, and I could not bear to see him won away from me by a creature whose very existence is an insult to Heaven, and whose origin must bring the blush to every honest cheek.

JONES. [*Shrewdly*] It seems strange, señora, you did not think of this when you made her your child, gave her your name and the place of your own offspring in your house.

INEZ. Señor, could I refuse the last request of that old man as he lay there dying? He had always been kind to me, although he knew I could not love him. He had given me position, title, almost boundless wealth. Could I do less than share the name and fortune I owed to his bounty with the child he loved? My gratitude to him was stronger than my scruples. You cannot dream how hard it is for me, even now, to betray his secret! Had her love fallen on anyone in the world but Carlos, the secret should have remained buried forever.

JONES. [*Aside*] What a lawyer she would have made! [*Aloud*] I will tell Carlos what you have said, señora.

INEZ. [*Giving her hand*] Señor, you are so good! Tell him all, and then let him judge me calmly and honestly.

JONES. [*Rising*] Well, señora, I must be going. [*Aside*] Perhaps the padre can unravel this snarl of lies. [*Aloud*] Good-day!

INEZ. [*Shaking hand*] Señor, I thank you for this call, as it has given me a chance to save Carlos and vindicate myself. Good-bye! [*Exit Jones. She laughs triumphantly*] There! I have made Carlos' pride my ally. He will not wed a child of shame! Ah, Padre Domingus! I told you I would conquer yet! Woman's wit against man's power! It is a desperate game, but I have won! Aguila's lips once sealed, no one can disprove my story. [*Goes to door R.3.E.*] You may come out now. [*Music, tremolo, pianissimo, till Isadora on*]

Isa. [*Entering*] Mother, if you have one kindly feeling, if your heart is not stone, do not torture me any more! Do not threaten me with this hated marriage with Count Pedro! Or, if you are merciless still, why, kill me! I am ready to die!

Inez. Perhaps I may if you do not obey me. You marry Count Pedro at once!

Isa. [*Falling on knees*] Oh, mother! Have pity! Mercy!

Inez. [*Throwing her off*] Child, it is time this farce was ended! Listen! You are not my child! You are the child of my husband by a slave! You are a thing of shame!

Isa. [*Defiantly*] It is a lie!

Inez. [*Sneeringly*] Indeed! How do you know? I have reared you as my child, but you are not. You are a stain upon the family whose name you bear! Carlos knows this now, and he would cut off his right hand before he would disgrace his noble name by giving that hand or name to a thing like you!

Isa. You have lied. But I will use your own weapons against you. I shall tell Count Pedro Martinez this story, and he will refuse the child of your husband's slave!

Inez. [*Fiercely*] Do it if you dare! I will declare you insane. I will send you to a private madhouse. Do not think to trifle with me! You cannot escape from this room. Aguila cannot help you. I will put him beyond reach of you! You have no alternative, you must yield!

Isa. Never! I can die!

Inez. Fool! You are a feather in my hands! There is no foe this side of death to match a woman who wars for love and hate at once! Kill yourself if you will! You only serve my purpose. [*Going R.3.E.*] Beat your wings against your cage if you will, you cannot escape. [*Exit door R.3.E., laughing. Music, tremolo, till Aguila enters*]

Isa. [*Throwing off restraint*] The child of a slave! A thing of infamy! A living shame! And he believes it! He loathes, despises me! My last hope gone, a helpless captive, branded with infamy, Carlos lost to me forever. My only choice that hated marriage or a madhouse! No! There is always one hope left to despair. Death! [*Prays R.C.*] Santa Madre! Forgive me, if I do wrong! I, who have no mother! Better death than dishonor, and a marriage unsanctified by love is nothing less! Think how I am goaded to despair! Thou, who knowest all suffering, forgive my sin and take me to thyself! [*Sobbing. Goes to toilet-table up L. on which is cushion with bodkin for hair*] Oh, for some means! [*Sees bodkin*] The desperate wretch is never without a weapon against himself! This bodkin! One quick thrust will reach my heart—[*Aguila springs from panel, seizes her wrist. Chord, fortissimo, as Aguila enters*]

Ag. Child! What would you do?

Isa. [*Falls in his arms*] Aguila!

Ag. Yes! Why don't you trust me? I have sworn to guard you as my soul!

Isa. Oh, but Papa Aguila! She has told me all! Has told Carlos, and he hates and despises me now!

Ag. All! All what?

Isa. That I am not her child!

Ag. [*Astonished*] What! That you are not her child? How did she know that! I thought I alone knew the secret.

Isa. That I am a thing of shame! The child of her husband's slave!

Ag. [*Fiercely*] It is a lie!

Isa. [*Eagerly*] Oh! Is it, Aguila? Is it a lie?

Ag. Yes, my child! She herself does not know you are not her own child, but I do!

Isa. Tell me, Papa Aguila! What do your words mean? Who am I then?

Ag. Not now, my child! In time, you shall know all. 'Tis enough to know now that you are her equal. Your blood as pure as hers! Fear not Carlos' faith! He loves you too well to doubt, or give you up for a lie from lips that he knows are false as Hell!

Isa. Go to him, Aguila! He will believe you. Tell him I am not the thing she would make me! And if she tries to force me to marry Count Pedro, I will kill myself rather than be untrue to my love!

Ag. Listen, child! You need not die. You see that secret door? No one but me knows of its existence. It was built by your—by Señor Juan Alvarez, the former owner, as a hiding place for his vast treasures. I discovered it three years ago. There is a secret passage leading to the room below. There is a spring of water there, lamps and oil enough to last for weeks, and food and bed for you, my little one!

Isa. Oh, good Aguila! You have saved me!

Ag. I foresaw the coming storm, and knowing you might need a refuge, I hastened here before the countess, and stocked it with all things needful for your comfort. Now hear me, child! Only use it as a last resort. Not a word to anyone of it or what it holds. Trust old Aguila, he will not fail you! Now promise me one thing, little señorita—that you will not attempt to destroy yourself again!

Isa. But should she succeed in forcing me into this union with Count Pedro—

AG. [*Interrupting her*] Have you not a safe retreat? Even should they seize you, aye, though the priest had said the words that made you his wife, I will save you at the eleventh hour. Believe and trust me, mea alma! Has Aguila's word ever failed you yet?

ISA. But suppose she should, as she has threatened, imprison you. How could you save me then?

AG. Our good padre thought of that, and gave me this phial. 'Tis an acid that can eat away all bolts and chains. She may cage my little dove, but not the eagle!

ISA. She has some dreadful plan against you, Aguila.

AG. I know it. I was skulking amid the flowers in the garden, when I heard her bid that yellow wolf, Manuel, to stab me while I slept.

ISA. [*Appalled*] Oh, horrible!

AG. [*Fiercely*] Let her beware how she opens the gates of the hurricane, lest the tempest crush her! Fear not, Mariposa! That slimy snake will never crawl into the eagle's nest! I'll give his carcass to the kites before tomorrow! But do as I bid you, and we are safe. But as you love Carlos and trust me, never raise your hand against yourself again! Promise me, promise!

ISA. [*Kissing him*] I promise, Aguila.—I will do as you bid me to the last! I will trust you always! [*Hurry, pianissimo, to suit action till curtain*]

AG. [*Clasping her to his heart*] Bless you, my darling child! [*Looks through window*] Ah! What is that? The assassin who tried to kill Carlos? El Capitan's servant! [*Closing shutters*] The secret panel! The lion's mouth the spring! In! In!

ISA. [*Terrified*] Who can shelter us now?

AG. [*Back against shutters*] The wings of the eagle! [*Battering against shutters*] In, I say, in! [*Isadora enters panel and closes it after her. Shutters are struck, Aguila staggers; shutters burst in. Aguila falls down stage. El Capitan and robbers enter, masked. At window. Aguila staggers to his feet and strikes El Capitan in breast, felling him. Bernal and robber seize him from behind and force him to his knee*]

BERN. [*Raises machete*] Strike him!

EL CAP. [*Stopping him*] Hold, you fool! He knows the secret of the hidden treasure! He shall tell us where it is or I will flay the red dog alive! Where is the girl? Speak!

AG. [*Laughs defiantly*] Go! Seek her! Within the convent's walls! Safe from your grasp, you robber!

EL CAP. Away with him to the cave!

AG. [*Throws off robbers*] Do your worst! Ha! Ha! I defy you!

PICTURE

ACT IV.

SCENE 1: *Eight bars pathetic. Cave scene in 2. Can be braced to run off back of 1. so that R. and L. may be left clear for sea-cloth. Tropic island set back of scene before curtain goes up. Phillippe dozing on bench R.2.E. Set door R.2.E. Wing boxed L.2.E.*

JUAN. [*Chained L.2., talking to himself*] They'll not find it there! Ha, ha, ha! Oh, how my head pains me! He struck me here. I can't remember since then. No, no! I forget where I hid it! Did they kill Aguila? I saw him cut El Capitan here! Ha! Ha! It was no child's blow! Yes, yes! Where is my child, my baby Isabella? Mercedes! Wife! Where is our little sunshine?

PHIL. Shut up, ye old fool! I want to sleep!

JUAN. I won't!

PHIL. [*Starts up. Crosses L.*] What! Ye won't? Take that! [*Kicks him*] And that! [*Same business*]

JUAN. You may kill me if you want to. I will not tell. I cannot! I have forgotten!

PHIL. Silence, ye chattering old monkey! [*Crossing R.*] He's thinking of his buried treasure. There's where the Capitan's temper cost him something. When the fool wouldn't tell where it was hid, the Capitan hit him on the head, and he went crazy. Now he can't tell! El Capitan might have starved the truth out of him. But now his only hope is that he may get his wits some day and tell where it is. Damn the money anyway! Give me aguardiente and I am happy. [*Drinks*] Ah, that's the stuff! Drink fit for a saint! [*Knock—he listens*] What's that? El Capitan and the rest back so soon? [*Voices without*] Who's there?

BERN. [*Without. Music, hurry, till all on*] The wolf's litter!

PHIL. [*Unbolting door*] Back so early? [*Enter robbers with Aguila bound and blindfolded. They take off the hoodwink. Throw him C. at back*]

EL CAP. Yes, but without the girl. [*Aguila laughs*] But we have you, you dog of an Indian! He shall be of some services to us. He can tell us what that crazed fool has forgotten. And by Satan he shall, or I'll have him skinned alive at sunrise!

AG. You can tear the flesh from my old bones, but you cannot tear the secret from my heart!

EL CAP. We shall see! Listen, Aguila! I will spare your young mistress and let you and that crazy old idiot go free, if you tell the truth. Refuse, and I will torture the secret out of you or kill you!

JUAN. Aguila? Who said Aguila? You are not Aguila! No! He killed you in the pass. You are Aguila's ghost. How came you here among devils? This is not your place.

AG. What! Señor Juan, my old master, alive? Thank Heaven!

EL CAP. Yes, and you can save him and yourself by telling where the treasure is hid. Refuse, and he shall be tortured with you!

AG. [Aside] I dare not tell him, not even to save Master Juan, for it would betray her hiding place!

EL CAP. Answer me, you old fool!

AG. I don't know!

EL CAP. [Music, hurry, till Aguila chained] You lie, you dog! Men! Chain him to the wall! [They chain him, ring bolt C. at back. Phillippe locks chain, keys in belt]

JUAN. I'll tell you! It is hidden behind the fourth stone. [Pauses]

AG. [Aside] Saints of Heaven! If he remembers, she is lost!

JUAN. The fourth stone—the fourth toward the sea. It is in the sea! I know! No, I have forgotten all! All! I cannot tell!

AG. [Aside] Thank Heaven!

BERN. [Threatening Aguila] You stole my knife in the garden. You struck me. I always pay my debts. [Strikes him in face] Take that! [Chord!]

AG. Coward! If my hands were free you would no more dare do that than you would dare knock at the gates of Hell!

BERN. [Laughs] You said, when we met, you'd make a buzzard's feast of me! Do it! I'll make a handsome saddle of your hide, tomorrow! [Seizing Aguila by the throat] Ha! Ha! I'd like to throttle you!

AG. Would you? Why don't you do it, then? You need not be afraid, I'm chained.

EL CAP. Never mind him, "Alacran," he can wait till morning. Come here, I have work for you. Go back to the casa of Señora de Oro, watch for the señorita. I believe that old knave lies. She must be there! If you see her, seize her and bring her to me at the island. I will be there by evening.

BERN. [Points to Aguila] What about him?

EL CAP. He will keep till we get back.

JUAN. Aguila, call Mercedes and bring little Isabella. It is time to go.

PHIL. [Springs at him with whip] Shut up, you old parrot! [Cuts him twice. Chords at whip cuts]

AG. [Tugging at chains] If I were but free of these cursed irons, I'd make a stairway of your bloody corpses!

PHIL. Oh! You want your share, eh? Take it, then! [Cuts him. Chords at whip cuts]

JUAN. [*To himself, gloatingly*] Oh, if he would only fall asleep within reach of my chain! He'll do it sometime—then—Ha, ha, ha!

PHIL. What! Ye want more? [*Cuts him again. Drops keys on blanket. Juan sees them and covers them with corner of blanket. Gets them later*]

EL CAP. Here, matador! You make more noise than he does! Be quiet!

PHIL. [*Crossing R.*] All right, Señor Capitan.

EL CAP. [*To Bernal*] If you capture her, take her to the island, as I told you. There are two black rocks on the north side, and a narrow, deep channel between them. That is the safest and most hidden landing place. [*They drink*]

AG. [*Quickly, aside*] Black rocks, narrow channel? He means El Toro! Oh, if I were only free!

EL CAP. Once there, tie her and come off with the boat for me, you hear?

BERN. Yes, Señor Capitan. But I may need aid to seize her.

EL CAP. Take Vasquez, Miguel and Sancho with you then. Mind! No harm to the girl, or El Alacran and the rest of you shall answer to me!

BERN. [*Crosses R.1.*] Have no fear of us, Señor Capitan, you know I am always faithful to you.

EL CAP. [*To Aguila*] With the girl in my power, I think I can bend your stubborn will.

AG. [*With assumed calmness*] You will not find her, señor. She is in the convent of Santa Madre, safe from harm.

EL CAP. [*Laughs incredulously*] Perhaps. But we shall see. If we do not find her at the casa, we will storm the convent.

JUAN. Give me back the locket! It contains the picture of Mercedes, my wife.

EL CAP. [*Striking him*] Silence, you fool!

JUAN. [*Points to his head*] There is where you struck me before. It aches yet, and that was a long time ago.

EL CAP. [*Seizing him by the throat*] Be quiet, I tell you! [*Throws him down*]

AG. Have mercy! He is an old man, and mad!

EL CAP. Mercy? Ha, ha! You talk like a fool! [*Turns R.*] See here, lads! Go to the lower pass. There is a rich prize coming today. An old rich señor and his servants. Pluck the pigeons, and, if they are well behaved, let them off with whole skins. He is a fat sheep, and we may have a chance to shear him again when his new fleece has grown. So don't kill him this time, mind!

ROBBER. All right, Señor Capitan.

EL CAP. Vasquez—you, Miguel and Sancho go with "El Alacran." The rest to the Pass! Vicente, Chico and Gonzales to the lower bridge; Pancho with the others wait at the gorge above, and follow the game to the bridge, to attack them in the rear. I must go first to my hacienda, then to meet you, Bernal, at the island.

BERN. [*To two robbers*] Come, boys, let's be off! [*They exit door R.2.E.*]

PHIL. And me, Señor Capitan, shall I go with the others?

EL CAP. No, Matador, you stay here to watch your pets and guard the cave. Don't get your head so full of aguardiente that you lose your brains.

PHIL. Trust me, Señor Capitan, I am not such an ass as to put my neck in a halter.

EL CAP. Be careful that you don't. There are soldiers in the neighborhood, and your love of liquor will be the death of us all someday, I fear.

PHIL. I'll not touch another drop today, Señor Capitan.

EL CAP. Come, boys, be off now, and good luck to you! Make a quick and clean job of it, and don't let the grass grow under your feet when it is done. Be careful you are not watched, and if you are, remember—"dead men tell no tales!"

ROBBER. All right, Señor Capitan. [*They exit door R.2.E.*]

EL CAP. [*Mockingly to Aguila*] Adios, friends! I hope soon to bring a guest who will unseal your royal lips.

AG. Heaven grant you may not!

EL CAP. Watch close, Matador.

PHIL. Adios, Señor Capitan.

EL CAP. And remember, no more liquor.

PHIL. Not another drop, Señor Capitan. [*Exit El Capitan, door R.2.*]

AG. [*Remembers phial*] Ah, the good padre's gift! The phial! [*Phillippe, as he bolts door and sees all safe, sings. During song, Aguila gets phial from hair and puts acid on ringbolt. Turns quickly as Juan calls Phillippe's attention*]

PHIL. A woman to love and a bottle of brandy,
          A good game to play and a good song to sing,
       When fat purses travel, a machette handy,
          And I wouldn't change with an abbot or king!

JUAN. They say swans sing before they die!

PHIL. Here! I want to sleep. If you make a riot and wake me, I'll fan you with this! [*Shakes whip*] I'll have another drink first, and damn the Capitan! [*Drinks. Throws himself on blanket R.2.E.*] I'll tame the cattle! I'll—I'll— [*Sleeps. Aguila bursts chains. They fall from wall with noise. Phillippe wakens. When chain breaks, hurry music till Phillippe falls*]

PHIL. Eh? Hello! What's this? [*Seeing Aguila*] What! Broke yer tether, eh? [*Draws knife*]

AG. [*Raises chains over head*]   Back, I say! Or my path lies across your grave!

PHIL. [*Springing at him*]   Ye will have it, eh? [*They fight. Phillippe draws knife. During fight Juan works wildly on his chains with keys*]

JUAN. [*Wild and exultant*]   Kill him, Aguila! Kill him! Ha, ha, ha! Down with him! [*Aguila gets Phillippe's wrist in his teeth. With a howl of rage he drops knife. Juan bursting from his chains, picks it up and stabs him in the back*] Ha, ha! I knew I'd pay him back! [*Gets whip, cuts corpse with it*] Take that! And that! Ha, ha, ha! He drops his keys and I hid them there, in the blanket! [*Cuts corpse. Music, hurry, till Jones on*]

AG.   Master Juan, where are the keys? [*Knocking at door. Aguila runs to door, raising chains as weapon*] Who's there?

JONES. [*Without*]   Open in the name of the law!

AG.   Señor Jones?

JONES.   Yes, with my American bulldog and the Mexican army! Open this rat's nest or we will open it for you! [*Aguila draws bolts. Enter Jones followed by soldiers*] Aguila?

AG.   Yes, señor.

JONES.   A dead man and a maniac. Who is this?

AG.   Señor Jones, that is my old master, Señor Juan Alvarez. [*Soldiers unlock Aguila's chains. L.C.*]

JUAN. [*Courteously. R.C.*]   Your servant, gentlemen! Excuse me! I am killing a snake. [*Juan throws dead body off*]

AG. [*Rapidly*]   Señor, the password is "The wolf's litter." They will be back by night. Take Señor Juan with you.

JUAN. [*Interrupting*]   No, no! I am free! Free! [*Springs back with knife. Tremolo, pianissimo, suit action till curtain*]

AG. [*Trying to conciliate him*]   Master Juan, give me the knife!

JUAN.   No, no! I will not!

AG.   Yes, señor. I am old Aguila, your faithful Aguila.

JUAN.   So you are! [*Slowly gives knife*]   Did they kill you? He struck me here. See the dent?

AG.   They will take you to your friend, good Padre Domingus, and to little Isabella.

JUAN.   Yes, I'll go to Padre Domingus. [*Points to Jones*] Is he the señor, your friend?

AG.   Yes, master. [*Puts Juan's hand in Jones'*] Take him to the good padre, he will cure his head. [*Soldiers take up body ready for change. Tremolo*]

JONES.   But you, Aguila, where are you going?

AG. Send guards to Casa de Oro, and to El Toro after me. I go to save the little señorita, or die defending her! [*Exit followed by Jones and guards. Scene moves down to 1st grooves, followed down by sea-cloth, then runs off back of 1st grooves*]

SCENE 2: *Tropic island drop in 5. Padded platform across stage in 5. Shore-piece in 4. Cut wood and set tree on platform. Flats obliqued off in 3. to show sides of island and sea beyond. Grooves in 2. empty. Concentric turntable device for shark fight. Sea-cloth, scrim. Sand-bar foreground to hold edge of sea-cloth in 1. Bernal appears L.4. in boat with Isadora bound. Lands L.C. at back*]

BERN. [*Lifting her*] Come, señorita. Here we are. You must wait here for the Capitan.

ISA. Oh, señor! Have you no mercy? What would you do? By the memory of your mother whom you must have loved, I beg you to let me go!

BERN. [*Doggedly*] Can't do it I tell you! I must obey orders.

ISA. Oh, spare me, señor! You are a brave, strong man. You cannot fight with women!

BERN. Come! No more of your whimpering! I shan't harm ye, and if ye don't put on airs with the Capitan, ye'll live like a queen.

ISA. [*Appalled*] What awful fate is hidden in your words? Oh, señor! In mercy, kill me then! Kill me! I will kiss your hands, red with my blood, and die blessing you! [*Sinks half fainting*]

BERN. Shut up, I tell ye! I must see all safe around here, and then go back for the Capitan. [*Going R.4.E.*] She's a devilish pretty one. I'd like her for myself if it wasn't for stealing her from the Capitan. [*Exit R.U.E.*]

ISA. [*Bound to tree*] I am lost, lost! Is there no hope? Santa Maria! Hear and save me! Poor old Papa Aguila! Would they had killed me as they have you! How gladly would I lie dead now in your kind, strong arms where I slept so often when a child! Come to me, Aguila! Come to me! [*Aguila appears swimming L.2.E. Chord segue, hurry till curtain*]

AG. I am coming!

ISA. [*Cries joyfully*] Aguila!

AG. Still! Or we are lost! [*Shark appears C.*]

ISA. See! Aguila! The shark! The shark!

AG. Hush, I say, or you will ruin us! Fear not for me!

ISA. [*Praying*] Santa Madre Maria, save him, my old Papa Aguila! Oh, Aguila, thank Heaven! Oh, I dare not look! Ah! There he comes! [*Aguila stabs shark, who turns over and sinks. He lands*]

AG. My child! My darling child! [*Cutting her bonds*] Thank Heaven I am here to save you!

ISA. Are you hurt? Tell me?

BERN. [*Out R.U.E.*] What riot is this? Has the little fool gone mad? [*Enters, sees them*] What! Free?

AG. Yes! [*Springs on him before he can draw machete. Fight with knives. Aguila down. Bites Bernal's wrist, he drops knife. Aguila stabs him, turns and stabs him again. Bernal front. Throws him out in water. During fight, shark's fins show above water. When Bernal strikes water, the fin disappears. Isadora faints in Aguila's arms*]

AG. The shark steals the buzzard's feast!

PICTURE

ACT V.

Same as Act III. Eight bars triumphant. Night backing in 4. Countess seated R. by table. Pedro C.

PED. [*Offering hand*] So, countess, our feud is ended! We are friends once more, eh? You pardon me?

INEZ. Fully, señor, and more. I ask your pardon. I am very grateful to you for using your influence to have her returned to me.

PED. Not at all, señora! I had just received your treaty of peace, this letter, when the news of her abduction was brought to me. Of course I was almost driven wild. I ordered my horse and was off at a madman's pace to find the alcalde. Half way to town, whom should I meet but the alcalde himself, with the rescuing party. Among them that infernal Indian and that prying American. Of course she remonstrated against being returned to your house.

INEZ. [*Sneeringly*] I do not doubt it! She probably threw herself on the protection of that red traitor, Aguila, and that quixotic Jones.

PED. Yes, señora, and they espoused her cause and tried to hold her, but I told the alcalde that, as you were her mother, to deliver her into the custody of anyone else would be unlawful and equivalent to abduction. He took my view of the matter, and sent her back to you.

INEZ. You have worsted our enemies. Now, if we use our time, the day is ours. I learned that Señor Castillo was not dead, and my anger against you softened. I wrote you that letter, asking your pardon for my hasty words, and requesting an interview. I wished to tell you that if you so desired, we will proceed with this marriage at once.

PED. Señora, it is my dearest wish.

INEZ. This marriage once accomplished, we are masters of the situation and our enemies are completely outgeneralled.

PED. Yes, señora. Once in my house, as my wife, they will take their lives in their hands if they attempt to meddle with my household.

INEZ. I will bring in your bride. You will doubtless find her cold and distant at first, but firmness and kindness will soon teach her how useless it is to sigh for a lost lover, and she will soon see that her only chance of happiness is in courting the favor and esteem of her husband.

PED. Trust me, señora! I shall manage her when she is once my wife!

INEZ. [*Going R.U.E.*] Pardon me a moment, señor, and I will bring her here. [*Exit D.R.*]

PED. [*Alone*] So, I shall accomplish my purpose at last, and all legally! She shall be mine, body and soul! No human will has ever yet opposed me that I have not crushed! I will not now be balked by a puny girl! As for her lover, I can have him removed; we shall see who wins!

INEZ. [*Entering with Isadora. D.R.U.*] Señor, here is your promised wife. [*To Isadora*] Child, prepare yourself, at once, to be married to Count Pedro.

ISA. [*C. Aside*] Will Aguila keep his word? [*Aloud*] Señor, I do not love you—

INEZ. [*R. Aside. Clutching her wrist*] Beware! You know me!

PED. [*Smiling*] You will learn to in time, señorita.

ANN. [*Entering L.3.*] If you please, señora countess, there is a holy father out here who fears to go down the Passo at night, and asks permission to wait here till morning.

INEZ. A holy father? [*Aside*] Most opportune! [*Aloud*] Bid him come in.

ANN. [*At door L.3.*] Enter, father!

PRIEST. [*Entering*] Benedicite, my children! Señora countess, pardon my intrusion, but I am belated on my way to Puebla. My mule is lame, and the night is on me. These passes are infested by El Capitan and his band. I am forced to ask your hospitality till daylight, when I can continue my journey in safety.

INEZ. You are most welcome, holy father! This is Count Pedro Martinez of Puebla. [*Pedro bows*]

PRIEST. Benedicite, my son!

INEZ. Father, we need your good offices to celebrate the union of this gentleman and lady at once.

ANN. [*Aside*] I wish I had set the dogs on him!

ISA. [*R. starts up defiantly*] I will not marry him! You may kill me if you will, I care not!

PRIEST. [*Crossing R.*] Calm yourself, my child! [*To Inez*] Is she your daughter, señora?

INEZ. [*L.C., with Pedro*] Yes, father. Though a most wilful and disobedient one. She is infatuated with a young and worthless adventurer. I have selected a worthy, wealthy and honorable husband for her. One who can give her position, title and luxury. And you see how the ungrateful child opposes my love and care!

PRIEST. My child, you owe obedience to your mother! You should let her wisdom guide your impetuous youth.

ISA. [*Appealingly*] But, father, I do not love him! Would you have me make a mockery of Heaven's blessings, by letting you bestow it on a loveless marriage?

PRIEST. Have faith, my daughter, that Heaven will send you love. By faith the dead have been called back to life. Remember the story of Lazarus; though dead, he yet lives.

ISA. [*Surprised. Aside to him*] Those words! Who are you?

PRIEST. [*Warning her*] Sh! [*Smuggles letter to her. R.*]

INEZ. I thank you, father, for your holy counsel to my wayward child. We will leave you with her, while I give orders for your entertainment. And I trust she may profit by your good advice. Come, count. [*Exeunt Pedro and Inez D.R.U.E.*]

ANN. [*Half hidden in curtains*] I don't believe he's a holy father at all, or he would not try to marry poor Señorita Isadora to an old monkey that she hates!

ISA. Who are you?

PRIEST. Fear not, my child. I know your story. I am the friend of Padre Domingus, your friend. Passing his parish the day your mother brought you here, he commissioned me to prevent her placing you in a convent here, and to be your friend in need, as he would be. But read your letter!

ISA. [*Opens letter and reads*] "Trust the Holy Father. He is our friend. Let them go on with the wedding. You are surrounded by friends. We will be there at the proper time. Carlos." [*Kisses letter*] Dear, brave Carlos! [*Annetta comes down from curtains*]

PADRE. [*To Annetta*] You are her friend, are you not?

ANN. Friend! I would die for her, father!

PADRE. You are a good girl! The American señor—Ah! you blush! You love him! Now I know I can trust you. A woman may always be trusted where she loves.

ANN. Yes, padre! What are Señor Jones' wishes?

44   CLARENCE BENNETT

PADRE. He sends word that you should have the dogs tied on the other side of the house, away from that window. Let no one see you do it. You understand?

ANN. Yes, father. [*Exits door L.3.*]

PRIEST. There, poor child! Prepare for your wedding, and, at the final moment, there shall be a change of bridegrooms!

ISA. [*Clasping his hands*] Heaven bless you, father! [*Countess and Pedro enter D.R.U.E.*]

PRIEST. [*Signals their presence to Isadora*] There! Calm yourself, my child; go and dress for your marriage, and leave the result to Heaven.

ISA. [*Seemingly yielding*] I will do as you bid me, father! Heaven grant it may be for the best! [*Exit R.3.E.*]

INEZ. I am much indebted to you for the wonderful influence you have gained over her, father.

PED. It seems wonderful that you could so completely have subdued her opposition!

PRIEST. Kind words will lead a child where death could not drive her. I have a nephew who can be ruled by no other means. He is kind-hearted, but such a wag. I believe he would play his pranks on the saints! Here are some candles he gave me as I started. [*Unrolling package*] I tremble to use anything from his hands without first testing it, and I mistrust these innocent looking candles. [*Annetta seen peeping on at door L.3.*]

PED. Those candles? Mistrust them? And why?

PRIEST. [*Drily*] His candles do not always burn evenly! For fear that these are not staid, sober and well behaved, I will, with your permission, light one outside of the window. As its capers, if it be frolicsome, will do no harm there.

INEZ. [*Laughing*] The young rogue! To play tricks on his uncle, thus.

PRIEST. [*Preparing at window*] It is a young rascal, but I love him for it, after all; I was a boy myself, once. Heaven forgive my wild pranks! [*Lights rocket candle*] Ah! I thought so! The young monkey! Ha! Ha! Ha! [*Inez and Pedro laughing heartily. Distant pistol shot and whistle. Aside triumphantly*] They see it! [*Closes window. Isadora enters D.R.U.E. dressed as a bride. Music tremolo till Aguila on*]

ISA. Well, father, I am ready.

PRIEST. [*By table L.2., candles on it*] Ah, my child! You are a good and obedient daughter. [*Annetta crosses to R. of window*] Give your hand to this gentleman. [*She obeys. Countess R.C. Pedro C.R. Isadora C.L. Priest by table L. Whistle outside. Priest with back to others, puts out candles. Lights down. Glass crash. Guards, Carlos, Aguila on*] How stupid of me! [*Lighting candle.*

Lights up. Aguila L.C., Isadora in his arms L. His sword at Pedro's breast. Jones getting in window. Chord, fortissimo]

PEDRO. [*Amazed*] What does this mean?

JONES. It means that we are about to reverse the rule, and give away the bridegroom!

INEZ. Señors, leave my house! I am mistress here, and this intrusion is most insolent! More! It is a violation of the laws for which you shall answer.

JONES. Señora, we are here on business of the state, and can't accept your pressing invitation to take a walk. We can't tear ourselves away so unceremoniously.

INEZ. Such insolence!

JONES. Don't put your fingers in this mess of porridge, or you may burn them! [*Goes to Annetta*]

PED. Trickster! This is your work! Who are you?

PADRE. [*Throws off disguise*] Padre Domingus, who has assumed this disguise to save this poor persecuted child from the clutches of a robber!

PED. A robber! What do you mean?

CARL. It means, Pedro Martinez, you are our prisoner.

PED. Upon what evidence?

CARL. Mine, and these gentlemen's. I accuse you of being El Capitan, the noted robber chief. This locket, stolen from the body of your victim, Juan Alvarez, you lost where you fought with me, by the river. I accuse you of robbing him, attempting his life, and of all the countless crimes that have made you the scourge of the Republic for so many years.

PED. [*Laughs defiantly*] Is this your proof? Ha! Ha! I'll show you how worthless it is. I bought that locket, years ago, from a Jew in the city of Mexico. It bore so strange a resemblance to the little señorita, whom I loved even as a child. You see, señors, your evidence is trash!

CARL. [*Triumphantly*] Stay! Not so fast! Here is a witness whose evidence you cannot so easily gainsay! [*Leads Juan on L.U.E.*]

PED. [*Quickly*] What testimony do you expect to gain from him? He is mad!

JONES. [*Quickly*] How do you know?

PED. [*Confused*] Well, I could see by his eyes that he was not sane.

PADRE. He is as sane as you! You struck him on the head, and dented his skull. The blow made him insane. I have relieved the pressure on his brain, and his reason has returned. So you see, señors, he had no way of knowing but his knowledge of his previous condition. [*Pedro attempts to rush out. Stopped by guards*]

CARL. Your attempt to fly is almost enough to condemn you! [*To Juan*] Is this man El Capitan?

JUAN. Yes, señor.

PED. 'Tis false! This man is mad, I tell you! Even though he fancied he saw a resemblance, that proves nothing. Your evidence is worthless!

AG. But mine shall crush you!

PED. [*Sneeringly*] Indeed? Since when has the evidence of a dog of a slave been sufficient to crush a man of wealth, rank and noble blood?

AG. Noble! In years gone by, in this fair land, my fathers ruled. Their gentle sway lay like a happy maid, that, smiling, slept upon a bed of roses, her fair hands clasped by either sea! The stranger came, a man like you; a robber and a murderer, who wore the cross of God above a heart where coiled things of Hell! You are the whelp of that robber! I am the child of a King!

PED. Well, wretch! What can you tell?

AG. Fourteen years ago, señors, I gave El Capitan a slash with my machete, across the left shoulder. Let us see if the noble Count Pedro bears the mark of Cain! [*Springs on him. Pedro draws knife. Aguila tears it from him and forces him to kneel. Tears open shirt and exposes scar*] Behold! [*Throws Pedro up C. into arms of guards*] Bind him, señors, and away with him.

PED. [*Struggling with guards, as they take him L.U.E.*] Curse ye all! You've trapped the lion, see that you hold him! If I break my meshes, beware!

JONES. We've clipped your claws! Your band are all killed or captured to the last man. We've got the whole business. Don Pedro, Sancho, High Low Jack and the game! [*Throwing him to soldiers*] Gentlemen of the Guard, guard the gentleman. [*Exit soldiers with Pedro*]

INEZ. Señors, now that you have disgraced my house with this scene, I trust you will relieve us of your presence! [*To Isadora*] Come here, my child!

AG. She is not your child!

ALL. Not her child?

AG. No! Your child died in its cradle the day you turned your sister Mercedes starving from your door. I told her of its death, and she begged me to save her baby's life by putting it in the dead one's place. You have reared your sister's daughter!

INEZ. [*Furious*] This is a lie! A wicked lie!

PADRE. No. It is Heaven's truth! Your sister told me the story as she was dying. How you loved Juan and hated her that she had won his heart. And of the deception practised on you. But I never knew that Aguila was her assistant. [*To Isadora*] My child, you are not Isadora de Oro, but Isabella Alvarez, and this gentleman is your father!

JUAN. [*Clasps her*] My child!

Isa. Father, Carlos, my dear old Aguila—I have you all, all! [*Tremolo, pathetic, pianissimo, till curtain*]

Inez. [*With wild laugh*] Yes, all! All! Ha, ha, ha! And I have lost all! Carlos, you were all to me, as he once was! And I have lost you! I sinned to gain you, Ha, ha, ha! Fool that I was! Fool! Fool! [*Buries face in her hands*]

Carl. [*L.C.*] Merciful Heavens, she is mad!

Inez. [*C. Starting up*] Mad! Am I mad? Oh, tell me, Carlos! You hate me now, but you will forgive me when I'm dead. Yes, and kiss me just once! Just once. I loved you so! Just once that I may know that you forgive me. Good-night, Carlos! Ha, ha, ha! [*Snatches bodkin from her hair. Stabs herself. All spring forward to prevent her. She waves them back*] Stand back, señors! [*Hands on breast*] See the roses—beautiful red roses! They are your gifts, Carlos! See how the petals fall off! No, it is blood! My blood! [*Staggers. Aguila supports her*] Aguila, don't let Carlos forget to kiss me when I'm dead. [*Gasps*] Carlos! Carl—[*Dies in Aguila's arms*]

Ag. Poor Inez! Heaven forgive and pity thee! [*Padre, Inez and Aguila C. Juan and Isabella L.*]

PICTURE

CURTAIN

THE GREAT DIAMOND ROBBERY

By Colonel Edward M. Alfriend and A. C. Wheeler

CHARACTERS

Dick Brummage

Frank Kennet

Mr. Clinton Bulford

Grandfather Lavelot

Mario Marino

Dr. Livingstone

Senator McSorker

The Count Garbiadoff

Sheeney Ike

Jimmy McCune

Philip

Jack Clancy

Mickey Brannigan

Policeman

Mrs. Mary Bulford

Mary Lavelot

Mother Rosenbaum (Frau)

Mrs. O'Geogan

Peggy Daly

Mme. Mervaine

Incidentals: heelers, clubman, salvation army lass, messenger boy, barkeepers, waiters, street gamin, blind musician, guests.

ACT I.

SCENE: *Small cosy breakfast or supper room in Mr. Bulford's house on Lexington Avenue in New York set in 2. It is tastefully furnished with grate fire burning, and an easy chair and table in front of·it. Room lit by gas or lamps, but not glaringly. There is a sofa R. with buffet in corner C. It is furnished with glass, silver, decanters, etc. There is an entrance R.2.E., another L. in back flat. Bitter storm outside—howling of wind heard with banging of shutter. See fire lighted and red medium for rise.* TIME: *Nine o'clock at night, late winter or early spring.* DISCOVERED: *Mrs. Bulford at half open door L. in flat. She is listening intently at door and is nervous. At the expiration of half a minute, she goes to a little table and strikes bell. Crosses R.C. and to R., then listens. Enter Philip L.*

MRS. B. Philip, that shutter in the parlor is banging.

PHIL. [*L.C.*] Yes'm. [*Is about to go*]

MRS. B. Where is my brother, Marino.

PHIL. In his room, ma'am. I smelt his cigar in the hall.

MRS. B. Tell him to come here.

PHIL. Yes'm. [*Is about to go*]

MRS. B. What have you in your hand?

PHIL. It's·a letter, ma'am. It came by messenger a few minutes ago. It's for Mr. Bulford. I couldn't give it to him because he's got parties in the reception room. [*Puts letter on table*]

MRS. B. Did you see the people in the reception room?

PHIL. Yes'm. I let 'em in.

MRS. B. What did they look like?

PHIL. Like foreigners! [*Mrs. Bulford starts*]

MRS. B. Did they bring anything?

PHIL. Yes'm. One of them had a hand bag.

MRS. B. Go and fasten that shutter and tell my brother to come here.

PHIL. Yes'm. [*Exit leaving door ajar. Mrs. Bulford stands a minute in perplexed attitude looking at letter, then places it on table and going to buffet, takes a drink of water and composes her face in the glass. Enter Marino, L., with book in hand*]

MAR. Hello, dear!

MRS. B. Are you going to the club tonight? [*Crosses to L.*]

MAR. [*Yawning*] Heaven forbid! It is almost as dull there as it is here. I was reading Daudet and smoking.

MRS. B. [*Shutting the door*] Did you see the men who are with Mr. Bulford in the reception room?

MAR. See them? No, I didn't know there were men there. [*Crosses to sofa*]

MRS. B. [*Relieved*] I was going to ask you to go out in the storm and execute a commission for me. You will object, of course?

MAR. [*Sitting on sofa R.*] Santa Maria, my charming sister, why do you insist on making me uncomfortable?

MRS. B. [*Petulantly*] You would be comfortable on the edge of Hades. As for me I wish we were in Rio tonight. Think of it! They are celebrating the feast of St. Catherine with flowers. [*Lights cigarette at buffet C., then crosses to fire L.*]

MAR. Aye—and the streets are filled with black eyed señoritas, who have tropical faces all the year around. I detest this northern climate. But you, who have spent a winter in St. Petersburg, ought to be comfortable in New York.

MRS. B. [*Facing him*] I should be more comfortable in New York if I had never been to St. Petersburg. I made the mistake of my life there.

MAR. I only know of one.

MRS. B. What's that?

MAR. You got married. [*Rises, crosses to C. up to buffet*] Most adorable of sisters, you did not send for me to tell me this.

MRS. B. [*Sits by fire*] Why not? I have been telling it to you for months. You think because I wear a calm face I am comfortable. My heart is like a volcano covered with snow, but wearing a core of fire! I can play at respectability, but the play must not be too long or too tedious.

MAR. Well, if I were going to play the respectable thing, I'd get rid of that senator you keep hanging about. It makes me feel sorry for your generous old husband.

MRS. B. Senator McSorker is the most powerful and influential politician in New York.

MAR. [*R. of table, L.*] And one of the most disreputable, I fancy.

MRS. B. Nobody is disreputable in New York, unless they are unsuccessful.

MAR. Oh, but he dresses so damnably and smokes such rank cigars.

MRS. B. [*Seated at fire L.*] Bah—you are a child. I shall never make a man of you. In Europe we have to fight brains, finesse and diplomacy to get on. [*Rises, crosses to L.C.*] Here the canaille are the supreme rulers and we ought to be princes among them. Instead of going to St. Petersburg and marrying a respectable old gentleman because he was attached to the American Legation there, and who keeps you in cigarettes and pays your club bills to please me, we should have come direct to New York; for here every politician is a gold mine and every clever woman can defy the law. [*Crosses C. at back of sofa*]

MAR. By Heavens, if you were single, I believe you would marry that senator.

MRS. B. No. But I should like to have the chance for six months to make him think I would. [*Leans over back of sofa*]

MAR. Well, you have been scheming for six months. I hope you will not do anything to disturb our respectability and comfort. For my part, I rather like this sort of thing. [*Wind. Enter Mr. Bulford door L., evening paper sticking out of his pocket—jewel-case under his arm; looks at the pair on the sofa, shivers and places jewel-case on the table*]

MR. B. Boo-oo. I am chilled through. That reception room is like a vault. [*Wind*] Listen to that wind! Now, this is cosy. [*Warms his hands at grate fire L.*]

MRS. B. Your visitors must have had business of great importance to bring them out on such a night.

MR. B. Importance? Yes, I should say it was. It's the most extraordinary thing I ever heard of.

MAR. [*Seated on sofa; eagerly*] Why, what is it pray?

MR. B. [*Back to fire*] Do you remember the robbery of the Garbiadoff diamonds in Europe? It took place just before we left there, a year and a half ago. It was all in the papers, but I did not pay much attention to it, although I knew Garbiadoff well. We are friends in fact.

MAR. I remember it very well. They were stolen in Cracow by—

MR. B. [*Stands back to fire L.*] By the cleverest thief in Europe. They were said to be worth fifty thousand pounds. [*Mrs. Bulford C., standing*]

MAR. Fifty thousand pounds?

MR. B. The thief, who is known as Don Plon, has operated in both hemispheres. He was in this country once, I understand, but incurred the deadly enmity of a powerful criminal who is a woman, for he betrayed her son to the authorities, and she swore to be revenged. He accomplished this robbery in Cracow by introducing a handsome woman in the count's house, and while the count was carrying on an amour, the diamonds disappeared with the woman. After chasing the jewels through Europe, the Russian police got upon their track in this city and succeeded in negotiating with some of the conspirators and getting the jewels back, but so afraid were those agents of Don Plon or this woman that they came to me tonight with the property and wanted me to go to the bank with them and have the jewels deposited. There they are in that case.

MAR. [*Going to table*] Why, this beats Daudet! Fifty thousand pounds! [*Sits at head of table L.*]

MR. B. I told them I wouldn't go out tonight for all the jewels in the Russian Empire, but they assured me that it was in their interest that they should get them out of their hands into the safe keeping of a responsible party. [*Mrs. Bulford crosses and leans on back of sofa R.*]

MAR. [*Seated at head of table L., looking at the case*] But do you really mean to say they are worth fifty thousand pounds!

MR. B. [*Sitting L. of table by fire*] Yes—that is the estimate put upon them by England. There is said to be a ruby in that case worth five thousand pounds. It was known along the upper Ganges as the "heart of fire."

MAR. [*Rises*] You are assuming a great risk by accepting the property in this way.

MR. B. The men appeared to think they were lessening the risk by getting the property into my hands.

MRS. B. And none know they are here, but those men?

MAR. [*Turning to Mrs. Bulford*] Don't you wish to see them, Maria?

MRS. B. [*On sofa R.*] No. It has given me quite a sensation. I can fancy the mysterious Don Plon hanging about our house tonight when we are asleep, and, if they should disappear—

MR. B. [*Seated L. of table, interrupting*] Oh, nonsense! Don't say anything to the servants and I'll be responsible for them until morning. I've the count's order and I will see the jewels deposited carefully.

MAR. [*Seated at head of table, taking up case*] Can't we see them?

MR. B. [*Seated by fire*] No. It is sealed. You see, there is some difficulty in identifying the diamonds, owing to the absence of the count. Nobody but Don Plon or that woman of his could identify them and it would be a very easy matter to change them. [*Marino returns to the lounge thoughtfully, stands at back of it. Mr. Bulford turns around in his chair again. Enter servant L., hands card to Mr. Bulford, then stands by door L., L. of it*]

MR. B. [*Looking at card*] Kennet—Kennet—Frank Kennet? What does he want to see me for? It's no use.

MRS. B. Who is Frank Kennet?

MR. B. It's a young man I put in the bank six months ago. He's got into some kind of trouble with his accounts. I feel sorry for him but it's no use running after me here.

MRS. B. [*Music for Kennet's entrance until well on*] Oh, you had better see him. Perhaps he wishes to confess.

MAR. I'll be in the way, please excuse me, I'll go back to Daudet. [*Exit, L.*]

MR. B. Well, I am not going into that cold reception room again. Tell him to come here. [*Servant bows and exits*]

MRS. B. [*Rises*] Perhaps I had better retire. [*Crosses a little to C.*]

MR. B. [*Rises*] Nonsense—sit still. Confound it—why can't young men go straight.

MRS. B. [*R.C.*] What is the trouble?

MR. B. There's something crooked. I've got to lay it before the directors. A case of bad habits and worse companions, I suppose. [*Enter servant L., stands R. of door L., showing in Frank Kennet who wears a great coat with collar turned up and carries a soft hat in his hand. Servant exits L. Kennet stops at entrance, disturbed that Mr. Bulford is not alone*]

FRANK. [*Up C.*] I expected to see you alone, sir. [*Mr. Bulford doubles his newspaper and places it carefully over jewel-case on table*]

MR. B. If you come into my family this way, sir, you must expect to see some of the members of it. [*Points to Mrs. Bulford*] Whatever you have to say—you can say it here [*Mrs. Bulford goes to window, looks through*] but make it short. [*Sits L. of table*]

FRANK. [*Goes slowly down to Mr. Bulford*] I came to appeal to you, sir, not to make public the charges against me until they are investigated. I am innocent.

MR. B. [*Seated L. of table*] Hum-ph! I hope so, but the business of the bank must be carried on regularly. I must report the matter to the directors tomorrow.

FRANK. [*L.C.*] Tomorrow? A day or two cannot injure the bank, but it may give me time to vindicate myself. There are others who will suffer from haste.

MR. B. Ah, there are others—of course—your associates.

FRANK. [*L.C.*] No sir—I have no associates.

MR. B. Come—come—this is idle talk. What do you mean?

FRANK. [*L.C.*] I am engaged to be married. I thought that perhaps that fact would incline you to listen to me kindly.

MR. B. Oh, there's a woman at the bottom of it, is there? I thought as much.

FRANK. Pardon me, sir, you are going too far. Some women cannot stand even the rumor of dishonesty and Mary Lavelot is that kind of a woman.

MR. B. [*Impatiently*] Well, this is all very fine, but as a bank officer, I've got to stick to the accounts. I am responsible to the stockholders.

FRANK. [*R. of table L. above it*] I did not come here as a culprit, sir. I only ask you to satisfy yourself of the injustice of these charges before making them public. Once that bank sets in to prosecute me, I have no means to fight it and no friends. I am not thinking of myself as much as others. [*Mrs. Bulford is listening from window, R.*]

Mr. B.   If you are innocent, you need not fear an official examination—in fact, there is no other way whether you are innocent or not.

Frank. [*At head of table L.*]   But sir, what if some of the directors, in order to save the real culprit, should desire to make me appear guilty?

Mr. B. [*Rising*]   What's that? What's that? You have a warm temper young man. It is sheer folly to accuse me of unkindness. I have done a great deal for you.

Frank.   It is that which hurts me, for you are undoing it all now.

Mrs. B.   What's the matter? Is he faint? Let me offer him a glass of wine? [*She turns to buffet C., back to audience and pours glass of wine*] We can afford to be generous as well as just on such a night.

Mr. B.   Nobody ever accused me of being either ungenerous or unjust.

Frank.   But you intend to take this action tomorrow?

Mr. B.   Young man, I shall do my duty tomorrow, if I live, as I have always done. [*Mrs. Bulford hands Frank the glass of wine, R. of him*] But you needn't go away with any hard feelings to me. Maria, you can give me a glass of sherry. [*Mrs. Bulford comes to table with glass of wine in a cut sherry glass, gives wine to Mr. Bulford, looks at them a moment and goes to window R.*] Drink that young man—it will warm you. [*Frank and Bulford drink*] Let us hope matters will not be as bad as they look. [*Frank drinks the wine, places glass on table, stares at Mr. Bulford a moment, goes to door L. where he stands irresolute*] Good night! [*Goes and sits L. by fire. Frank attempts to speak, breaks down and exits. Mr. Bulford sighs, takes newspaper from table L. and resettles himself in his chair. Fifteen seconds elapse. Mrs. Bulford tries to appear unconcerned. Business ad lib*]

Mrs. B. [*Coming from window R., crosses to table L.*]   Oh, there is a letter for you—did you get it?

Mr. B.   No. Where is it?

Mrs. B. [*R. of table at head of it*]   Philip placed it here on the table. Here it is. [*Gives envelope. Mr. Bulford tears it open and takes out enclosed foreign letter*]

Mr. B.   Why, this is a foreign letter sent to the care of the Russian Consul here, and by him delivered to me. It must have come by messenger. [*Opens letter and looks at signature*] It is from Count Garbiadoff himself.

Mrs. B. [*R. of table—eagerly*]   Garbiadoff! [*Goes back a step or two*]

Mr. B. [*Seated next to fire*]   Yes. There is his signature—Garbiadoff. It doesn't look like the signature on the order. What did I do with that order? [*Feels in his pockets*]

Mrs. B. [*Eagerly*] Never mind about the signature. Read the letter.

Mr. B. [*Looking at the two names*] Yes, the letter must be genuine. There is the count's coat of arms in the corner. I remember it very well—and there's the Imperial postmark on the envelope. Do you see Maria, do you see?

Mrs. B. [*R. of table, agitatedly*] Certainly it must be genuine. Why do you not read it?

Mr. B. [*Seated L. of table, L.*] But if the letter is genuine, the order cannot be. It must be a forgery! Why should any one forge an order to get the jewels into my hands? There is something wrong here.

Mrs. B. Let me read the letter for you.

Mr. B. [*Holding letter open and reading*] No! No! I will read it myself! "Dear Sir:

"Recalling our pleasant acquaintance while you were in St. Petersburg, I venture to address you. If in this communication I give you pain you must not blame me—necessity compels me to write as I do. You will remember that for a few weeks prior to your departure from Russia I was absent from home. I returned to find that you had married, resigned your position as Attache of the American Legation and departed for America. Curious to find whom my good friend had honored with his name, I made inquiries at the Embassy and elsewhere, but beyond the fact that you had married somewhat suddenly, a woman supposed to be French, I could learn nothing. In point of fact your old companions seemed somewhat reticent and so disinclined to impart any information upon the matter that I dropped it entirely. More than a year has passed, and today it has been brought back to me by an occurrence at once remarkable and painful. You know all about the theft of my diamonds, how I was tricked out of them by the wiles of a woman, at the time the mistress of that supreme scoundrel calling himself Don Plon. Happily for the world this villain never lived to enjoy his plunder, for he died in Paris eight months ago. I have employed the best detectives to find my property, and while I have been unable to recover it, so closely have I been on its track that a sale of the diamonds by the thieves in any of the markets of Europe has been made impossible. Today, however, a woman formerly a servant of Don Plon's mistress, was arrested by the Russian police on some petty charge, and sent for me in prison, saying if I would procure her release, she would give me information that might aid in the search for my lost property. The information she gave me was startling—even tragic. It was that the diamonds had been recently sent to America and that the wretch who had tricked me, Don Plon's partner in the theft, was"—My God!—"Marie Marino, the same woman who had married my American friend Bulford." [*Bulford starting up in great agitation—stop music*] Is this the truth? Speak, or I shall kill you where you stand. You do not answer. You cannot. Ah, I see it all now. The men who brought those diamonds here tonight were not the police but your tools! The order was a forgery and you are—you are—Plon's woman! [*Mrs. Bulford stares at him for a moment or two, goes to buffet, puts poison in glass then pours in wine, with back to audience, turns, brings glass to Bulford, behind him on his R., pours it down his throat*]

Mrs. B.   Take this, my dear it will revive you. [*He drinks*] Oh! [*Steps a step back with look of triumph then looks frightened*]

Mr. B.   Oh! My God, my God, the shame of it! The shame of it! It will kill me! It will kill me! Oh—Oh!—[*Falls, struggles in chair, dies. Mrs. Bulford stands a moment horrified, then goes around to front of chair, presses his head back with her hand. It falls on his breast. She goes to his R. at back takes the letter out of his hand, puts it in her bosom. Taps bell on table. Enter Marino L.*]

Mar.   What's the matter?

Mrs. B.   Quick, a doctor! He is dying! He says the young man who was here poisoned him, but I think it is apoplexy. [*Imperatively stamping her foot*] Why do you stand? Go! Go! [*Music till curtain is well down. Wind and rain outside. Exit Marino hurriedly L. Mrs. Bulford watches him off, clasps her head in her hands for a moment as if bewildered and listens. Then staggers and facing audience goes to table and gets sherry glass—quickly seizes it with left hand and with the right grasps jewel-case through the paper—staring wildly into space. Quick curtain*]

ACT II.

Scene: *Old Lavelot's house and shop in Houston Street. Three days later. An old-fashioned apartment littered with old clothes and personal effects on pegs and tables. Stove rear, window L. and curtains showing street. Children's shouts. Doors L. in back flat, R.1. and R.3.* Time: *Morning.* Discovered: *Old Lavelot sitting at stove doubled up, with poker in his hand. Dr. Livingstone and Mrs. O'Geogan down front C.*

Dr. L.   I'll give you a powder to put in his tea at night to keep him quiet.

Mrs. O'G.   Tay, is it? If I put tay in the medicine he wouldn't take it. He'd taste the water in a drink if it was a foggy mornin'. Sure tay is for the strong-minded sex, like meself, doctor.

Dr. L.   [*R. at head of table*] I'm sorry to find the old man such a wreck. It was lucky I happened to be in the neighborhood.

OLD L. [*At stove*] Oh, you come here too much, damme! Fire him out—fire him out! [*Strikes the stove viciously with the poker. They disregard him entirely*]

MRS. O'G. Don't mind him, don't mind him. It's very good of you, doctor. To think of the loikes of him, and you havin' so many rich people to attind.

DR. L. Don't mention it. I knew the old man when he was a political influence in his ward.

MRS. O'G. I mind it well. That was in the Fourteenth, and he ought to be goin' to Albany this blessed minute. I hear, doctor, that the women do be takin' the politics in their own hands, thank God!

DR. L. You always had your share of political influence in the Fourteenth I believe.

MRS. O'G. But nary a job did I ever get. If I'd had the scrubbin' of the City Hall and the Court House as long as Mrs. Dooley, I'd be a ridin' in me coach meself, this blessed minute. [*Goes to door L.*]

OLD L. [*Seated R. of stove*] Lay for'ed—lay for'ed. [*Strikes the stove with the poker*] How long is this thing going to last?

DR. L. [*Crosses to C.*] You had better give him two powders Mrs. O'-Geogan.

MRS. O'G. I'll give him half a dozen and choke him at wanst. It's yourself cud be doin' an honest widdy a good turn by spakin' to the senator.

DR. L. [*R.C.*] Oh, you have more influence with him than I have.

MRS. O'G. Influence, is it? May St. Peter fly away with him! He has a heart as big as his fist, but his tongue ought to melt in his mouth with his own blarney. Aha, is that you, Mrs. Dooley—you'll be comin' up to see me in my new house on the Avenoo, says he, and drink a glass of champagne with the boys, at election toime. The devil an invite do I get to the house on the Avenoo and me workin' like a nager with the gang on election day. I'm thinkin' I'll put on me trousseau at the next blow-out, and march into the house on the Avenoo. [*Imitating him with hands on her hips*] A-ha—is that you, sinator? You'll be givin' Biddy O'Geogan a mug of champagne I don't know, or divil another whack will you git of election day.

DR. L. Where is Pop Lavelot's granddaughter, Mary. I saw the girl once —in fact, I assisted at her début.

MRS. O'G. She never had it. A healthier baby I never saw.

DR. L. [*Smiling*] I mean, her first appearance. [*Music till Mary is well on*] She promised to become a very handsome girl.

MRS. O'G. She is a good girl and kept her promise. Didn't ye see her, doctor, she must have stepped out. I'll call her. [*Goes to door R.3. and calls*] Miss Mary—whist—here's the doctor.

MARY. [*Outside*] I'm coming in a moment.

MRS. O'G. [*Coming down*] It's no place for the loikes of her with her schoolin' and tinder sinsibilities. But the old pelican there has got a pot of money, and she's the only one who can manage him. [*Going up to door R.3. Enter Mary R.3. Coming C.*] This is Doctor Livingstone, miss. He knew your mother.

DR. L. [*Advancing to Mary*] It's no use my telling you we have met before. You wouldn't remember it. [*To Mrs. O'Geogan*] She has kept her promise indeed! A little pale, however—and—[*Regarding her closely*] I don't like the look of worry on your face.

MRS. O'G. Bedad she's breakin' her heart, doctor!

MARY. I need exercise, doctor.

MRS. O'G. [*Aside*] Exercise—listen to that. Does a cat need fur?

DR. L. Well, you will have to let me come over and look after you a little. It will never do, your eyes are red.

MARY. It is nothing, doctor. I took a little cold in them. [*Crosses L.*]

DR. L. [*Going toward door L.*] Mrs. O'Geogan, don't forget two powders at night and one in the morning. Miss Lavelot, let me advise you to take care of your health. Good-bye. [*Exits L.*]

MRS. O'G. Good-bye! He's the foinest doctor in New York. I'll speak to Senator McSorker about him. He ought to be on the health board—his medicines are so tasty.

MARY. You are very careless with your tongue and I am surprised at you.

MRS. O'G. When you have killed me with your trouble, I'll not be able to speak of it.

MARY. I don't want it spoken of to anybody.

MRS. O'G. You're killin' yourself entoirely and there isn't a man on earth that's worth it.

MARY. [*Going to window*] Oh, why does not Frank send me some word. I seem to be wandering about in a ghastly dream.

MRS. O'G. It's that young man Frank Kennet, that's wanderin' about with the police at his heels. [*Mary opens window and looks out; laughter; children's voices heard*] Listen to that, and our hearts are as heavy as a hod of bricks.

MARY. There is a girl dancing for them. She is a brazen thing. [*Speaks to some one outside*] Yes, this is Pop Lavelot's. You'd better come inside, I can't hear what you say. [*Opens door L. Enter Dick Brummage and Peggy Daly.*]

Door is left open. Brummage is roughly dressed as a longshoreman—pea jacket and cap, muffler, etc. Peggy wears a short coarse skirt, cheap waist tucked into it, coarse jacket, yarn stockings and heavy shoes. She is eating an apple with juicy exuberance]

BRUM. [*Laughing. To Mary*] I promised the girl to buy her a frock if she'd shake a horn pipe and blow me if she didn't kick it out on the flags like a boatswain's mate. She's got a foot like a ripple and a leg like the spar on the commodore's yacht. Shake them out a shuffle, old gal.

MRS. O'G. Oxcuse me. This is a respectable man's house!

BRUM. Well, she's respectable round the ankles. Wait till you see her.

MARY. [*L. at back of sofa*] Do you wish to buy something?

BRUM. Yes. I got to buy the girl some togs.

MARY. [*L.*] You had better go to a store. We've nothing but odds and ends.

PEG. Say, old man, will you buy me a sweater?

MRS. O'G. You had better hold your whist and get out of here. [*Mrs. O'-Geogan and Peggy scowl at each other*]

PEG. [*To Brummage*] Wait till I eat me apple and I'll take a rise out of the old woman. [*To Mrs. O'Geogan*] Say, old lady I'm the champion contortion-east.

MRS. O'G. [*R.C.*] You are, are you? Well you'd better take a tumble to yourself. I'm the Columbian terror from the Fourteenth when me rules and regulations is interfered with. [*Gets broom*]

BRUM. [*C.*] If you don't dance she'll lather you.

PEG. Lather me? Wait till I show you how I can dance? [*Wild dance ad lib; Arapahoe spasm*]

BRUM. Now, old woman—fetch her frock out.

MRS. O'G. You don't need no decent woman's frock. You'd better go over on Broadway and buy yourself a set of tights. [*Peggy goes up L.C.*]

MARY. [*Coming down from window*] Oh, get her what she wants, Mrs. O'Geogan and let her go. There's a lot of stuff in that back room. [*Crosses to R.*]

MRS. O'G. It doesn't become me to be waitin' on the loikes of her.

MARY. [*Going to door R.3.*] Very well. I will wait upon her myself. [*To Brummage*] Wait a moment, sir.

BRUM. All right. Take your time. [*Crossing to R. Peggy dancing up stage C. Mrs. O'Geogan follows Mary to the door*]

MRS. O'G. Oi wouldn't ruin me reputation by stayin' alone with them. [*Exit Mrs. O'Geogan and Mary R.3. Brummage immediately shuts door L. and returns to Peggy, who is dancing very quickly*]

BRUM. [*L.*] Now then, Peggy Daly, what are you doing in Houston Street when your beat is in Canal Street? Come, straight out with it. I'm looking at you. The old woman sent you up here—what for?

PEG. [*Frightened*] Who be you?

BRUM. You ought to know me pretty well. I'm Dick Brummage.

PEG. Dick Brummage. [*Takes a step or two towards R.*]

BRUM. I got you out of the Oak Street station, but I'll put you back there pretty quick if you don't give it to me straight—you were sent up here by Rosenbaum to watch this house.

PEG. [*R.C.*] I hope to die, if I've done anything. A gal can come to Houston Street, can't she?

BRUM. Yes, and she can go to Blackwell's Island when I've got a through ticket. The old woman sent you here to see who was hangin' about this house.

PEG. [*Beginning to cry. R.C.*] She'd broke my back if I hadn't come.

BRUM. That's all right. Keep your mouth still and I'll stand your friend yet. The old woman never bought you a frock since you've been with her. [*Peggy crosses to table R. Enter Mrs. O'Geogan and Mary R.3. Mrs. O'Geogan carries a bundle which she puts on table R. Group to table examining clothes. As Brummage speaks to Mary, she goes to window, leaving Mrs. O'Geogan and Peggy facing audience at table. While the conversation is going on between Mary and Brummage, Peggy picks up a lorgnette from table and hides it in the folds of her dress, going up R.C.*]

BRUM. [*To Mary*] I want to get some duds meself.

MARY. I don't think you'll find what you want here, sir.

BRUM. Oh, that room is full of odds and ends. I'll get the old lady to let me pick out what I want.

OLD L. Oh, take him down the cellar and give him some oats. [*Peggy looks sharply around*]

BRUM. Well, gal, you got your frock?

MRS. O'G. [*R. of table R.*] Yes; sir, there's the frock. It will cost you a dollar.

MARY. [*At window; to Mrs. O'Geogan*] The gentleman wishes to buy some things himself. You'd better show him what you've got.

MRS. O'G. [*Resignedly*] Oh, very well. Step this way, sir.

BRUM. Good-bye, Peggy. You can start a dancing school now.

PEG. [*By door L.*] So long—so long—I'm goin' to the Eyetalian Opera. [*Exit Peggy L. Mary comes down and sits L. of table R.*]

MRS. O'G. [*At door*] This way, sir.

BRUM. [*To Mary*] I'll see you again, lass, before I go. I might have something to say to you. [*As Mrs. O'Geogan and Brummage exit R.3. Mary drops her head in her hands*]

OLD L. Get over—get over. Stand round. What's the matter with you? Whoa! [*Strikes the stove with a poker as if it were a horse then rises and exits grumblingly and slowly R.3. Enter suddenly Frank Kennet street door L.; he turns, locks the door and comes C. quickly*]

FRANK. Mary! [*Going to her*]

MARY. [*Seated L. of table R. Looking up*] Frank! [*Covers her face with her hands*]

FRANK. [*L. of her*] Look me in the eyes. I'm hunted! Tell me if I am a murderer?

MARY. [*Staring at him*] Where have you been these three days?

FRANK. Trying to get to see you to see if you believed in me, for that was the only thing worth living for. [*Puts hat on table R.*]

MARY. You were hiding.

FRANK. Do you believe that?

MARY. [*Rises*] They were looking for you everywhere—why did you not face this terrible charge of murder and robbery if you are innocent?

FRANK. [*Turning away aside*] My God! Even she suspects me. [*Goes up to window*]

MARY. You do not answer me. [*Crossing to L.C.*]

FRANK. [*Comes down R.C.*] I will tell you. When I left Mr. Bulford's house on that fatal night, I started to come to you. My senses became bewildered. I was numb with cold. I must have fallen down somewhere. When I recovered my senses, I was on the deck of a South American ship, and was being carried out of the country. I waited till dark set in, cut loose one of the boats and escaped from the vessel. A strong ebb was running—no effort was made to pick me up. Almost dead with cold I succeeded in reaching the Jersey shore in the grey of the morning. When I saw the papers and saw the crime with which I was charged [*Mary sits on sofa L.*] one desire influenced me. It was to see you first and then give myself up and demand a trial. I have made my way to you to tell you I am innocent and to hear you say you believe me. The rest is fate. [*Crosses to table, takes up hat and steps up a little. Reenter Brummage dressed as Old Lavelot. Seats himself R. of stove*]

MARY. [*Rising*] What are you going to do now?

FRANK. I am going to the nearest station.

MARY. [*L. back of sofa*] Can you prove your innocence?

FRANK. [*R.*] Is that worth proving which no one will believe in?

MARY. [*L. back of sofa. Approaching him*] Frank, this is a terrible mystery. The blow has numbed me—my heart tells me that you are innocent, but the dreadful facts stare me in the face. If you are innocent, we must prove it. [*Crosses to C.*]

FRANK. [*R. at head of table*] Mary, I can fight adversity, and poverty and keep my spirit, but I cannot fight fate. [*Throws his hat on table, R.*] What cursed luck was it that sent me to that house that night and put me in these toils? [*Comes down R.*] I'll tell you what it was. [*Back to C.*] I was thinking of your happiness.

MARY. You can never make me unhappy if you are innocent.

FRANK. [*R.C. Turns Mary to his R.*] I am innocent and you are the only friend in the world that I thought would believe me. [*Crosses a step to L.C.*]

MARY. [*R.C.*] Oh, no! You must have a friend who can advise you and help you.

FRANK. [*L.C.*] I thought so before I came here.

MARY. [*R.C.*] Well, in Heaven's name think so yet.

FRANK. [*L.C.*] There is not a person on earth who will not believe me guilty after reading the newspapers. [*Goes, looks out of window*]

MARY. [*R.C.*] I don't want to believe the newspapers. I want to believe you.

FRANK. Mary!

MARY. [*Looking into each other's eyes*] Let me look at you—yes—you are the same Frank to me—no matter what happens. There is no murder in your eyes. [*Embrace, C.*]

FRANK. [*L.*] No, my darling, I could not put these arms around you again if they had committed a crime. All that I want you to do is to believe in me.

MARY. Oh, I must do more. I only wish that I knew how. [*Marino gives a loud knock at street door, L. They are both startled*] Go in there. [*Pointing to door R.1.*] You must not be taken yet, I have so much to say to you. Go! Go! [*Knock again. Exit Frank R.1. Mary goes to street door and, unlocking it, admits Marino*]

MAR. Are you Miss Lavelot?

MARY. Yes. What do you wish? [*Crosses L. to behind sofa*]

MAR. I am in search of Frank Kennet.

MARY. [*Aside*] He has followed him here. [*Direct*] What is it you wish to know?

MAR. [*Coming down L.C.*]· I will be frank with you. I have learned that you are engaged to be married to Frank Kennet.

MARY. Well, sir—

MAR. He is suspected of murder and the theft of valuable jewels.

MARY. But he is innocent of both.

MAR. You think so?

MARY. I am convinced of it.

MAR. [*Quickly*] Ah, then you have seen him since the murder and he has convinced you.

MARY. [*Aside*] He does not know he is here. [*Direct*] He has not convinced me.

MAR. I assume that you know where he is.

MARY. But you must not assume that I would betray him if I did.

MAR. I came here to open negotiations with him through you for the recovery of the diamonds, and to discover the murderer.

MARY. I, too, am anxious to discover the murderer.

MAR. [*Eagerly*] Has the murderer wronged you? [*During the speech they are standing one each side of the table, facing each other*]

MARY. Yes, he has.

MAR. Then we ought to be able to act together.

MARY. [*R. of table R.*] To what end?

MAR. To the discovery of the murderer. If Frank Kennet is that murderer, you would like to know it, wouldn't you?

MARY. I am anxious, as I have told you, to discover the murderer.

MAR. Then we can be of some assistance to each other. Now put me in communication with him. It is much the best way. He will be caught in time and then it may be too late for us to recover the property. Think it over and I will come back and see you again. It is not my intention to annoy you. [*Goes to door, L. Politely*] I beg your pardon for this intrusion. [*Bows and exits L. Door left unlocked*]

BRUM. [*Getting up from stove, looks out of door L. Coming down C.*] Well, you got rid of him very nicely, my girl.

MARY. [*Astonished*] You? Who are you?

BRUM. An officer from Headquarters, and I am waiting to see Kennet.

MARY. [*Overcome*] Oh, Heaven! Then it's no use. I have betrayed him!

BRUM. Well, don't go to pieces. Frank Kennet is suspected of two crimes, you know that?

MARY. [*At head of table R. back to end of it*] Yes, I know it, but he never committed them.

BRUM. [*C. up a little*] He went to the Bulford's house full of revenge. He was left alone with the old gentleman. They had an angry conversation. They drank wine together, and Mrs. Bulford says that when she returned to the room, Mr. Bulford was dead and the diamonds had disappeared. Have you read the papers?

MARY. Oh, yes—everything is against him—but—he is innocent—I know it.

BRUM. It is one thing to know and another thing to prove.

MARY. Everything. [*Covers her face with her hands*]

BRUM. No, not everything. Sit down here, you are trembling. [*Mary sits on L. of sofa*] Now listen to me. The coroner said Mr. Bulford was poisoned. But the inquest could not tell with what. It might have been in the wine he drank and the belief is that Kennet slipped it in the sherry glass when Mrs. Bulford went out. He drank it out of a cut sherry glass. That is in evidence. Are you listening to me carefully?

MARY. Oh, yes.

BRUM. [*R. of sofa L.*] Mrs. Bulford in her examination said that the two glasses were on the table when she returned to the room. But the police were in the house before twelve o'clock that night looking for the diamonds. Something had disappeared.

MARY. Yes, yes, the jewel-case.

BRUM. The cut sherry glass.

MARY. Let me think. Yes. Go on.

BRUM. Somebody had made away with it, and it could not have been Kennet. Don't you see that? [*Mary jumps up*] Don't excite yourself. Why was that glass made away with, and who made away with it?

MARY. I understand. What do you intend to do?

BRUM. I am going to save Frank Kennet if I can.

MARY. Who are you?

BRUM. I am Detective Brummage of the Central Office, the one friend that the newspapers haven't convinced. When I was a poor man and a friendless boy, Frank Kennet's father befriended me and helped me. What are you crying for? [*Goes up, opens door L., looks out*]

MARY. I suppose it is because he's got such a good friend.

BRUM. [*Comes down C.*] I suspect there is some kind of deviltry at work in that house of the Bulfords. Do you know who that man was that just left here? It was Mrs. Bulford's brother. [*Mary rises, goes L. around sofa at back of it*] But he will not suspect that Kennet is in town when he discovers the mistake he has made.

MARY. [*Behind sofa L.*] Oh, tell me what do you want me to do?

BRUM. It isn't much. [*Takes newspaper from pocket, points to paragraph*] Read that. [*Goes up, opens door L.*]

MARY. [*Taking paper and reading*] "Wanted—a neat maid to attend a lady—must not be over twenty-three; with good penmanship and a knowledge of hair dressing; apply in own handwriting to No. 400 Lexington Avenue." [*Speaking*] What does it mean?

BRUM. It means that Mrs. Bulford has discharged all her old servants and is hiring new ones. Can't you apply for that place?

MARY. I? In that house? [*Crosses to R., sits L. of table*]

BRUM. There are some things in that house I want to find out. Once inside of it you can help me.

MARY. [*Seated L. of table*] But you forget that Mrs. Bulford's brother who has seen me here will see me there and betray me.

BRUM. No. I don't forget. You must take the risk of meeting him in order to help me.

MARY. [*Gets up and approaches Brummage*] I will take all risks and encounter all perils.

BRUM. [*Going to her—placing his hand on her shoulder and speaking tenderly*] You must be guided by me. We must not let it be known that Kennet has returned. The conspirators think he is out of the country and that makes them careless. I will take care of him and be responsible for him. [*Door L. opens softly and Marino looks in and listens*] You must trust me. I don't want to be known. [*Marino beckons to someone outside*] If you betray me we may lose everything.

MAR. [*Aside*] The very man! Frank Kennet!

MARY. I will believe in you and trust you. [*Marino closes door and disappears L.*]

BRUM. Good! Keep your counsel. Frank shall not give himself up to anyone but me, until this is settled. Now I'll go and get these things off, or your grandfather will think his double is walking about. [*Goes to door R.3.*] Brave girl! Keep your spirits up. [*Exits R.3.*]

OLD L. [*Outside R.3.*] Mary! Mary! [*Enter Old Lavelot from door, growling; he reseats himself at stove and takes poker*]

MARY. Yes, grandpa, dear, I'm coming. I'm coming.

OLD L. I want my bran, damn it! Been chewing on my manger ever since sunrise.

MARY. Grandpa, dear, I'll get you something to eat right away. [*Enter from L. door Marino and officer. Marino advances and points to Lavelot*]

MAR. There's your man. Ah, Kennet!

MARY. Kennet!

MAR. [*With quiet triumph*] This is better than we expected. You're a pretty sly bird but your game is up.

OLD L. [*By stove*] Throw 'em down the hay-loft stairs—I'm getting tired of this.

OFF. It's no go. Will you come quietly or shall I put you out? Don't be a fool any longer.

MAR. [*Down to table; to Mary*] It is not too late. Ask him where the diamonds are. [*Crosses to C. Mary indicates by her manner that she understands the mistake and to save Frank is willing to keep it up*]

MARY. Frank—[*Breaks down; officer seizes Lavelot; business of absurd struggle in which officer succeeds in getting him out of L. door followed by Marino. The moment they are gone Mary runs to door and locks it; calls in suppressed voice*] Frank—[*Frank enters R.1.*] We have only a few moments. They have taken the old man by mistake and will be back as soon as they discover it. [*Enter Brummage R.3.*]

BRUM. I'll be responsible for you. If they lock you up now, you can't help me. I've the superintendent with me, but the people we are going to fight have only the commissioners and politicians.

FRANK. And I, God help me, have nobody. [*Brummage is between Mary and Frank*]

BRUM. Nonsense! You've got two of the best friends that any man ever had on this earth and they are going to help you.

MARY. Yes, we are going to help you.

FRANK. *You?*

BRUM. Yes, she! [*Puts their hands together*] We've got a big fight, but if you'll be steered by Dick Brummage, we will run the real culprit to earth. [*Quick curtain*]

ACT III.

SCENE: *Two days later. Dining room in Mrs. Bulford's house. Two entrances—one at portieres in rear wall L. with screen in two folds, the other a hall door well up R.3. Buffet back C. Table with cloth up C. with chair R. and L. of it. Large mirror L.* TIME: *Early morning.* DISCOVERED: *Mary at buffet with back to audience looking at glasses. She wears a white apron and is plainly but tastefully dressed as a maid.*

MRS. B. [*Outside L.*] Susanne!

MARY. [*At buffet, startled*] Yes, madam.

MRS. B. [*Outside L.*] There is a man coming with flowers—let him in and see who they are from. I am not dressed yet.

MARY. Yes, madam. [*Mary goes to hall door R.3. Enter Dick Brummage disguised as an Irishman and carrying two bouquets—one large and the other small*]

BRUM. [*Coming to table and looking around*] Where's your mistress?

MARY. You can put the flowers on the table.

BRUM. How the divil then do Oi know I'm givin' them to the right person?

MARY. Mrs. Bulford is dressing. It's all right.

BRUM. Drissin', is she? Begorra it's yourself that needs no drissin'.

MARY. You may leave the room.

BRUM. Av course I'll lave the room. D'ye think I'd be takin' it wid me? Let me speak a word in your ear, my darlint. [*They go around the table; Mary goes to hall door and opens it*]

MARY. Leave the flowers and leave the room.

BRUM. There, me darlint. [*Puts flowers on the table, approaches her, changes voice*] Lass, don't you know me? [*Goes to door L.*]

MARY. [*Astonished*] You?

BRUM. Sh-sh-sh, not too loud. Where is she?

MARY. She is dressing.

BRUM. There's something going on here tonight. Keep your wits about you. Have you discovered anything?

MARY. Nothing.

BRUM. Well, you will tonight. Keep your eye on that portiere—if you see it move signal me at once and I'll stop. I've brought these flowers so as to keep you in sight. I am going to pretend that I have brought the wrong bouquets, so as to come back again with the right ones. Do you understand?

MARY. Yes; you frighten me.

BRUM. Keep your courage up, my little woman. If anything should happen to you tonight in this place and you want to communicate with me— write a line and put it in this small bouquet. I will leave it here and when I come back, I'll get it. Is it perfectly plain to you?

MARY. What can happen to me?

BRUM. Well, not much—if you keep me informed. You haven't found out who made away with that glass?

MARY. No, I have found out nothing, yet.

BRUM. Well, keep your ears open tonight. A girl's instinct is better than a man's reason when she's got a man to save.

MARY. Yes—poor Frank. Has he given himself up yet?

BRUM. Yes—to me. I am responsible for him. [*Mary suddenly looks right at him and starts. Crosses L. Portieres move; Brummage's voice and manner change*] Phat the divil, then, do I care for the trouble. I'd carry the blissed flowers forty toimes to git a look at a pretty gurrl loike yourself, so I would. [*Enter Mrs. Bulford through portiers*]

MRS. B. [*C. up stage*] What's the matter?

BRUM. [*At table*] The divil of anything's the matter save meself who's brought the wrong flowers. Axin' your pardon, I'll have the right ones here before a billy goat cud eat them.

MRS. B. Very well, you may leave the room.

BRUM. [*Taking up large bouquet and leaving small one*] I'll lave that to sweeten your room anyhow. [*Going at door*] But with two such beauties, it's too sweet already for an Oirishman. [*Exit through hall door R.3.*]

MRS. B. [*Looking at flowers at head of table C.*] Who sent the flowers?

MARY. The man was so rude I could not find out and as you heard, he brought the wrong bouquets.

MRS. B. Never mind. Attend the door—I expect Dr. Livingstone. [*Turns down R.*]

MARY. [*Starting*] Dr. Livingstone?

MRS. B. [*Turning quickly*] What's the matter—do you know him?

MARY. No—o. But, are you ill?

MRS. B. No. He calls on business. [*Door bell rings*] There he is now. Show him in here. [*Takes bouquet from table, smells it and places it on side table L. Mary opens hall door R.3; timidly screening herself with it, and Dr. Livingstone enters, walks straight in without perceiving her. He comes down hat and cane in hand; Mary exits door L.*] I am glad you obeyed my summons, doctor. [*Doctor puts hat and cane on table. Mrs. Bulford at sofa L.*]

DR. L. [*Taking off gloves*] Yes, you have summoned me for what?

MRS. B. Will you be seated? [*Indicating chair*]

DR. L. [*Still standing*] Proceed, madam—why have you summoned me?

MRS. B. [*Crosses to sofa end of it L.*] I have a woman's curiosity and I wish to ask you some questions.

DR. L. [*Gravely*] I trust, madam, that you will not occupy my time in gratifying your curiosity.

MRS. B. [*Sits on sofa*] I pray that you will be seated, doctor. [*Indicating chair. Doctor sits easy chair close to Mrs. Bulford*] On the night that Mr. Bulford died, you told me that he died of apoplexy and that you would give me a certificate, but you changed your mind and notified the coroner.

DR. L. You are correct, madam. Proceed!

MRS. B. What I wish to know is, why you changed your mind after leaving my house. [*Dr. Livingstone gets up and walks toward door R.3. and does not immediately reply. Mrs. Bulford goes to the portiere L., looks through, and returns to sofa*] We are entirely alone so you may be confidential. Why did you change your mind after leaving my house? [*Mary appears at L. door listening; Dr. Livingstone sits on sofa L.*]

Dr. L. [*Speaking deliberately*] Madam, I changed my mind because I saw you.

Mrs. B. [*On sofa L.*] Not after you left the house, doctor.

Dr. L. Yes.

Mrs. B. I did not leave the house that night.

Dr. L. [*Looking at her and speaking slowly*] No, but you came to an upper window. [*Mrs. Bulford starts but recovers herself*] You lifted the sash and threw something out. [*Mrs. Bulford clutches arm of sofa involuntarily but smiles and looks the doctor in the eyes*]

Mrs. B. What a curious hallucination. You must have seen my ghost.

Dr. L. Madam, that which you threw out of the window could not well be an hallucination, for I picked it up. It was a cut sherry glass with a monogram on it. It fell upon a heap of rubbish and was unbroken. [*The two look at each other for a moment. Mary, in her eagerness to hear, has pushed herself in at door*]

Mrs. B. This is really interesting. What did you find in the phantom glass, doctor?

Dr. L. A little of the wine adhered to the bottom of the glass.

Mrs. B. And you sent it to the chemist?

Dr. L. That was not necessary—I tested it myself.

Mrs. B. And of course—in all such romances—you found—

Dr. L. Poison.

Mrs. B. [*Still seated on sofa*] But, doctor, of course you didn't know what kind of poison it was?

Dr. L. Fortunately, I am one of the few who are familiar with it. It was the deadly Para poison made only in South America. It was that fact that defied the coroner. [*Mary closes the curtains and disappears*]

Mrs. B. Capital! And what did you say when you made this charming discovery?

Dr. L. I said to myself—a woman will undo the craft of months with the impulse of a moment. [*Rises*] Instead of washing the glass you threw it out of the window. It is by such miscalculations that crime is detected.

Mrs. B. [*Rises*] No, it is by such fairy stories that detection is misdirected.

Dr. L. I scarcely understand you.

Mrs. B. [*Taking a few steps to C. with assumed lightness of manner*] I mean—that a disinterested person hearing your story would say the doctor was a confederate of ghosts and that phantoms threw the glass out to him, especially when he acknowledges he is one of the few persons familiar with the poison. [*Goes and stands by sofa*] Besides, he went away the next day so as not to be present at the inquest. Then too he was, in all probability, on intimate terms with the phantom and may have made her visits extra professionally—just as you are visiting me tonight. [*Crosses to C.*] Doctor.

Dr. L. [*Bitterly*] Madam, you are not only a clever, but an unscrupulous woman.

Mrs. B. But not so clever as you are, doctor, at inventing stories. Let me ask you—have you told this to anyone? [*Dr. Livingstone walks up and down R.*] Try and compose yourself, doctor. Let me beg of you to be seated? [*Sits L. of table C.*]

Dr. L. I was called away early in the morning after Mr. Bulford's death by a professional appointment at Montreal, and have only returned this morning. I have had no opportunity to give it much thought.

Mrs. B. Well, now, doctor, don't you think that in view of your own peace of mind and your future success in New York (I understand you have an eye on the position of health officer of the Port, which is a political gift— I believe), don't you think, doctor, that for your own interests it would be well to abandon these ghost stories and thus save some estimable people from a great deal of annoyance? You are so eminent in your specialty of compounding medicines that it seems a pity to assume the risk of a romancer at your age.

Dr. L. [*Seated R. of table C. After pause—looking at her*] You are right, madam, I have compounded medicines for many years, but I never compounded a felony.

Mrs. B. Now you are angry, doctor; I beg your pardon.

Dr. L. If you had studied faces as long as I have, madam, you would know that what you call anger is only a man's pity.

Mrs. B. Not pity for me, doctor, I hope.

Dr. L. No, madam—pity for an innocent man somewhere who is accused of a crime he never committed.

Mrs. B. But who, if the papers are correct, ran away from the crime?

Dr. L. [*Turning*] But I am informed that he had a friend who has not run away.

Mrs. B. Are you referring to yourself, doctor?

Dr. L. No, I am referring to a woman. So far as I am concerned I have been trained to the rigid performances of two duties—one to my patient. [*Pause*] The other to the public.

Mrs. B. [*Rising*] Then, doctor, I hope that you will always permit me to be your patient. [*Mrs. Bulford goes L. Doctor R.C., watching her*] Doctor, would you mind telling me who is the woman in your fairy story so interested in this matter? [*Doctor is surprised, but does not answer. Mrs. Bulford calls through portiere*] Susanne! I have a morbid desire to meet her. [*The doctor has turned toward audience and does not see her*] You and this woman both know of the phantom glass I suppose?

DR. L. [*Annoyed*] Madam, I have already told you that I just returned to town and have as yet communicated with no one. She therefore could not know it—unless—unless she had been listening to our conversation. Madam, as I can be of no further service to you, I think it would be well for you to change your physician. [*Bows. Mary enters L. Doctor goes to table to take his hat and cane and comes face to face with Mary across table. Doctor starts as he recognizes her. Mary appealingly puts her finger to her lips and signals him not to betray her; all of which Mrs. Bulford sees in the mirror L. and turns quickly in blank dismay to watch them. Doctor hesitates a moment, looks from one to the other, takes his hat and cane and comes down C. With dignity*] Madam, I wish you good evening. [*Mrs. Bulford is speechless and only glares at him. Doctor exits hall door R.3. Mary glides quickly out at R.3. Mrs. Bulford comes down to table in great agitation*]

MRS. B. [*Leaning over table C.*] What does it all mean? Let me think—let me think? They know each other—what were his words? What were his very words? Unless she has heard our conversation. There are two of them who know. I have been spied upon in my own house. Where are my wits—where are my wits. What I do now must be done quickly. Who is this woman? [*Enter Mary R.3.*]

MARY. Madam, the senator.

MRS. B. Ah! [*Mary holds door R.3. Enter Senator McSorker dressed in Prince Albert coat; wears a large diamond; typical well-to-do New York politician*]

SEN. [*Heartily*] Ah—ha—there you are, lovelier than wax. Madam, yours obediently. You look like a four-year-old.

MRS. B. A four-year-old. Do I look childish, senator?

SEN. No, no, no—I mean a horse.

MRS. B. Look like a horse—Heavens, senator.

SEN. I beg your pardon—of course not—of course not. You know what I mean—an angel.

MRS. B. [*Still L. on sofa*] I see, when you say a horse—you mean an angel.

SEN. [*Front of sofa*] What's the matter? You look as though you'd been nominated and withdrawn.

MRS. B. We all have our troubles.

SEN. [*Seating himself in chair*] I'll buy your troubles at your price and carry them around for a pocket piece. What's your price?

MRS. B. [*Coquetting with her foot*] Yes, I dare say a man with your influence could soon end my troubles—if you were sufficiently interested in me.

SEN. [*Seated R. of sofa L., looking at her foot*] Say, that's good. I like that —interested in you—do you want me to get down on my knees like they do in the play? Lock the doors—I'll do it.

MRS. B. No, no—if there is any appealing to be done, I must do it.

SEN. Ha—ha—that's good. Now I particularly like that. You appeal to me? Say—that's rich. What'll you have?

MRS. B. You're a generous man, but I want too much.

SEN. *Name it! Name it!*—put up your scale. If I haven't got it, I'll borrow it.

MRS. B. Ah, what would I have given to have met a man like you earlier in my career—how different my life would have been.

SEN. [*Slapping his knee*] Better late than never. Call off your wants.

MRS. B. You're like all men when you're in a generous mood and would play the lover.

SEN. By Heavens, I would do anything else but play the lover.

MRS. B. I am afraid I want something more than a lover.

SEN. Anything you like—how would slave do?

MRS. B. What I want is a protector.

SEN. All right—I'll protect you from other lovers and I'll begin now. [*Sits down on sofa beside her and puts his arm about her*]

MRS. B. I want protection from powerful enemies. The man that wins my favor must shield me from scandal if he has to stop the law and defy the machinery of justice. Are you able to do that?

SEN. [*Attempting to rise*] Ain't you drawin'—a—it a little strong?

MRS. B. [*Attempting to rise*] I see—your power and your devotion are not boundless!

SEN. [*Pulling her back*] Don't go off that way—I'm yours. Do you want me to start something—or stop something?

MRS. B. I want something stopped. That dreadful affair of Mr. Bulford's.

SEN. But you didn't have anything to do with it.

MRS. B. [*Snatching his hands*] I don't want anything to do with it—that's the point. I have enemies who hope to drag me into court.

SEN. Look here—I'm gone to pieces on you—see? I don't know what you want me to do, but I'll do it if you don't play me.

MRS. B. I want you to stand between me and my personal enemies when the time comes, no matter who they may be, you will crush them with all the influence and power that your position gives you. Now do you know?

SEN. [*Fondling her*] It's a go. I'll show you how we handle these things in New York. [*Seizes her hand*]

MRS. B. You are hurting my hand, senator—I have a sharp ring on it.

SEN. [*Looking at ring*] Gee—willikens—where did you get that blazer? You must have been. in politics yourself. I've carried the district attorney's office in one pocket and the Central Office in the other, but I never had a stone like that on my finger. [*Mrs. Bulford pulls her hand away quickly*]

MRS. B. Senator, I'm going away in the morning to a quiet place in the country.

SEN. [*Rising*] Going away! Oh, come now, you can't do that. Damn it—I beg your pardon. I've made all arrangements. [*Sits on sofa again*]

MRS. B. Arrangements for me?

SEN. Now see here, I told you tomorrow is election day and if things go right, I'm going to give the boys a blow-out at my house on Madison Avenue and I want you to be there.

MRS. B. Oh, but senator, I should dislike to appear in public at this time.

SEN. 'Tain't in public—it's my private house. I'm going to give a banner to the Fourteenth and I wanted you to give it away. I made all calculations.

MRS. B. Who will be there?

SEN. Only my friends, the politicians, and they're your friends. See? And you have to stand in with them. You needn't come till late. I'll take you away as soon as it's over.

MRS. B. You don't have to announce me by name?

SEN. No—we'll call you the glittering Goddess of Liberty—anything you like. I'll waltz you through and take care of you. That's the way to see whether I can protect you or not.

MRS. B. [*Rising*] I suppose I must earn my protection by obeying you. [*Enter Marino hurriedly from L.*]

MAR. How-de do, senator. [*To Mrs. Bulford*] Was Dr. Livingstone here half an hour ago?

MRS. B. Yes, yes. What's the matter? [*L.C. senator L.; goes round sofa up L. to C.*]

MAR. He is killed! A fire truck run into his carriage on the Avenue and threw him out on his head. I happened to pass at the time and the ambulance attendant, who had the doctor's book, said that his last call was here. [*Mrs. Bulford clasps her hands and shivers*]

MRS. B. Dead!

Mar. What's the matter?

Mrs. B. [*Laughing hysterically*] Nothing—it is so sudden. Give me a glass of water—dead—then there is but one.

Sen. [*To Marino, coming down C.*] Young man, go and sit down. [*Takes Mrs. Bulford over to sofa*]

Mrs. B. Gentlemen, I shall have to ask you to leave me. You have undone me for the moment. [*Sits on sofa L.*]

Sen. Don't forget tomorrow night, dear. Get yourself in your best— good-bye. [*Goes to door R.3.*] Young man, you're too damn sudden! [*Exit R.3.*]

Mrs. B. Come here and sit down.

Mar. [*Sits on sofa*]   What is agitating you so? You don't usually take on in this way.

Mrs. B. Did you send the message to the old woman, that I gave you?

Mar. Yes, I did.

Mrs. B. I must have some money and I have a few jewels that she will pay me a better price for than any one else. Is she coming?

Mar. Yes, but I don't want to see her.

Mrs. B. No, I will spare you this humiliating business, but I must have some money. You know more about this woman than I do.

Mar. I know too much about her to have her name linked with yours.

Mrs. B. Did you understand that she is the woman who hates Don Plon?

Mar. Yes, he is said to have betrayed her son who was executed. What are you asking me this for, now?

Mrs. B. [*Sotto voce*] And she has threatened to be revenged?

Mar. Yes. What has got into your head?

Mrs. B. That is all. I wanted to be sure I had not dreamed it.

Mar. [*Rises*] You look as if you had a fever and a bad dream. If I were you I'd go and lie down before she comes. [*Bell heard*] There she is now. I'm going to skip. [*Music. Enter Mary R.3.*]

Mary. Madam, a lady in black—she would not give her name.

Mrs. B. Let her in. [*To Marino*] You must be at the senator's house to-morrow night, I may need you.

Mar. [*Going*] Yes, but I don't like the crowd—I'm not a politician. [*Exit Marino L. door. Enter Mother Rosenbaum R.3; she advances to C.*]

Ros. [*Down to C.*] Ah, madam, you will not come to see me in my little store, so I must come to you, when you have something to sell.

Mrs. B. [*Fastening back the portiere*] Sit down, madam. I did think of selling my few family jewels, but I have changed my mind as I am going to remain in the city. [*Both seated on sofa*]

Ros. You have not many diamonds? Ah, madam, you are too modest. I think you have the finest jewels in America.

Mrs. B. [*Sits in chair next sofa*] What makes you think so? I am not a rich woman.

Ros. Ah, it is not the rich woman who has the most diamonds.

Mrs. B. I have a few jewels that were presents—

Ros. [*Interrupting*] They were presents to you—heh?

Mrs. B. I said—presents, but I have concluded to keep them.

Ros. Are they diamonds?

Mrs. B. Yes, but of no great value.

Ros. Have you not a ruby?

Mrs. B. [*Face to her in chair by sofa*] Now if we are to do any business, let me beg of you to be at least respectful.

Ros. Respectful, madam? I very much respect the woman who has a ruby and a large ruby—what you call—u-m. Mein Gott, woman, I could not, at my time of life, ask where people get things.

Mrs. B. You are affected with the same suspicion that besets other people, and that is that I have the Garbiadoff jewels. You and your friend Plon are both of one mind. I sent for you to get you to help me against his plot.

Ros. The dog! You say Plon is my friend and he and I are of the one mind? Oh, madam, do not say that again, or you will make me your enemy for life. Plon—the hound! It was he who made my poor and only boy suffer. The dog! I wish I had my fingers on his throat.

Mrs. B. The miscreant has a woman whom he employs to obtain his plunder.

Ros. Yes, yes—I know, I know.

Mrs. B. [*Seated R. of her*] She is here in my house. She obtained service as a maid. I caught her tonight telegraphing to a visitor. She has been eavesdropping here for a week.

Ros. [*Eagerly*] Where is she now?

Mrs. B. She is at the other end of that passage and she cannot approach without my seeing her. [*Rises and crosses to end of sofa L.*]

Ros. [*Going up and down. Hesitates, then eagerly*] How do you know that she is Plon's woman? [*Down by sofa R. of it*]

Mrs. B. [*Hesitating*] Because I discovered a letter from him in her room.

Ros. [*Viciously*] Ah—the sweet little creature—give her to me.

Mrs. B. How can you take her?

Ros. I will not take her—she will go herself—just as gently—you shall see. What is she here for? Is she not looking for the diamonds?

Mrs. B. Yes, yes—well?

Ros. Will she not know that I come to buy the diamonds—anybody can tell by my poor dress that I buy diamonds—I do not wear them. You shall tell her to go in my carriage and bring the diamonds here from my place. She will think they are the Garbiadoff's and to get them in her hands, she will be so eager she will go. [*Viciously*] But she will come away not again.

Mrs. B. But I cannot consent to any step that will imperil my character.

Ros. Gott in Himmel. If I did not respect your character, I would not be seen in your house. I have a character myself.

Mrs. B. But my friends—Senator McSorker.

Ros. If you did not have Senator McSorker for your friend then would I not do it? Of course you will marry the senator.

Mrs. B. Marry the senator?

Ros. Aye. Aye. You will marry the senator. You will go to his party to-morrow night. You will put on all your jewels and your fine dresses and when he sees you come down the staircase, he will think you came down from Heaven, like the angel you are. Now if you do not fix the senator to-morrow night, not even Rosenbaum can save you. Now let me see the jewels —the diamonds.

Mrs. B. Let you see the jewels? What for?

Ros. What for? Mein Gott! Woman, do you think I make a bargain with a cat in a bag?

Mrs. B. You are a queer creature. You are erratic.

Ros. Am I? Well, I see, I see, Rosenbaum cannot do any straight business with madam—so I'd better go. [*Starts to rise*]

Mrs. B. Stop! Sit down.

Ros. Well, I sit! Well?

Mrs. B. I cannot lay hands on the jewels at the present moment—

Ros. Yes, you can.

Mrs. B. How?

Ros. Because they are here.

Mrs. B. Here? Where?

Ros. On your person. Get them out. To save you I must see the jewels. [*Mrs. Bulford goes to portieres, pulls curtains together, then goes to chair L. of table, takes up cloth with back to audience at C. table in front of it, and pretends to take jewels out of her bosom—then goes down L. of Rosenbaum, who is on sofa. Mrs. Bulford sits, unwraps cloth. While Mrs. Bulford is at table*] I always thought she killed old Bulford, and now I know it. [*Mrs. Bulford goes down to Rosenbaum. Examining jewels*] Now shut them up. [*Mrs. Bulford rises, goes to C. table. Business*] And now let me see Plon's woman. You shall send her in my coach to my house on an errand.

MRS. B. *Very well!* [*Goes to portiere and calls*] Susanne! Susanne! [*To sofa*] Be careful, or she will suspect. [*Enter Mary L.*]

MARY. [*Down C.*] Yes, madam.

MRS. B. Susanne, pay attention. I have some jewels which this lady took to her house to sell for me, but as I have changed my mind, I want to get them back again. Can you get in this lady's coach—go to her house and bring me the jewels?

MARY. Yes, madam. [*Aside*] Heavens—the jewels! [*Direct*] Do you wish me to go now? [*Mrs. Bulford at back of sofa*]

ROS. [*Seated on sofa L.*] Right away, my dear. What a beautiful child you are. You must be careful and come right back—heh—while I wait here for you.

MARY. Yes, madam.

ROS. Come here, my child. [*Mary crosses to head of sofa, Mrs. Bulford crosses to C.*]

ROS. [*Taking her hand*] What a beautiful hand! [*To Mrs. Bulford*] Madam, it is not right to send a child on such an errand—I will go myself.

MARY. [*Nervously*] I can do it, madam.

MRS. B. There is no danger that I can see. Give her a note—she will get the package and come straight back. I would not have her take any risks. [*To Mary*] Go bring paper and pencil, Susanne. [*Exit Mary at L.*]

ROS. [*Clutching Mrs. Bulford by the arm*] I will save you, but how will you save me?

MRS. B. Save you—what do you mean?

ROS. Mein Gott! Woman, do you think I save people for the amusement?

MRS. B. [*In chair next to sofa*] What do you want?

ROS. [*With her face close to Mrs. Bulford and with hissing intensity*] I want the "Heart of Fire."

MRS. B. [*Rises and suddenly with dignity*] Why?

ROS. If we cannot understand each other, then what for do I come here? Do you think I have no heart? I have, my dear, I cannot take a young lady from such a nice home—it is too cruel. [*Sits again on sofa*]

MRS. B. I must have my jewels to wear tomorrow night at the senator's. The day after I will talk to you. Can you trust me?

ROS. I do not have to trust you when I have the young woman. [*Enter Mary at portieres with paper; place it on side table front L.; crosses to C. table and takes bouquet from table and goes to buffet with it where she is seen by audience putting a folded paper into the bunch of flowers, which she places on table while Rosenbaum is writing on side table. Mrs. Bulford is watching Rosenbaum*]

MARY. [*At C. table, aside*] If anything happens to me he said he would get this.

Ros. Come here, my dear. [*Gives note to Mary who comes down*]

MRS. B. [*Behind Rosenbaum without turning around*] Do be careful of yourself, my child.

Ros. [*Rising and crossing to Mary*] I will tell my coachman to be very careful of her and bring her right back. [*Exit R.3. Rosenbaum and Mary. Mrs. Bulford watches them off nervously and the moment they disappear, she jumps up and walks stage to C. Enter Marino from L.—the two face each other*]

MRS. B. You! Why have you come back?

MAR. Did Susanne go out? [*Goes toward portiere*]

MRS. B. [*Quickly*] Yes, why?

MAR. I wish to speak to her.

MRS. B. [*Controlling herself*] Try and behave yourself in my room— what do you want of Susanne?

MAR. [*Going up a little*] Do you know who she is?

MRS. B. What do you mean?

MAR. I have been thinking of her a great deal. She may know something of the murderer of Mr. Bulford.

MRS. B. [*Sotto voce*] Yes, she may.

MAR. [*Catching Mrs. Bulford by the arm impressively*] Maria, are you sure that when you returned to the room that night the jewels were gone?

MRS. B. What are you talking about? Have you lost your wits?

MAR. Where is the girl? [*Enter Rosenbaum at R.3.*]

MRS. B. [*Hesitating and looking at Rosenbaum*] She is gone.

MAR. [*Astonished*] Gone where?

MRS. B. [*Impressively*] I do not know. [*Walks rapidly*]

MAR. [*Excitedly*] But I will know. [*Rosenbaum and Mrs. Bulford to front L. together*] I am going to find the murderer of Mr. Bulford. [*Marino takes bouquet from table and mechanically sniffs it as he walks. Enter Dick Brummage from R.3. with flowers*]

BRUM. Oi've brought ye the right flowers. [*Looks at bouquet in Marino's hand disconcertedly*] And Oi'd thank you to give me that one.

MAR. [*Walking, carelessly*] Oh, I'll keep this one—I like it. Leave the room.

BRUM. [*With comical distress*] Shure you wouldn't have a man lose his place, by lavin' the flowers wid ye that belonged to some one else.

Mrs. B.   Oh, give him the flowers and let him go. [*Marino throws bouquet to Brummage, who seizes it eagerly and goes to door behind screen, faces audience, looking into bouquet for paper. Marino continues walking*]

Ros. [*To Mrs. Bulford*]   You will bring me the "Heart of Fire" on Thursday.

Mrs. B. [*To Rosenbaum*]   You are sure that when she left this house, she could communicate with no one?

Ros.   Ah, when she go away from here, no one shall ever know one word from her. [*Brummage pulls Mary's note from bouquet deliberately, putting it in his pocket*]

ACT IV.

Scene: *Hoffman House Café. The set represents the room as if seen from Twenty-fourth Street. Square bar in C. with fixtures; barkeeper dealing liquors. Groups ad lib. Large frame of Bouguereau's Nymphs seen in profile L.C. lit from above. Statuary, plants, etc., and six tables arranged at equal distances in front and up R. Time: Eight o'clock in the evening. Brummage seated at table L. Enter countryman L.C., comes down slowly and stops in front of picture. His attention is fixed. He is amazed—looks intently, looks furtively away and looks back at the picture in the same way. Enter Mrs. O'Geogan looking at picture and then to Marino who is at the bar.*

Mrs. O'G.   Is Senator McSorker here? I came here to find him.

Mar.   No, I have not seen him.

Mrs. O'G. [*Looking at picture aghast, pointing to it*]   What's them?

Mar.   What do you mean, the picture?

Mrs. O'G.   *Yes.*

Mar.   The picture is called the Nymphs and the Satyr.

Mrs. O'G.   Please say that agin to me, I didn't catch it.

Mar.   The Nymphs and the Satyr.

Mrs. O'G.   That's a funny name for them women. Why they ain't got no clothes on. Why don't they put some dresses on them?

Mar.   They are painted natural.

Mrs. O'G.   Yes, they's mighty natural. There is no mistake about that. It ought not to be allowed. It is sinful. [*Pauses*] But they are daisies you bet.

Mar.   Why do you look at them, if it be sinful? [*Crosses down below*]

Mrs. O'G.   I can't help it, they fetches me so. Them gals is peaches, ain't they? Why, I can't just take my eyes off them. Natur is natur, and I'm just as natural. Air you still hungering for the flesh pots of Egypt? If you see the senator tell him his old friend Mrs. O.'G. is looking for him. Good-bye. [*She *and Marino exit L.2. Enter Count Garbiadoff R.; he comes down front. Dick Brummage, who has been seated at table L. since rise, sees count and approaches him*]

BRUM. Well, Count Garbiadoff, you are, I observe, taking in all the sights of the city.

COUNT. [*Surprised*]   Who are you?

BRUM. [*Opening coat and showing badge*]   Detective Brummage. We met at the Central Office today.

COUNT. Oh, yes. I remember now. Haf you tell me something?

BRUM. Yes. Sit down. [*They sit L.*]

COUNT. What is it, speak. I am anxious to hear.

BRUM. Could you identify your diamonds if you saw them?

COUNT. Every stone.

BRUM. Even if on the person of the woman we suspect and at night?

COUNT. Yes, under any circumstances.

BRUM. The politician under whose protection this woman is, gives a party at his home, No. 1360 Madison Avenue. You must be there.

COUNT. What for?

BRUM. The woman will be there, and I think will wear your diamonds.

COUNT. Wear my diamonds? The audacity—it is not possible!

BRUM. I think she will wear them. A woman's vanity is always greater than her caution. She does not believe that anybody can identify them, and as she does not know the Count Garbiadoff is here. Be careful, remember you are sent there only to see them.

COUNT. Oui. I came all the way from Cracow to see them and to see her. [*Aside*] I will tear them from her—the pitiless wretch.

BRUM. Let me warn you not to be rash. If you can identify your jewels on her it will be all we can do tonight. If you are not prudent you may ruin us both, and destroy all chances of recovering the property.

COUNT. Mon dieu! Do you tell me I shall take only ze look and go back to Cracow with vat you call ze tail between ze legs? Pah! You shall call the gendarmes.

BRUM. Everything will be gained for the courts if you can identify the woman and the jewels. That is enough. Everything else would be madness. You do not understand this politician's power.

COUNT. Canaille, I do not understand.

BRUM. Calm yourself and meet me at the senator's tonight. Any cabman will carry you there.

COUNT. The entrée? How will I get that?

BRUM. Walk boldly in. The company will be so mixed that the senator will not know his guests and you will not be recognized. Now we had better say good-bye for the present, as I have other work to do.

COUNT. Au revoir. [*Exit door off R. at back. Brummage waves his hand and sits L. reading paper. Enter senator L.2., followed by Marino, Clancy, Brannigan and others. He is greeted cordially by several as he comes on to front of bar*]

SEN. Well, well, boys, as I was telling you, I have always depended on the Fourteenth. She deserves the banner and tonight she gets it—see? The handsomest woman in New York, my friend Mrs. Bulford, will make the presentation. Gentlemen, Mr. Marino, her brother. He is going in politics. [*To bartender*] Set 'em up, councillor. [*The two heelers shake Marino's hand, boisterously*]

CLAN. There's nothing the matter wid the Fourteenth. She gits the banner, dat's all right; and I get me brudder out of Sing Sing, eh, senator?

SEN. You bet. Have some cigars. [*Business with cigars. First heeler takes a handful from the box and puts them in his coat pocket, conversation in dumb show*]

BRAN. Ah, what d'ye know about the Fourteenth? You was brought up in de Sixth.

CLAN. De men in de Sixth learned the trade of votin' before de Fourteenth was made.

BRAN. Ah, de Fourteenth don't depend on no votin' when dey can do de countin'. What's de Fourteenth care for voters when dey got de inspectors?

COUNT. I am very anxious to learn the political methods of New York, but I don't know at present what I am to do to help on the glorious cause.

BRAN. Well, you kin do the drinkin' can't yer, like the rest of us?

CLAN. Ah—what does the Sixth know about drinkin'? [*Sheeney Ike appears L. coming down R., stops at corner of bar L. and tries to catch the senator's eye. Brummage moves so as to see Sheeney Ike over his paper*]

SEN. [*Laughing*] You'll have to take my friend down in the Sixth and show him the ropes. [*Sees Sheeney Ike*] Excuse me a minute, gentlemen. [*Goes to corner of bar, conversation of heelers continues in dumb show*] Are you looking for me?

IKE. Yes, Mother Rosenbaum sent me up from Canal Street.

SEN. What's the matter with her now?

IKE. She says there's a special from the Central Office a workin' the Bulford lay.

SEN. Well, it's none of his business. I'm takin' care of that. Tell the old woman to brace up. What's she got to do with it anyhow?

IKE. She says they're a tryin' to fix it on the widder—Mrs. Bulford.

SEN. Oh, they are, are they? Well, it don't go, because I'm lookin' out for the widder, and he can't work no lay there for I'll call him down. I've got a party at my house tonight—going to have Mrs. Bulford present the banner to the Fourteenth. You tell the old woman to rest easy in her mind—I will see her tomorrow—they can't work no lay without me. You bet. [*Marino going. Senator and Ike's dialogue continues in dumb show. While this conversation has been going on, the two heelers have got into violent altercation in dumb show which Marino absurdly tries to prevent, and both rush to senator for a decision, coming to the corner of bar L. and opposite table where Brummage sits*]

BRAN. [*With great excitement*] Well, I'm bettin' me pile on it. [*Pulls an enormous roll of bills from his hip pocket and slaps the roll down violently on table. First heeler pulls a still larger roll from pocket and imitates defiantly*]

CLAN. Say, your money was born deaf and dumb. Here's the money what talks. [*Brummage gets up, disgustedly holding paper. Business continues between heelers in dumb show, Marino showing absurd anxiety and astonishment, senator leaning against bar and laughing at them. Senator and Ike move away from heelers*]

SEN. [*To Ike*] Who's the officer that's meddlin' in this matter?

IKE. She says it's Brummage.

SEN. Well I'll break him tomorrow, see? Have a drink, have some wine? [*Heelers coming promptly to bar again. At this moment great shouting is heard in the office and a crowd of Princeton and Yale boys shouting college cries and waving flags, singing songs, come crowding into room. Everybody yells, scenes of confusion, students cluster around the bar or sit at tables and pound bells ordering drinks. Senator and his friends form a group at bottom of bar, drinking and looking amusedly at boys. Frank is seen coming on at back mingling with the crowd. The moment he is well on, Brummage spies him and rushing across to him, takes him well R. and in a low voice but excitedly, says*]

BRUM. My God, what are you doing here? I told you not to leave the house.

FRANK. I know, I know. But I couldn't stand the suspense any longer. So I came here hoping to see you, and hear something of Mary and my own fate.

BRUM. Well, I have something to say to you, and not much time to say it in.

FRANK. Where is Mary?

BRUM. Don't look around—we may be watched. Mary's kidnapped.

FRANK. My God, then what are you doing here? [*Ike's attention is attracted by Frank's manner*]

BRUM. Do you want to tell everybody in the place what we are talking about?

FRANK. [*Dropping back in his chair*] Kidnapped on my account and I am helpless!

BRUM. I respect your feelings, but just now they are damned risky, for we've got work to do.

FRANK. Why don't you tell me—where have they taken her? Who are the miscreants?

BRUM. Well, don't shout—I'm trying to find out. I've got a letter from the girl. If you'll keep quiet I'll show it to you. [*Produces note that he took from bouquet. Subdued laughter in bar, rear. Brummage and Frank listen a moment. Brummage then hands Mary's note to Frank*]

FRANK. [*Reading with difficulty*] "I am going to Madam Rosenbaum's to fetch the diamonds to Mrs. Bulford—don't know where. I am suspicious and nervous. I depend on you if anything happens to me." [*Direct*] What Madam Rosenbaum, where has she gone?

BRUM. There's only one old woman in New York that's likely to be mixed up in this, and she's a desperate character protected by the politicians and rolling in ill-gotten wealth. She has never hesitated at murder when it served her ends, for she goes to that senator there for protection. There stands the senator and there's the old hag's man talking to him.

FRANK. [*With gesture of impatience*] My God! What iniquity!

BRUM. Well, don't telegraph it. It must occur to you that in any case they wouldn't send the girl to fetch the diamonds and if they made her believe it, it was to trap her.

FRANK. Go on—you've got the knife into me—turn it around. Is there no living show for innocence in this city?

BRUM. Well, there is if you've got patience, and if you've got your facts right. But there's something else on that paper I couldn't make out. [*Frank looks at paper*]

FRANK. Yes, there's something else, but it's rubbed. [*Holds paper to light*] Oh, yes. It says "I know all about the glass." What does that mean?

BRUM. [*Starting*] Does it say that? [*Snatches paper and looks at it*]

FRANK. What does it mean?

BRUM. It means that she knows something and they've tried to make away with her.

FRANK. For God's sake, tell me what you're going to do.

BRUM. I'm going to get the information tonight. Tomorrow it will be too late. They are celebrating that politician's power now. Tomorrow he will stand between us and justice.

FRANK. We are wasting time—it may be too late now.

BRUM. Try and be cool and listen to me. The only way to save her is to get that information. [*Ike leaves senator and comes slowly and guardedly toward picture back of table where Brummage and Frank are sitting. Senator goes up R. to other groups*]

FRANK. Very well, man, let's be quick about it.

BRUM. The old woman has two places—one in Rivington Street—that's her store. The other in Canal Street near the river. That's her den. We've got to get in those two places tonight. If we only see Mary for a moment and get that information. [*Brummage and Frank have their heads down intent on the subject and Ike goes past them trying to listen just as Brummage has uttered the last speech*]

FRANK. Yes, yes.

BRUM. I am going to one place and I want you to go to the other. You can do just what I tell you. I'll write the number of the place in Canal Street on this card. [*Writes on card*] And on this side of it—[*Turns card over*] I'll give you a line to the patrolman on the beat. He will know it and will keep his eye on you. [*Hands card*] I will go to the other place. If the girl isn't there, I will be in Canal Street almost as soon as you are. We may not save the girl, but we may get the information that will save you. [*Ike is approaching the table and trying to listen*]

FRANK. I will not be saved at such a sacrifice.

BRUM. Never mind the rescue. See the girl—[*Brummage stops suddenly and eyes Ike fixedly. The latter seemingly does not turn his head—cowed by Brummage's gaze slinks off hurriedly at back*]

FRANK. Well—well—why do you stop? You wanted me to go to Canal Street to this old woman—

BRUM. But I don't want you to tell it to that ruffian who has just passed us. [*Marino, who has been intently watching all this, goes to senator and points to Brummage and Frank. Senator starts and looks in their direction*]

BRUM. Wait a moment. Is that sheeney still there?

FRANK. No. He has gone, but the senator is watching us closely. Does he suspect?

BRUM. Yes, very likely. We have got to act quickly. The girl, if you can get to her, will tell you all, and if you can get away with the information, we will hang the right person.

MAR. [*Motioning his head in direction of Brummage*] Senator, there's your friend the detective, I am sure.

SEN. [*Astonished*] Brummage?

MAR. Yes, and the young fellow with him is startlingly like that young fellow Kennet I saw that fatal night at Mr. Bulford's.

SEN. You don't mean it! He would never dare—

MAR. 'Tis he. I would swear it.

SEN. [*Amazed*] I'll make a bluff and have him taken and spoil Brummage's game whatever it is. [*Senator beckons to Clancy and Brannigan. They join him. Senator talks to them in dumb show. They shake their heads knowingly and affirmatively. Frank and Brummage rise—they start towards door L.2.*]

SEN. Hold on! Both of you! Don't be in a hurry. I want you, see?

BRUM. Are you talking to me, sir?

SEN. Well, I am talking straight at you. See. I am on to you!

BRUM. Sir?

SEN. Oh, "sir" don't go, I won't have any frills. You are meddlin' in something that's my business. [*Tapping his breast*] And I'm going to call you down right here.

BRUM. You are drunk, sir, and I have no time to waste with you. [*Senator gets squarely in front of him*]

SEN. You're a liar. What are you doing? Where are you going?

BRUM. I am going out of that door.

SEN. Not yet, you ain't. You are going to stay here where my eye is on you.

BRUM. I am going. [*Slowly*]

SEN. And I am going to stop you.

BRUM. Oh, no. Remember you can't stop me tonight. You may tomorrow. [*Music till curtain*]

SEN. I'll stop both of you now. That man there with you is a murderer. [*Frank shudders*] And I am going to have him taken in. [*Motioning head toward Brannigan and Clancy. Brummage looks over his shoulder cynically at them*]

BRUM. Touch him if you dare. He is in my charge, by order of the superintendent, and while there, no man can arrest him. I represent the law, and don't you dare to put your hands on him.

SEN. Not a step shall he move until I get an officer. Patsy, Shorty seize him. [*Patsy and Shorty start to seize Frank; Brummage puts himself between them and Frank, one hand behind him on his pistol, the other on Frank, making picture*]

BRUM. Stop! I'll make daylight shine through the man who puts a finger on him.

SEN. [*As if to draw pistol*] You dog, I'll make an end of you here, and now, and I'll take in that murderer.

BRUM. *Draw!* I dare you. I am prepared for that. I am doing my duty and I shall protect this man unless you kill me. [*Places himself between senator and his men, shielding Frank completely. Senator and his men make picture standing at bay*]

SEN. Damn you—if I didn't have a party on my hands tonight, I'd have the buttons pulled off of you—you infernal hound.

BRUM. [*With intensity and deliberation*] Your party will be over by midnight; I'll report to you at twelve o'clock. [*Goes to door L.2.*] You'll have your friends around you. That hour will be yours—till then the hours are mine. [*Arm about Frank, pistol in hand, forcing way through crowd L.C. They give way in fright*]

CURTAIN

ACT V.

SCENE: *Canal Street. Exterior of Mother Rosenbaum's house, front scene. Old fashioned house, brick with green blinds. Alley in drop with practicable door. One practical window. Music for rise until curtain is well up.* TIME: *Nine o'clock at night.* AT RISE: *Old man playing harmonica. Peggy Daly dancing to his music. Four boys looking on; they have shinny sticks; clapping hands and keeping time with their feet. Enter Jimmy McCune with girl on his arm. She is leading a dog. He wears a silk hat and the girl carries a satchel.*

PEG. [*L.*] Where are you goin', Jimmy McCune, with your consort? How's yer sore eyes?

McC. Don't you gull me, Peggy Daly. Here, take me dorg into the alley. I am going down to Lumpy Kidney's.

PEG. Dere ain't no free lunch at Lumpy's today. [*Exit L.1. with dog. While they are talking, one of the boys snatches the satchel; Jimmy makes a dash at him, his hat falls off. Immediately the boys begin playing shinny noisily with it, two on a side. Peggy reappears from the alley and finally rescues the hat and gives it to Jimmy*]

McC. I'll make the old woman pay for that. Tell her I'm down to Lumpy Kidney's. [*Exit L.1. with companion. As he goes off there is a sound of rushing wheels and a gong. Boys all strike listening attitude and boy No. 1 shouts*]

BOY No. 1. Hi, fellers, there's a fire!

Boys. Fire! Fire! [*Exit hurriedly L.I., followed by Peggy. At the same time Sheeney Ike comes on R.I., goes to entrance of brick house. The blinds of practicable window open cautiously and Mother Rosenbaum's head appears with shawl thrown around it. Noise stops here*]

Ike. Is that you?

Ros. Yes, what's the matter?

Ike. [*Looking guardedly around*] There's something up. I just came from the Hoffman House.

Ros. Is the senator all right?

Ike. He's all right. Where's the gal?

Ros. I've got her here—she's all safe.

Ike. They are coming for her.

Ros. Who's coming?

Ike. A young fellah's coming down here fer to get word from her. I got onto it straight in the Hoffman House by listenin'. He's to spot the cop on his beat who's a goin' to look out for him.

Ros. Who's the nice young gentleman who's a comin' to visit the old woman?

Ike. [*R. of window*] I think it was Brummage was puttin' him up. But I steered the senator onto Brummage, and he'll take care of him. What we've got to look after, is the other one.

Ros. And the other one is coming to the pleceman on this beat?

Ike. That's the way I heard it.

Ros. And if he don't see the pleceman and comes in—

Ike. Then they'll never know he come.

Ros. Quick—where's Peggy?

Ike. There she comes—she's been down to Lumpy Kidney's. [*Pointing to L.I. Enter Peggy L.I.*]

Ros. Come here to me and mind what I tell you. [*Peggy to window*] Where's Jimmy McCune?

Peg. He's down to Lumpy's now. [*Takes a dancing step and hums*]

Ros. Stop that! Go back there and tell him to put on the cop's dress and lay for the young man what's a comin' here. Be quick about it. He's to steer this young man in here and not let the regular cop see him. Do you understand? Here's the shield—the coat's in the saloon. [*Hands out shield*] Tell him to keep out of the patrolman's sight. Go on now and if you make a mistake I'll skin you! [*Exit Peggy L.I. dancing. To Ike*] Go up to Cahill's saloon and tell the boys to keep the regular patrolman there till this is over. Here's the money. [*Gives money*] Buy whiskey, will you—no wine. Go on and come back here—I want you. We will give my young friend a chance to see [*Music till she closes window*] the old woman at her best. [*Ike takes money and hurriedly exits R.1. Rosenbaum looks up and down and then closes the shutters. Enter Peggy L.1., crosses to R. and exits through door. Enter Frank Kennet, R.1., looks about him*]

FRANK.   This must be the place. I wonder if Mary is in that dismal hole—and I am the cause of her misfortune. My God! She may be dead before this. [*Walks L. and looks about*] I wonder where I'll find the patrolman. [*Looks off L.*] Thank Heaven, here he comes. [*Music tremolo till change of scene. Enter McCune, L.1., disguised as policeman. He walks guardedly along drop. Frank advances*] Are you the officer on this beat? [*McCune assents inarticulately*] There's a card for you. [*Gives card*] I want to find Mother Rosenbaum's.

McC. [*Pointing to the house*]   You are right on top of it, see!

FRANK.   Do you understand this card? You are to keep your eye on the place if I get inside.

McC.   All right, I won't let go o' you, see!

FRANK.   If I do not come out in twenty minutes—

McC.   I'll fetch you. See? This is the way. Here, and I'll introduce you meself. See. [*Exit McCune followed by Frank through door. Dark change*]

SCENE 2: *Mother Rosenbaum's den. A large stone room in a cellar with one exit up a practicable swinging steps, C. of rear wall, with practicable door at top cut across in C., about eight feet up. On L. of room is a door to closet or dark room. Room is lit by iron grating. Small pine table extreme L. front, on which is a butcher's knife. Two wooden chairs at table. At extreme R. is a trap in 2. closed.* DISCOVERED: *Mother Rosenbaum seated at table L. Sheeney Ike and Peggy Daly half way down steps. Lights down.*

PEG. [*On steps*]   He's got the man—they're comin' in.

Ros. [*Seated at table, screaming*]   Go back to the front window and keep your eye out. [*Girl stands irresolute a moment. Mother Rosenbaum throws knife at her viciously and crosses a little to C. Peggy runs up steps and exits. Sheeney Ike picks up knife*]

IKE. [*R.C. crosses to Mother Rosenbaum*]   You'd better let me keep it. You'll have it into somebody while this fit's on.

Ros. [*Screaming*]   I'll have it into you if you don't mind your business. Give it to me. [*She clutches the knife and goes to table L. Ike shrugs his shoulders and relinquishes it*] Open that door. [*Pointing to door, L.*] I put some ointment on me beauty's head, and I want to see her. [*Comes to C. Ike unlocks door and opens it, pulls Mary out roughly. She is poorly dressed, has her head bound up and is terrified*]

MARY. [*Crosses to C., shrinking*] Do not kill me.

ROS. [*Striking knife on table*] Kill you, eh? Yes, I kill you easy enough. But first tell me who made you play the spy—who is he, eh? [*Seated at table L.*]

MARY. [*C.*] Let me go. I do not wish to play the spy. I am a helpless girl. [*Looks about piteously*]

ROS. [*Seated at table L., contemptuously*] Yes, you are a helpless girl. You have some friends, eh? Mebbe they come here and help you. [*Laughs bitterly*] Who put you up to this? You tell me who it is or maybe I cut it out of you this time. [*Viciously. Business with knife*]

MARY. You are mistaken. I do not know you. You brought me here yourself.

ROS. You lie! You were looking for the diamonds. You play the maid, eh? You shall play the maid for me. [*Rises and crosses to Mary advancing upon her*] You shall dress my hair. [*Clutching fingers*] No, I will dress your beautiful hair. You have a friend who comes to see you. I will show you what I will do to your friend. [*Mary shrinks terrified, Ike coming down and throwing Mary to R.*]

IKE. Oh, don't tear the girl to pieces. We've got enough to attend to without this.

ROS. [*R.C., swinging Ike, L.*] Don't you interfere—maybe I tear you to pieces.

IKE. [*Stepping back*] Oh, well I ain't murdering girls. You'll have the whole Central Office swarming over us.

ROS. [*Defiantly*] What does Rosenbaum care for the Central Office, you sneaking coward? If it was not for Rosenbaum you would be hanged long ago. It is Rosenbaum who has defended and released you when they had the rope on your neck, because you did what I told you. When you change your mind—pif! away you go. [*Goes up and turns*] You think Rosenbaum has no heart. Yes, you are right because it was torn out of my bosom when they killed my beautiful boy. I have lived with no heart waiting for Plon and his woman. I have laughed at the police and have bought the judges with my stolen money. And now when at last there comes to me Plon's woman, you think I will get my heart back again. Ha—ha—! you shall tear to pieces what I like. You shall do what Rosenbaum tells you or go like Red Leary and Scotty Jack. When you do not what I want you shall hang. [*Goes up, music*]

IKE. [*Astonished*] Plon's woman! Here? Why didn't you say so before. [*Crosses and seizes Mary. Crosses with her to door L. Half door at head of stairs opens and Jimmy McCune in policeman's uniform puts his head in and looks down. All start*]

Ros. Put her back there. [*Pointing to L. Ike seizes Mary and crosses with her*]

Mary. [*Piteously*] Oh, no—no—anywhere but in there. [*Appealingly to McCune*] Are you an officer? [*Ike roughly thrusts her in the dark closet and closes it*]

Ros. [*To McCune*] What are you grinning there for, McCune?

McC. [*At head of stairs*] De bloke's comin' in—here's de card he gave me. [*Throws down card. Ike picks it up and gives it to Mother Rosenbaum*]

McC. [*Looking back*] Look out for the steps. [*Frank appears at door, looks down and then slowly descends the steps. McCune leans on the half door. Ike up L.*]

Frank. [*Down R.C.*] Are you the woman they call Mother Rosenbaum?

Ros. [*Screaming*] Shut the door McCune and stay here.

McC. All right. [*McCune starts to shut the door, and gets behind it. Brummage, disguised as a policeman, substitutes for McCune. (NOTE: Brummage and McCune must be made up alike, and be of same size and height so as to successfully accomplish substitution) Brummage shuts the door and comes down steps as if drunk, goes to the extreme upper R. where he sits down sideways to the audience on a box. He is disregarded by Ike and Mother Rosenbaum who are occupied with Frank*]

Ros. [*L.C.*] Madam Rosenbaum, if you please.

Frank. [*R.C.*] You or some of your friends have a girl that I wish to communicate with. I come to you because—

Ros. You come to me, eh? Mebbe I brought you and you don't get away so easy.

Frank. It is useless to threaten me for I communicated with the police before I came in.

Ros. [*Spitefully*] Yes, you tried to. Well, I stopped you. There's the card you gave to my man. The piece don't know you're here [*Flips the card up to him, then up to Brummage. Frank picks it up with some astonishment*]

Frank. [*Aside*] What does this mean? I am trapped. [*Goes down R.*]

Ros. [*Up by Brummage, L. of him. To Brummage*] Jimmy, he thought you was a reg'lar. I'll have to be payin' you reg'lar salary pretty soon. [*Down C.—Brummage simulates drunkenness*]

Frank. [*Alarmed*] Madam, I come here with but one purpose—it was to see the girl. I only want to speak to her.

Ros. [*Striking knife on table. Sits*] Well, I'm going to let you see her. Ikey, bring her out. [*Ike goes to closet door, unlocks it, and brings Mary out. She puts her hands to her eyes as if the light dazzled her. Sees Frank*]

Mary. Frank Kennet! You here?

Ros. and IKE. Frank Kennet! [*Mother Rosenbaum starts to her feet*]

FRANK. [*Advancing to Mary*] Mary, my poor girl. What have these miscreants done to you? [*Music*]

IKE. [*Interposing*] Keep back!

Ros. Frank—ha—ha. Quick, Ikey, the steps. [*Rises and goes down R.C. presses button, throws steps up, cuts off retreat by means of a spring in the wall; at the same time Mary and Frank come together and the girl clings to him terrified*] So—o—o, you are Frank. You've been hiding from everybody since you killed the old man. Nobody knows you are in New York and nobody will miss you—and you set out to ruin the old woman. Let me look at you. For thirty years they have been trying to ruin Rosenbaum. They killed my boy. They put spies in my house. They set the police on me, they dragged me into courts. Because I am Rosenbaum. [*Goes to table and down L.*]

FRANK. You dastardly wretches—you are making a big mistake.

Ros. Ha—ha—ha! Rosenbaum makes no mistakes.

FRANK. Dick Brummage knows where I am. [*Music stops*]

Ros. The copper will tell him he didn't see you. If I were to let you run, you'd be tryin' to prove you didn't kill Mr. Bulford and we couldn't have that. [*Advances upon Mary slowly R.*] And I ain't going to let you run loose. [*Seizes Mary suddenly by the arms, pulls her away from Frank violently and thrusts her into chair L. As Frank attempts to interfere Ike catches hold of him behind by arms back; struggle; Frank throws him off and the three glare at each other. To Mary*] Now, you set there and see what we do with men who try to ruin the old woman. If you move an inch I'll put this into you. [*Picks up knife. Mary drops her head into her hands piteously and shudders*]

FRANK. Hellhounds! If you think you can murder me without a fight for it, you've made the mistake of your lives. [*Takes his coat off and throws it behind him. Music*]

MARY. [*Half rising*] No, no, they will kill you.

Ros. [*Thrusting her back in chair*] Set down or I'll settle you first. [*Ike goes to trap R. and lifts it up (be particular about carpenters attending to steps—they fall when button is pushed). Brummage appears to be in drunken sleep*]

FRANK. Mary—tell me—have you anything to say to me—what about the glass?

MARY. [*L.*] Mrs. Bulford threw it out of the window the night of the murder and Dr. Livingstone has it.

Ros. [*By Mary, L.*] Ha, that settles you—when you're both dead, the madam will be free. Ikey, open the trap. Jimmy, you drunken dog, get up. [*To Mary*] Now you sit still. [*Men struggle up and down the stage and*

Frank gets the better of Ike. Ike calls on Mother Rosenbaum; women watch the fight intently. Mother Rosenbaum goes R. Mary also rises and goes L. and thence to steps. The action of the two women must be so timed that Mary arrives at the spring in the wall at the same time Mother Rosenbaum reaches steps a second after they fall. Mary touches the spring and they have come down with a bang. All three of the group turn sharply around and Mother Rosenbaum makes two impulsive steps toward Mary and stops undecidedly. Mary runs up the steps but the door at the top is locked and she pounds on it with her fists. The two men glare at each other] Can [*On foot of steps C., to Ike*] you get away with him?

Ike. [*Struggling with Frank*]   Can I? Give me the knife. You take care of the girl. [*Mother Rosenbaum tosses the knife to Ike. It falls on the floor. Ike instantly goes toward Brummage to pick it up*]

Ros.   Quick, finish him—you are man to man and even. [*Ike stoops to pick up the knife when Brummage leans forward, presenting pistol; stands up R.C. above Ike*]

Brum.   But what are you going to do with the old man? [*Change music till curtain. Tableau*] How are you going to get away with Dick Brummage?

TABLEAU. CURTAIN. RING.

2ND CURTAIN: *Mary comes down the steps, stops at bottom. Frank jumps to her, they embrace.*

Frank.   Mary!

ACT VI.

SCENE: *Senator McSorker's house on Madison Avenue. Music off R.2.E. for rise. Interior showing handsome corridor and grand staircase C. coming well down stage, with lamps at bottom on either side flanked by heavy tropical plants. Arcaded entrances to salon L.2.; smoking room and hall R.2. Guests in evening dress standing at salon entrance looking at guests and conversing. At rise soft chamber music heard. Burst of laughter from group.* TIME: *Eleven o'clock at night.*

Clancy. [*L.*]   Yes, if it ain't Lumpy Kidney I hope to die.

Brannigan.   Well, I never expected to see him in a dress coat. He wears it like an epileptic fit. Say, boys, there won't be any eating until twelve o'clock. Let's go over to the chophouse and get a welsh rarebit. [*All come down C.*]

Clan.   Oh, you'll miss the show. He's going to trot out her royal highness.

Bran.   That's what we're here for. We've got to throw our posies at her. It's a go-as-you-please. Grand entrance. Procession of maids. Burst of music

—lights up—shower of bouquets. Three cheers for the flag and the senator on top.

CLAN. Well, I like it. No invites. No airs—no introductions.

BRAN. Say, if you don't keep your mug shut, I'll shove this into it. You act as if you were on Eighth Avenue instead of Madison. De Sixth ain't cele-bratin' tonight. [*Music stops*]

CLAN. When I get me brudder out of Sing Sing and he's a sheriff, I'm agoin' to move on de Fifth meself.

BRAN. Yes, I hear the whole Sixth is goin' to move up. [*Both go to salon entrance L.2. Bursts of laughter from guests*]

CLAN. She's a rich widow, I hear, from South America.

BRAN. Well, what's the matter with havin' her over to the Chowder Club? Come, let's go in. [*Move toward salon entrance and group themselves. Enter Mrs. O'Geogan from R.2. She is fantastically dressed and has a feather fan*]

MRS. O'G. I wonder if the senator calls that a party. It's more like a soree. [*The male guests laugh and exit R.2.*]

BRAN. No, madam, it's a levée.

MRS. O'G. I thought a levee was something that kept the flood out. Where's the cook room? [*Going R.C. Enter second heeler*] It's yourself that's cuttin' a fine shine this evening, Mr. Brannigan, with your shwaller tail.

BRAN. Oh, I ain't cuttin' no shine. We wuz to hang around the edges for a call. But it's all guzzle and munch and no jumpin'.

MRS. O'G. I have a stick in my mind a soakin' for the senator.

BRAN. I heered you was on the school board Mrs. O'Geogan.

MRS. O'G. You did? The same to you Mr. Brannigan. I heard you was workin' a reform ticket on the Fourteenth. You'll be goin' to Albany wid your shwaller tail, I don't know. [*Enter first heeler from R.2. with his coat on his arm*]

BRAN. [*To second heeler*] Say, dere is one of the dry dock tarriers in the crowd. We don't want no dry dock tarriers among us gents, do we?

CLAN. Oh, put your coat on; why can't you act like a gent in a gent's crowd and stop for de word before you do any mussin'.

BRAN. [*Putting his coat on*] I ken tump him, if it wasn't fer de coat. What's the good of our bein' here. [*Two heelers cross toward R. When they reach R.2. they encounter Count Garbiadoff and Madame Mervaine who are entering R.2. Heelers exit R.2., Count and Madame Mervaine cross L.*]

MME. M. Thanks, count, it is so close in there that, but for your kind at-tention, I should have fainted.

COUNT. I am only too delighted to be of service to you, madam. You say Mr. Brummage asked you to guide me through this strange assemblage.

MME. M. Yes—but take care how you mention that name here. [*Indicates that Mrs. O'Geogan might overhear them; then quickly to Mrs. O'Geogan*] The senator has all his friends here tonight?

MRS. O'G. Yis, ma'am. Shure it would be a little more lively if some of his inimies were on deck.

MME. M. Are you one of his friends?

MRS. O'G. Of course I am—one of his best friends. I knew him when he tended bar in Tim O'Shaughnessy's and had to mix drinks in a buttoned up coat while I washed his shirt. He's got to be a great dude, has the senator.

MME. M. Will the lady who is to make the presentation come down those stairs? [*Pointing to stairs C.*]

MRS. O'G. Well, I'm thinkin' she wouldn't come down the fire escape, with her diamonds and starched skirts. I wonder if that door has a kitchen behind it. Sure it's starvin', I am. [*Exits R.2. Count and Madame Mervaine laugh heartily at Mrs. O'Geogan's remark and at her exit*]

COUNT. Is zis ze sort of canaille which your mansions are filled with at evening parties?

MME. M. Oh, count, when you are the guest of an American politician you must wonder in silence and endure silently. Fretting about your environment is quite out of order. Let's take another stroll and see if we can find Mr. Brummage.

COUNT. Yes, I must find him. [*Aside*] And I must see zat woman. [*They exit L.2. Enter two heelers from R.2. and two college boys*]

2ND H. Break away, here comes de drum corp. [*Enter senator L.2. He is fussy, anxious and exuberant, followed by several male and female guests*]

SEN. Ah, ha, gents, enjoying yourselves, I hope. Don't forget to go to the saylong before the horns go off. I've arranged everything on schedule time and that's the signal that the lady's coming downstairs. I don't want you to miss it. Have you got your flowers? [*Looks around at them. The two heelers and two college boys raise their bouquets as if to throw them*] Stop! All right. Don't throw them until she gets at the bottom of the stairs. [*Looks at his watch*] Half past eleven. Great success, eh?

2ND GUEST. Perfectly paralyzing. Beats the Wild West, senator.

1ST GUEST. Regular coop—de-e-tat. [*Senator moves fussily toward smoking room R.2. looks in and calls*]

SEN. Gentlemen—everybody in the saylong. The ceremony is about to begin. [*Looks at his watch again. To guests in front of stage*] Now then, gents—all in the saylong. [*Male guests move to entrance L.2. Senator crosses to L. and meets Marino, who comes from salon L.2.*] Is the lady all ready?

[*Looks at his watch*] I expect them horns to go off every minute. How does she look.

MAR. Like a goddess—she always does, senator.

SEN. [*Slapping Marino on back*] Damme! I'll make her the Goddess of Liberty. I'll have her walk in roses knee deep. It's going to be the proudest moment of her life, my boy. Just go up and see she is ready, will you? [*Marino goes up stairs and exits. Senator exits into salon L.2. followed by guests. Coutche-coutche polka. Enter Mrs. O'Geogan R.2. She is noticeably under the influence of wine. She carries a large fan and has an elaborate head-dress with two feathers*]

MRS. O'G. Oh, my! Oh, my! I've been havin' the greatest toime out there. Shure I don't know what's the matter with me. I wuz hungry just now, and —now—I'm loaded with everything good to eat and drink—ah! that pink stuff in a great glass christian bowl, with strawberries and pineapple all thrown in gratis. And they give it to you for nothin'. They kape fillin' your glass whenever it's empty, and just don't give you toime to get thirsty. [*Enter senator L.2., approaches her, and goes with great rush. Business, while senator is talking to Mrs. O'Geogan, of her leaning forward and bowing her head in acknowledgment of what he says, and the headdress feathers tickling his nose and face—he trying to escape*] It sounds like the Midway of Plaisance, I heard at the World's Fair. [*Business. Crosses to L and sits on sofa. Business*] Oh! my, oh, my. Oh, this is like the cable car, without the bumps.

SEN. [*To guests*] Mrs. O'Geogan—one of my constituents—what the devil brought her here?

MRS. O'G. Mister Conductor! Mister Conductor, please let me off at Forty-Second Street. [*Business. Senator coughs, comes down C. Mrs. O'Geogan turns on sofa; sees him, rises, crosses to C., bowing*] I'm here, senator, I'm here.

SEN. Yes, I see you are.

MRS. O'G. How do you like me get up?

SEN. Gorgeous! Gorgeous! I'm glad to see you on this glorious occasion. [*Crosses L.C. turns and faces her*] The Fourth of July ain't anywhere; music —fireworks—illuminations, beautiful women. And you, Mrs. O'Geogan, are queen of beauty and the jewel among women. The Kohinoor ain't in it with you.

MRS. O'G. [*R.C.*] Oh, thank you. I don't know Mrs. Kohinoor. But, senator, I'm wid you every toime.

SEN. [*Shaking hands*] I know you are, Mrs. O'Geogan. [*Aside*] How the devil am I to get rid of her. [*Goes up L.C.*]

Mrs. O'G. Oh, I'll always be wid ye, senator, you are the one man of my affeshuns. Come here, sinitor. [*Senator comes down to her, L.C.*] Mrs. O'-Dooley tould me that you are a great flirt.

Sen. Damn Mrs. O'Dooley. [*Goes up L.C.*]

Mrs. O'G. [*Sings*] "You're the only man in all the world for me," etc. [*Goes up R.C.; business; comes down*] Come here, senator. [*Senator comes down L.C.*] I can sing better than that if I like.

Sen. Well, I hope so.

Mrs. O'G. But, senator, I've always loved you. Senator, pardon my blushes.

Sen. [*L.C.*] Where did she get it? [*Turns away; steps up a little; turns facing her*] Mrs. O'Geogan have you had something to eat?

Mrs. O'G. Eat, is it? Shure, I've been down in the kitchen to see Mary the cook. Shure, Mary's an old friend of mine, and she had an elegant christian bowl full of punch, with strawberries, all floating on the top of it, and I helped myself—ah, shure I didn't have time to get thirsty. Senator—I'm loaded.

Sen. Eh?

Mrs. O'G. Wid the supper—wid the supper. Ah! Senator, you keep iligant liquors.

Sen. How d'ye know?

Mrs. O'G. Sure I imbibed—

Sen. What? [*Goes up L.*]

Mrs. O'G. I man, I inhaled—inhaled the aroma, and I intend to marry you—

Sen. [*Aside*] The devil you do.

Mrs. O'G. With your consent. You are—[*Business of patting him on the face*] my love's young dream. [*Business*] You are so beautiful, so fresh, so innocent. [*Putting her finger on his chin*] You're a daisy.

Sen. Oh, am I? [*She leans her head on his breast; business*]

Mrs. O'G. Sure, Mrs. O'Dooley told me. [*Putting her face close to his. He pushes it gently away. She puts her face to his again*] Senator, Mrs. O'Dooley tould me—[*Coutche-coutche polka*]

Sen. Damn Mrs. O'Dooley. [*Goes up, listens to music which plays off L.2.*] That's the way to get rid of her. Mrs. O'Geogan, I know you love music and dancing—

Mrs. O'G. Love music? The idea. Do you remember when we used to go speeling in Walla Walla Hall? Did you ever know an Irish lady that wasn't fond of music and dancing? Senator, will you dance a step wid me?

Sen. What? [*Looks off L.2. turns to her*] Not on your life.

MRS. O'G. Oh, come here, that or nothin'. [*She takes him by left hand; they dance a few steps toward R., turn facing L.2., dance and exit L.2., laughing. Enter Count Garbiadoff and Madame Mervaine R.2.*]

MME. M. Mr. Brummage has not come.

COUNT. Bah—the police Americans are what you call ze grande hoompoog.

MME. M. They are cautious, count. He probably did not want to witness this woman's triumph. Be careful, she is coming. If the earth does not open and swallow her before she gets to the bottom of the stairs, you will see the most magnificent victory of audacity. It was worth coming from Cracow to witness! [*Enter Marino from top of stairs, comes down past the sofa and speaks*]

MAR. The lady is coming. Will you not enter the salon? [*Exit Marino into salon L.2. Count rubs his glasses with his handkerchief, and leaving the sofa goes to stairs, standing off behind the plant. Mrs. Bulford appears at top of staircase in full evening dress, bejewelled and attended by maids of honor. She holds her head high and wears a triumphant look. Guests enter. The female guests are bending eagerly forward to see her, count is peering at her through his glass behind balustrade. When Mrs. Bulford has reached the middle of the stairway, Mary Lavelot suddenly steps out from behind the plants on L. of steps and stands like a statue under the lamps. At the same moment the trumpets are heard playing a fanfare. She is attired in the same dress she wore in Rosenbaum's den and her head is bound up in the same cloth. She is pale and distressed. Mrs. Bulford comes slowly and smilingly down steps, chatting and laughing to maids. When she reaches the bottom she is suddenly confronted by Mary. Fanfare stops. Mrs. Bulford starts, recovers herself and speaks, the maids forming a tableau of astonishment*]

MRS. B. Who are you?

MARY. Susanne!

MRS. B. [*Agitatedly*] What are you doing here?

MARY. Meeting you face to face for the last time.

MRS. B. [*Imperiously*] Stand aside. I cannot waste words with my servants now.

MARY. I have come out of a living grave to confront you in your triumph and to tell you that the God of Justice reigns even in New York. I cannot stand aside even if I would. [*Mrs. Bulford exhibits great distress*]

MRS. B. [*Almost at foot of stairs*] Who is this lunatic? Why is this outrage permitted? Where is the senator? Where are the police? [*Turns and looks R. Enter Brummage, R.2.*]

BRUM. Madam, the police are here and waiting. [*Mrs. Bulford turns her head and sees Garbiadoff standing a few paces down stage L.*]

MRS. B. Garbiadoff! [*Falls on steps, recovers, starts to go up steps and falls backward, falling in the arms of Garbiadoff, who is L. and Brummage who is R. Recovers again, goes up steps, struggling with Brummage who is holding her by the left wrist*] Don't touch me! Let me go! [*She is now on platform on top of steps*] My God! This is the end! [*Taking small vial from her bosom—puts it to her mouth—falls and dies. Brummage kneels by her a moment to see if she is dead. Takes the vial from her. (Brummage should carry a duplicate vial—she may lose hers.) Holds it in his right hand. Enter Marino quickly from L.2.; he looks about in wonder*]

MAR. What is the matter?

MME. M. The lady has fainted.

MAR. Fainted? Impossible! [*Rushes upstairs, looks at Mrs. Bulford in astonishment. Enter senator, L.2., followed by guests and Mrs. O'Geogan, L.2.*]

SEN. Well, what's the hitch? Where's the lady? Will somebody stop the music? [*Turning and looking off L.2.E., then turns to stairs again*] Where is she? [*Enter several other male and female guests R.2.*]

MAR. [*On top of stairs C.*] Dead!

OMNES. [*Solemnly*] Dead!

MAR. [*Kneeling by his sister*] Dead!—my God—dead!

BRUM. [*Holding up vial*] The Para poison! [*Senator takes a step or two towards stairs in rage*]

SEN. You damnable dog! [*Slight pause*] Here, Patsy, Shorty, where are you? [*Enter L.2., first and second heelers. They come left and right of senator. All the guests looking extremely anxious at stairs. Madame Mervaine at sofa looking at stairs, Garbiadoff a little above her, all looking to C. in suspense*]

BRUM. [*Who has come down a step or two holding up his hand authoritatively*] Stand back! The lady belongs to the law—her diamonds to the Count Garbiadoff! [*Pointing to the count*] Senator, it is twelve o'clock! [*Mary in Frank's arms L., a little above the senator*]

PICTURE

CURTAIN

FROM RAGS TO RICHES

By Charles A. Taylor

CHARACTERS

NED NIMBLE, *a newsboy who works his way from gutter to palace*
ALBERT COOPER, *his father under a brand of shame*
OLD MONTGOMERY, *a wealthy retired merchant*
PRINCE CHARLIE, *a gambler, his nephew*
CHINESE SAM, *a dog doctor*
MIKE DOOLEY, *a policeman*
BROWN, *the merchant's valet*
MOTHER MURPHY, *one of the real ol' sort*
FLOSSIE, *Ned's sister, who loves excitement*
GERTRUDE CLARK, *a trained nurse*
FLORA BRADLEY, *a fruit daughter of Eve*
WAITER
MESSENGER, CAB DRIVERS, DETECTIVES, POLICE, WAITERS, NEWSPAPER MEN,
   SOCIETY GIRLS, POLITICIANS, CIVILIANS
TIME, *The Present*
PLACE, *New York*

SYNOPSIS OF SCENES

ACT I.

*Mother Murphy's news stand and coffee counter on the Bowery—midnight.
Ned in poverty and rags. His playground the gutter. Meeting of the pauper
and the prince. Price of a sister's honor.*

ACT II.

*Library of the merchant's home. Plot to kill Montgomery. The abduction of
Flossie.*

ACT III.

SCENE 1. *Broadway after dark. On the trail of the kidnappers.*
SCENE 2. *Room in the Waldorf-Astoria. Ned as a messenger boy.*
SCENE 3. *Roof of Waldorf-Astoria.*
SCENE 4: *A cellar in Chinatown. At the eleventh hour.*

ACT IV.

*A palace on the Hudson. Ned as a royal host. Blood will tell. That which pays
best in the end. "On the road to the White House."*

ACT I.

*On the Bowery—midnight. Drop in 3. shows buildings with street in fore-
ground. Center arch doorway cut in drop; half-high swinging doors attached
to this doorway. Over and under swinging doors is seen the backing which
is drinking bar and sideboard with liquor bottles and glasses. Sign over doorway, "Concert Hall"; to the right of this doorway is painted a pawnshop; to
the left a lodging house. Set piece representing El track across stage directly
in front of drop. Profile electric train: windows illuminated to work back and
forth on this set piece. Set house representing tenement left. Doorway opening
upstage backed by practical stairway; hanging lamp over stairway; on transom over door "19." Lunch counter over which is dilapidated awning up- and
downstage in front of return piece L. On return piece is painted backing for
lunch counter—coffee urn, cups, plates, pies, cakes, and so forth. In front of
counter two wooden stools. End of counter downstage barrel on top of barrel;
wide board upon which are papers, magazines, and so forth. Sign on front of
awning, "Mother's Coffee House." From end of counter upstage to return
piece L. is small backing with open window. Flat with flipper wing R.—build-
ing "Chinese quarters." Door opening off stage in 2., sign over door, "Chinese
Sam, Dog Doctor." Set lamppost, on which are police, fire-alarm, and mail
boxes, in front of this door.*

*Curtain rises to drinking chorus and thumping of piano offstage in con-
cert hall. Discovers Flossie, girl of sixteen—plain petticoat off ankles—old
shirtwaist—kitchen apron—rose in her hair—behind counter—wiping coffee
cups with old linen towel; and Mike—policeman—middle-age—smooth-
shaven—neat uniform—Irish character study.*

MIKE. [*Enters L.3. as song ends—sticks head in window*] Ah, Flossie,
me darlin', how goes it with you this evening?

FLOS. It's not evening, Mike, it's morning. The clock struck one.

MIKE. I haven't struck one tonight, and haven't made an arrest. I never
saw the Bowery so quiet before. [*Crosses to C. Pushes open door and looks
in Concert Hall. Men and women seen drinking—shouts off—clinking of
glasses*]

FLOS. Stick around and you will find it noisy enough. Have a cup of
coffee, Mike?

MIKE. [*Comes down*] No, me darlin', much obliged. I'm looking for a drop of something stronger. Why don't you close up?

FLOS. I'm waiting for the old woman.

MIKE. And where is she?

FLOS. Looking for Ned.

MIKE. Who gave you the pretty posie that you have in your top-knot?

FLOS. Me feller.

MIKE. Truth and you have a hundred.

FLOS. But this one is the real thing, Mike. He rides in a cab and bought all of my papers—he dresses swell—has a big diamond ring. He told me I was pretty and would be a fine lady some day.

MIKE. Did he tell you anything else?

FLOS. No, but he said he would when he came back—

MIKE. So he is coming back, is he?

FLOS. [*Nodding*]

MIKE. Well, I don't blame him.

FLOS. He wanted to take me to ride but I had no one to leave with the stand.

MIKE. What's the matter? Won't it stand up alone? Going to take you to ride, is he? If he does I'll give him one in a patrol wagon! Mother Murphy should stay home and keep an eye on you.

FLOS. Don't tell her about the rich fellow, will you, Mike?

MIKE. I don't know about that. These chaps with fine clothes and pretty speeches don't visit this locality looking for wives. You're only a slip of a girl, Floss. You're well liked up and down the line and I for one would hate to see you go wrong. [*Crosses R.1.*]

FLOS. Oh, Mike [*C.*]

MIKE. What is it?

FLOS. You ain't mad, are you?

MIKE. No, but you have worried me. The old woman is a friend of mine—she's had a hard struggle to raise you and Ned. Remember you're not her children. Yu'd been in the gutter if it hadn't been for her.

FLOS. We work hard for what little we get.

MIKE. Yes, but it's a mother's care and good training. That's a whole lot, in a rough neighborhood like this. [*Exit R.1.*]

ALBERT. [*In rough clothes and under influence of liquor, pushed out of center door by man in shirt-sleeves and white apron. Reeling down C.*] That's right—when my money's gone—throw me into the street—much obliged. You're a gentleman—I don't think. [*Feels pockets*] I had it when I went in

—oh, well, it's gone like everything else—I ever had. [*Reels to counter, balances himself by stool*]

Flos. What's the matter, Pop?

Alb. Don't call me Pop. I'm nobody's papa. I'm a fool—

Flos. Oh, no you're not. It's only wise men who know when they have been foolish. Here's a hot cup of coffee. It will brace you up.

Alb. [*Getting on stool with difficulty*] I need it, girl. I can't pay for it.

Flos. That's all right—pay some other time.

Alb. They wouldn't stand for that in there.

Flos. We don't run that kind of a place. We don't burn as many lights as they do. We can afford to be generous—here's a sandwich. Mother made it for my supper—but you can have it.

Alb. Thank ye, girl. You make me ashamed of myself—I ain't had nothing but whiskey for two days.

Flos. Whiskey won't keep you alive.

Alb. No, but it helps me to forget.

Flos. Forget what?

Alb. The past, my dear, the past—helps me forget a little girl that would be just about your age if she's alive.

Flos. Was she your girl?

Alb. Yes.

Flos. Then why should you wish to forget her?

Alb. Because she may grow to be like her mother.

Flos. I don't understand you.

Alb. Her mother was bad. She ran away from me, left her two babies—ruined my life—made me a drunkard, an outcast; worse, made me a criminal. The prison brand is on me. My children lost to me forever.

Flos. Why don't you go home?

Alb. I have no home. When I got out of jail, my house was gone, my children were gone, all, everything.

Charlie. [*In long, stylish ulster, travelling cap, cane and gloves, enters L.3. Crosses rapidly to R.2.*] Chinese Sam, dog doctor. That must be the old devil I want. [*Pulls envelope out of pocket*] Yes, this is the number all right.

Flos. [*Steps downstage behind counter at Charlie's entrance, places hand upon her heart*] That's him—[*Turns and hangs head, walks*]

Char. [*Turning L.*] Hello there, neighbor—who has seen me? I'll square myself. [*Crosses L.*] Hello, Butterfly, you're up late. Time little girls were in bed.

Flos. You said you was coming back.

Char. Well, I'm here, am I not? [*Looking over shoulder at Albert*]

ALB. [*Engaged with his sandwich and coffee*]

FLOS. Yes, sir. [*Sinking down on doorstep*]

CHAR. I see you still have my rose. [*Bending over and scenting rose in Flossie's hair*]

FLOS. Yes, sir.

CHAR. Why don't you wear it over your heart? Then I shall place it upon your breast. Come, have you a pin? [*Removing rose from Flossie's hair*]

FLOS. Please don't. I must go now; mother will be back.

CHAR. Oh, hang mother.

FLOS. I don't think you could.

CHAR. Fat, is she? Well, I'm going soon as I adjust the rose. Are you going to give me a pin or—maybe you don't want this rose. Oh, very well, I'll keep it. [*Starts to place it in his button-hole*]

FLOS. Yes, yes, here's the pin. [*Pricks Charlie*]

CHAR. Ouch, you did that on purpose, you little mischief. Will you hold still! [*Adjusting rose on Flossie's shirtwaist*]

FLOS. I didn't mean to prick you—honest I didn't. [*Looks up into Charlie's face*] Mr.—Mr.—What's your name?

CHAR. Call me Prince—that's what the boys call me.

FLOS. And are you a real sure enough prince?

CHAR. Well, hardly. There now, you must pay me for that rose there. I must be going—[*Catching her by both hands and drawing her to him*]

FLOS. Pay you for it?

CHAR. Yes, give me a kiss, quick—no one's looking. Just one?

ALB. Hold on there. [*Slips from stool, staggers forward*] Let that girl alone.

CHAR. [*Turning and releasing Flossie*] You drunken fool, what right have you to interfere? [*Flossie enters door L., exits upstairs*]

ALB. No rights. No rights at all, old chap. But I interfered, didn't I? She's gone; now run home, sonny, and if you don't—well, I'm just drunk enough to put up a hell of a good scrap. [*Squares off*]

CHAR. [*Starts forward with arm drawn back to strike. Albert suddenly pauses, bends down and looks into his face, staggers back. Aside*] Albert Cooper—and he doesn't know me.

ALB. Come on, I'm not bluffing. My head's swimming so I can't see to punch straight—but I'll fight.

CHAR. Bah, I'm not fighting drunken men. [*Crosses R.*] If you don't go about your business I'll call an officer and have you locked up.

ALB. [*Staggering to counter*] Wish you would. I have no place to sleep tonight.

CHAR. He's too drunk to recognize me. I'm in luck. Curse the fellow, I thought he was in jail and out of my way. It won't do for us to come together just now. There is too much at stake. [*Exits into Concert Hall. Mike enters from R.1., crosses behind counter, watches Charlie. Goes up and pushes door open, looks after Charlie. Flossie enters from door L., crosses behind counter, watches Mike*]

BROWN. [*Plain business suit, enters L.3.*] Hello, Mike—did you catch him?

MIKE. Hello, Brown, what are you doing here?

BROWN. I'm after that fellow you're watching—[*They cross down R.*]

MIKE. Since you retired from the Force, I thought you'd given up watching crooks. Who is he?

BROWN. Don't you know him?

MIKE. Well, slightly. He poses as a gambler around here. He's known as Prince Charlie.

BROWN. He's the nephew of the man I'm working for.

MIKE. Old Montgomery, the millionaire?

BROWN. Yes, and his uncle wants to learn what he does out so late nights. You see there's a few hundred thousands coming his way when the old man dies.

MIKE. I see. And the young chap's getting his hand in so he'll learn how to spend them.

BROWN. He'll have none to spend if the old man learns what I know.

MIKE. I thought you was the old man's valet. So you've turned detective again.

BROWN. For a woman's sake, Mike. One that this man ruined and cast off—took from her husband and children, left them to die in the public hospital.

MIKE. Your heart was right when you was on the Force. Tell me more of this affair—you'll find I'm with you. Come, we'll keep an eye on the Prince. [*Crosses up with Brown through open door. They exit R.3. talking in byplay*]

ALB. Don't blame you for being angry, little girl. But somehow I felt that chap didn't mean right by you.

FLOS. They all get fresh if you give them half a chance. Men are all alike. [*Sighs*] But he seemed different than the rest. He said this rose reminded him of me. [*Crosses downstage end of counter*]

ALB. Let me see it. [*Flossie removes a rose from her dress, kisses it and hands it to Albert*]

ALB. [*Inspecting flower*] Pure white and a bud. Came from Bushman's and cost a dollar, I'll wager. Hum, buds like this one don't blossom in the hands of men like he is, my dear. They wither and decay. Killed by frosts of infidelity. [*His head falls on his breast and the flower falls from his hand*]

FLOS. [*Springing forward and picking up rose*] Oh, sir, you have crushed my rose.

ALB. Pardon me, little girl, I was thinking of my wife. You'll forgive me, won't you? [*Places his hand on Flossie's head, wiping eyes with sleeve*]

FLOS. [*Burying her face in the flower*] Yes, I'll forgive you because there are tears in your eyes. I know a big man like you don't cry unless he's had a lot of trouble. See, I'm going to give you this rose. I will pin it right here on your coat. Then when you look at it you will remember someone cares for you, and you won't drink any more, will you? There, when you find your own little girl [*Pins rose on Albert's coat*] you can give her the rose.

ALB. Thanks, child. You have put new life in me. Some day I'll come back here and hunt you up. Show you what a few kind words and a generous act will do for a man who is down on his luck. [*Crosses to R.*] From this night on I give you my promise I will keep clear of places like that. [*Points to Concert Hall and exits R.1. Laughter, shouts, and clinking of glasses in Concert Hall*]

MOTHER MURPHY. [*Stout good-natured Irish woman with shawl over her head, carrying a baseball bat, enters R.3.*] Flossie—I say, Floss—where the devil are you? Oh, there you are. What are them dirty dishes doing on the counter? Why don't you close up shop and go to bed? The Raines Law Committee will have us pinched for selling mint juleps after twelve o'clock at midnight. Is that brother of yours home yet? If I lay hands on him, I'll break this baseball bat across the soles of his two feet. What are you snivelling about? Has there been any of that Chatham Square gang around here making googlum eyes at yees?

FLOS. No, ma'am, I'm not crying.

MOTH. Then why are you wiping your nose on that dish towel?

MIKE. [*Enters R.3.*] Ah, Mother, so you've got home at last. Did you find Ned?

MOTH. Find him—you might as well look for a hole in the bottom of the East River.

MIKE. He'll come home all right. He's probably up around the Broadway Café, trying to get a few more pennies with his extras. Ned's a hustler.

MOTH. Yes, he'll work himself to death. I have to tie him in bed or he'd be on the street all the time. He's that way ever since I got him. Have some coffee, Mike. [*Crosses behind counter, draws coffee*]

MIKE. Thanks—don't care if I do. Did you ever try to look up the parents of these children? [*Flossie crosses down and sits on doorstep L.*]

MOTH. What time have I to look them up? It's a bustle to live. An old merchant who I used to scrub for down on Broome Street brought them to me when they was babies and told me he'd pay for their keep. Then he moved and I moved. It was a game of checkers between us, but they got into my king row and 'twas all off. I'm thinking it's the lad's move now. They do be saying, Mike, it's a wise child that can find his own father.

MIKE. Ned will find his if he's on earth. [*Chinaman Sam, in blue blouse, smoking Chinese pipe, enters R.2. Stands in doorway smoking*]

MIKE. What kind of joint does that fellow run? [*Pointing to Chink*]

MOTH. Who, the Chineser? That's me neighbor with the slanting eye. They do be saying he's a doctor but begorra I think he's a rat catcher. He must have swallowed one and the tail is growing out behind his head.

MIKE. His sign says he's a dog doctor. Do you ever see any dogs around here?

MOTH. Yes, two-legged dogs. Lots of 'em. And some of 'em wears petticoats. Hist, Mike, I think it's what you call a joint. Get an order from headquarters to raid it, Mike, and I'll give you free coffee for a month.

MIKE. Will you sign a complaint, Mother? [*Crosses R.1.*]

MOTH. Faith, Mike, and you know I can't sign my name. But I'll put my cross on that Chink the night of the wake. [*Mike exits R.1. El train from L. to R. Shouts from Concert Hall*]

CHAR. [*Enters from Concert Hall. Looks down and L. Crosses to R.2. Chinaman bows low, pushes open door. Charlie hesitates, sees Mother, crosses rapidly to counter L., throws leg over stool*] Give me a cup of black coffee. [*Flossie looks up from step as Mother's back is turned drawing coffee— shakes finger at Charlie. Places a finger on her lips*]

MOTH. There you are, sir—something else?

CHAR. No, thanks. When do you close up?

MOTH. This blessed minute, if me boy comes home.

CHAR. Then you have a boy to support?

MOTH. Yes, and a girl too. [*Pointing to Flossie*] She's more trouble than the boy.

CHAR. Why don't you find her a good husband?

MOTH. A husband? Faith, man, she's only a child. Stand up, Flossie, and show the gentleman how tall you be. [*Flossie arises, hangs her head*]

CHAR. [*Steps around end of counter*] Why she is quite a young lady. I'd give a good deal to have a girl like that.

MOTH. Have you no children of your own?

CHAR. Well, no. You see I have plenty of money and a beautiful house— but no children.

MOTH. What will you give for mine? You can have the boy and the girl if you give them a good home. You see I'm only a poor woman and this is no place for them.

CHAR. Well, really, I can't say. I've never seen the boy, you know. But the girl's appearance pleases me very much. My wife and I may drive down tomorrow and take her to our house for the afternoon. Then we will talk the matter over. [*Flossie turns and starts as Charlie says "My wife" but he winks and she again bows her head*]

MOTH. How about that, Floss? Would you like to go with the gentleman tomorrow?

FLOS. Yes, ma'am.

MOTH. But how do I know who you are, sir? Where is it you live?

CHAR. My home is on West End Avenue. My name is—there is my card.

MOTH. Thank you, sir. I guess you mean well by my girl. I will talk the matter over with her brother. He is younger than she is, but he's a good boy and the man of the house. He may go with her.

CHAR. Oh, the boy may come some other time. There is only room for three in the cab.

FLOS. Two's company and three is a crowd.

CHAR. There is the pay for your coffee. I must be going. I will call for the girl at ten tomorrow. [*Lays bill on counter*]

MOTH. Sir, this is twenty dollars, I have no change for that.

CHAR. You seem to be a hard-working woman and as I have plenty of money you are welcome to the change. And, by the way, I wish to give the child a gift to remember me by—[*Removing ring from his little finger, stepping forward and taking Flossie's hand*] This ring should just about fit her slender fingers. It is too small for mine. [*Slips ring on Flossie's fourth finger*]

FLOS. Look, mother, it's a diamond. A real sure-enough diamond! Isn't it beautiful? [*Kissing it, crosses R.*] It's an engagement ring. He placed it on my fourth finger. Oh, I'm so happy I could cry. [*Wiping eyes with apron, rubbing ring and kissing it R.*]

MOTH. Do hear how that child goes on. Don't mind what she says, sir, you'll be spoiling her. [*Crosses C.*] Engagement ring, you goose, the gentleman has a wife of his own. He's old enough to be your father.

CHAR. Yes, certainly. [*Winking at Flossie, crosses R.C.*]

FLOS. Oh, yes. I forgot—I'm to be his little girl.

NED. [*Enters R.3. Ragged cap and coat, bundles of extras under his arm. Comes down to center, looks from one to the other*] What's up, mother? What makes you all look so happy? Someone bought all your papers?

MOTH. That's him, sir. That's my boy. See, I bought him a nice baseball bat today, and he never came home to get it. [*Holding up bat and winking at Flossie*]

CHAR. How do you do, my lad? What's your name? [*Shakes hands with Ned*]

NED. My name is Ned, sir. The newsboys call me Ned Nimble because I move around and sell more papers than they do. Give us your hand again, sir—

CHAR. Certainly, what's the matter? [*Offers hand to Ned*]

NED. I didn't like the grip you gave me last time.

CHAR. The grip? Oh, I see—you're a Mason.

NED. No, I'm only a newsboy, but when a man shakes with me I don't want to feel that half-hearted squeeze as if he was shaking dice. Give me a good, hard grip, then I know you're right. My hands will stand it. They have seen plenty of honest work. [*They shake again*] That's right. Now I'll hear what you've got to say.

MOTH. Don't mind him, sir. He has the airs of a man.

CHAR. [*Aside*] Yes, and the impudence of the Devil. [*Aloud*] I suppose Ned will be a politician some day and run for office. Then he'll change his mind about handshakes.

NED. If I ever do get to the White House it will be hands of the working man that shakes mine.

FLOS. See, Ned, what the gentleman gave me. [*Removing ring and handing it to Ned*]

NED. What is it? A rhinestone? I wonder how much you could get on it. [*Blowing it and examining stone as an expert*]

MOTH. Yes, Ned, and he gave me twenty dollars.

CHAR. That's right, Ned, I mustn't forget you—[*Pulling roll of bills out of pocket*]

NED. Hold on, partner. Put that back. I've got to earn mine—[*Crosses L.*] What did you give the gentleman in return for twenty dollars, mother? Have you sold the stand?

MOTH. No, Ned—I gave him a cup of coffee.

NED. A cup of coffee. And you, Flo, what did you give him for this ring? That stone is a full-carat diamond.

FLOS. Why, you see, I—I—mother, you tell him.

CHAR. That's all right, Ned. It's only a trifle. It don't amount to much.

NED. It amounts to a good deal to us, sir; we are very poor.

CHAR. I know, and I am willing to help you. I've taken quite a fancy to your sister—and I—

MOTH. He's going to take her to his house tomorrow, Ned, a fine, swell mansion of West Avenue.

NED. Take Flo to his house?

CHAR. Yes, just for dinner and an informal call, that's all, Ned.

NED. Are you married?

CHAR. Don't I look it?

NED. That's not answering my question.

CHAR. Certainly. I have a very beautiful wife. [*Winking as he crosses to Flossie*]

NED. Then you should go home to her, instead of hanging around here making presents of diamonds to my sister.

MOTH. Ned, how dare you speak like that?

CHAR. The boy is insulting.

MOTH. Ned! Go up to bed, sir, or I'll take this bat to you.

NED. I'll not go to bed, mother, 'till this man leaves. Give me that money he gave you. Give it to me, I say—[*Snatching bill from mother*] There is your money and your ring, sir. I'm sorry if you think me rude but we can't accept them.

CHAR. No, no, Ned. Don't get mad. You don't understand. I've made arrangements to adopt your sister and you also.

NED. Adopt us?

MOTH. Yes, Ned, that's right.

FLOS. Yes, yes, Ned. We are to be rich.

NED. Rich—at what price? How can this man adopt us? Before God we are your children till we find our own parents. Mother, this man is not what he claims he is.

CHAR. You street arab! I've had enough of your insolence. How dare you speak to me like that!

NED. Because it's the truth. I've seen you in the gambling houses of the lower Bowery; at the race track, with fast women. Mother and I battle the world day and night to support our home in poverty. But if we are compelled to purchase riches at the cost of my sister's honor, we'll remain in rags all the rest of our lives—Go—[*Hurls money and ring at Charlie, who stoops and picks them up, crosses L.3., turns and doffs his hat. Flossie starts toward Charlie. Ned catches her hand and swings her left into Mother's arms, stands between them with arm uplifted. Enter Mike and Brown R.3. People from Concert Hall and Chinese crowd out of doorway C.*]

ACT II.

Library of the merchant's home. Next day. Arch doorway R.C.—conservatory backing. Arch doorway L.C.—plain hall backing. Hat rack with mirror against hall backing. Heavy portiere arch doorway L.C. Door opening off R.2., plain chamber backing. Door opening off L.2., plain chamber backing. Fireplace and mantel L.3. Armchair before fireplace; ottoman, cushion and so forth. Plain leather couch, R. corner. Chair, foot of couch. Plain flat-top office table, partway C. Chairs behind and R. of table. Plain small table, down L., containing water pitcher. Glasses, medicine bottles, and so forth. Books, writing material, on table Center. Chair, R. and L. of arch doorway L.C. Back wall painted to represent bookcases. Pedestals, stationery, bric-a-brac, plant, potted palms, maps and so forth. Sunlight in conservatory. Blue, hallway. Red glow in fireplace. Lights full up at rise.

BROWN. [*Enters L.C. at rise. Hangs hat on rack, comes down to table, picks up packages of mail, runs it over*] Here's the morning mail unopened —proves the old man's not up. I'm in luck. I learned enough about his rogue of a nephew last night to write a novel. What will he say when he learns that the woman who poses here in luxury as Charles Montgomery's wife is only an adventuress. Here is a letter for her now—"Mrs. Montgomery"—the brazen huzzy! It bears the trademark of Powell and Mason, the wholesale drug firm. Now what does she want with drugs? Can she be responsible for the old man's sinking spells—I've learned enough to warrant further investigation. I'll look this over. [*Puts letter in pocket*]

GERTRUDE. [*Enters L.2. Handsome, middle-aged woman as nurse. Dressed in black, white cap and cuffs, small lace apron. She has smoked glass goggles that disguise her face. Over one arm a blanket, bottle and spoon in other. Lays bottle and spoon on small table—throws rug over armchair*] Good morning, Brown.

BROWN. Good morning, Miss Clark. How's the old man?

GERT. He passed a bad night, Brown. He asked for you several times.

BROWN. He gave me permission to go.

GERT. Yes, I know. But he wants either you or I with him all the time. He grows weaker every day. He is suspicious of everyone else.

BROWN. I don't blame him. Did it ever occur to you, Miss Clark, that someone might wish to hasten the old man's end?

GERT. You mean his nephew?

BROWN. Yes, and that woman who poses as his wife. [*Pointing to door R.2.*]

GERT. No, no. I can't believe Charlie is as bad as that. [*Sinking into chair C., removing glasses, wiping eyes*]

BROWN. Not after the wrong he done you? Why a man who would ruin a woman's life as he did yours would be guilty of most any crime.

GERT. Silence, Brown. They must not know. I need this humble position I fill. Need it badly. Did they know who I was I would be out into the street.

BROWN. You have more right here than she has, and I don't believe Mr. Montgomery would turn you out. You have been too kind and good to him, Gertrude. Pardon me, I mean Miss Clark.

GERT. Call me Gertrude if you wish, Brown. One name is as good as another to me. They are both false—false as I am. [*Crosses R.*]

BROWN. Why don't you go to Mr. Montgomery and tell him all?

GERT. No, no, Brown. I am afraid.

BROWN. I've learned things about his nephew that he shall know, and I mean to stick by you, little woman, through everything.

GERT. Thank you, Brown—you've been a friend. God bless you for it.

BROWN. I would be more—no matter what your past has been. I love you.

GERT. No, no. Not that, Brown. Let us remain as we are. Remember I am a wife and a mother.

BROWN. Yes, but your husband is a convict in prison, and your children lost to you forever.

GERT. Don't say that, Brown. Every hour of my life I pray for their return.

BROWN. Suppose I could place them once more in your arms. What then, Gertie?

GERT. What are you saying, Arthur? Are you jesting with me? Speak, man! You know something, you have found them—my little girl and my baby boy? [*Sinking upon her knees sobbing*]

BROWN. Hush, Gertie—don't take on like that. We'll be heard. I don't wish to raise your hopes, but [*Raising her to her feet*] I'm on a clue that promises great results. Have courage, little woman. Fate had some object in placing you in the home of the man who ruined your life.

GERT. I expect every day that Charles Montgomery will recognize and kill me—I'm careful that he never sees me without my glasses.

BROWN. All the more reason to tell his uncle the truth and have him punished.

MONTGOMERY. [*Off L.2.*] Brown, oh, Brown. Is that you?

BROWN. There's the old man now.

MONT. [*Off L.2.*] Brown—

BROWN. Yes, sir—I'm coming. [*Crosses to door L.2.*] Give me that mail quick. [*Gertrude gathers mail from table, runs with it to Brown. Business.*

Brown keeps dropping papers and letters as Gertrude picks them up. Exits L.2.]

FLORA. [*Enters R.2. in handsome morning gown*] Good morning, Gertrude. Is my uncle better this morning?

GERT. [*Bending over small table L. and adjusting her glasses*] No, ma'am, he seems much weaker.

FLOR. Has his valet returned?

GERT. Yes, ma'am, he's with him now.

FLOR. Did you see a letter for me on the table? [*Looking on table*]

GERT. No, ma'am.

FLOR. Strange, I expected one. [*Walking to conservatory R.C.*] Get my uncle's wheeling chair ready, Gertrude. You will need to change the pillows. [*Crosses to table C.*]

GERT. [*Picking up bottle and crossing C.*] I must give Mr. Montgomery his medicine when his bath is over.

FLOR. I will attend to that. You may go. Do as I tell you. [*Gertrude sets bottle on table, exits R.C. Flora picks up bottle, shakes it, removes stopper, applies her nostrils*] This is not strong enough. It's too slow, all together too slow. If I only dared use something more powerful. With this I shall never be found out. [*Charlie enters L.C. Removes hat and coat. Tosses them to butler who hangs them on rack and retires. Flora crosses L., sits on arm of chair before fire*] Prince Charlie comes home to his little wife when he has no place else to go.

CHAR. You are right, Flo, always right. Where's the old man?

FLOR. Not up yet, my dear boy—indisposed as it were. It is about time he had his drops. [*Crosses to table C. and picks up bottle*]

CHAR. [*Clutching bottle and taking it from Flora*] You avarice-, money-crazed cat, you have no more heart than a stone.

FLOR. I might say the same of you, my dear Prince, but I wouldn't be so unladylike—did you get what I sent you for?

CHAR. No.

FLOR. Why didn't you?

CHAR. Because I will not be a party to your hellish plot.

FLOR. You are a coward, Prince. You are willing I should stay here and take the risk. When it's all over you will lay back in luxury and try and convince your conscience you are innocent.

CHAR. Where's the nurse—her eyes seem always on me.

FLOR. We are alone, my dear—have no fear.

CHAR. Flo, if the old man knew you were not my wife he'd cut me off without a penny.

FLOR. That's just why—the sooner it's over the better. This won't do. [*Handling bottle*] That Chinese doctor I sent you to can give me what I want. Did you see him?

CHAR. No, I didn't get a chance.

FLOR. It's only an opium pellet, Charlie. It will leave no trace to betray us. Your uncle is dying now with aneurism of the heart. It is only a question of a few weeks or months at most. In that time he may learn the truth and cast us into the street. I can't go back to the old life in the dance halls, and what would you do without money?

CHAR. I know that, Flo, but it would be murder. My God, woman, what are you asking me to do? We may be found out, go to the electric chair. No, no, you're a fiend from hell! Go 'way from me. I don't know why I ever brought you here. [*Gertrude with wheeling chair enters R.C. Stands in conservatory near doorway*]

FLOR. To pawn me off on your uncle as the wife of Albert Cooper, the man you wronged and sent to prison for a crime committed by yourself.

CHAR. Stop, Flo, for God's sake. Someone will hear. Do you want to ruin every chance we have to live a better life? [*Gertrude reels back as if fainting. Clutches handle of wheeling chair, supports herself, turns her back*] What's that? [*Turns suddenly, sees Gertrude adjusting pillows in chair as if she has not heard*]

FLOR. That prying, pale-faced nurse. She's always about when not wanted; Gertrude—Gertrude, are you deaf? You may go.

GERT. Yes, ma'am. [*Bows low and exits R.C.*]

FLOR. Don't look so scared. She didn't hear you. Are you going to get that for me? Or must I go to Chinatown?

CHAR. Go to hell for all I care.

FLOR. If I do you'll open the door for me. See here, "my dear husband in name only," there is no love lost between you and I. It's a cold business proposition of dollars and cents. Your uncle injects enough morphine into his veins every day to kill ten ordinary men. So much for habit; his system is filled with it. Opium is the same drug in another form. My friend the Dog Doctor compounds it to put crippled Chinamen out of the world without pain. Now what is twenty-four hours more or less in a man's life? You could hardly call an act of humanity by such a cruel name as was whispered here a moment ago.

CHAR. Enough! If I do this for you, will you do something for me?

FLOR. I think I am doing a great deal for you.

CHAR. There is a young girl I want, down in the Bowery. She is hardly of age yet and we must be careful.

FLOR. Oh, you hard-hearted man! So I am to take second place? And where are you to pitch her wigwam?

CHAR. I leave that to you, Flo. Is it a go?

FLOR. Yes, there is my hand. No use fighting, Charlie. We've too much at stake. If we pull a double oar we will reach the shores of wealth.

CHAR. Yes, or land in jail. Get dressed and we'll go for a ride. I don't feel like meeting the old man just now. [*Exits L.C. with hat*]

FLOR. [*Follows to L.C., looks after him, laughs and shrugs shoulders*] Poor weak miserable fool, how I abhor him. [*Crosses down C.*] And yet he placed me where I am. Was it not for him I would be in the lowest dives of this city today. Why have I no gratitude; why have I no heart? [*Picking up bottle*] Ask the men who have made me what I am. [*Brown and Montgomery enter L.2., Montgomery a refined old gent, white hair, dressing-gown, walks with cane and leans on Brown*]

MONT. Careful, Brown, careful. My old heart is thumping like a trip-hammer. Where is my nurse? Where is Gertrude? [*Brown leads Montgomery to chair before fire, assists him to seat*]

FLOR. I'm to be your nurse this morning, uncle. Miss Clark stepped out for a few moments.

MONT. I don't want you, I want Gertrude. It's time for my hypodermic and drops. [*Rolling back sleeve of his right arm*] See the scars on my arm, Brown, hardly a place can I find to insert the needle.

BROWN. Don't excite yourself, sir. I will administer the morphine. [*Crosses up to small table*]

MONT. Send that woman away. She annoys me.

FLOR. Now, uncle, don't be cross with me this morning. [*Pats old man's head, puts arm around neck*] I'm so sorry, so very, very, sorry for you. Won't you let me be your little nurse? See what a nice nosegay I picked for you this morning. [*Takes flowers from bosom and pins on old man's gown*]

MONT. Flowers, bah! [*Pulls off flowers, throws them on floor*] Save them for my coffin. I want my drops; bring my drops.

FLOR. [*Picks up nosegay; crosses to table, returns with bottle and spoon, pours out drops, offers to Montgomery*] Here they are, uncle.

MONT. I've changed my mind. Bring me whiskey. If I'm to die I might as well have my old hide filled with rum. Morphine, Brown, the morphine! What are you doing, man? You are slower than Balaam's ass. [*Lays back in chair, throws his naked arm across his breast and clutches at his heart*]

BROWN. [*Who has filled syringe from vial at small table; crosses up and after trying flesh several places on old man's arm, injects high up*] Steady, now—easy—you will soon be yourself. [*Flora has staggered back to table center with bottle and spoon and watches the above like a hawk*]

MONT. [*Gives sigh of relief*]   God bless you, Brown. That's a great relief. Heaven don't seem so far away as it did a moment ago. Flora, go get your marriage certificate. You promised to show it to me time and time again. Now I want to see it.

FLOR.   Yes, uncle, I'll go and search for it. I told you I mislaid it.

MONT.   Well, don't come back till you've found it.

FLOR. [*Aside*]   Old fool—he'll soon forget. [*Exits R.2., slams door*]

MONT.   My, that woman has a temper, Brown. She's a bad one. Did I believe what you told me I'd turn her out.

BROWN.   It's the truth. I'm going to furnish you with proofs today.

MONT.   You say that my nurse, Miss Clark, is the wife Charlie took from Albert Cooper fourteen years ago?

BROWN.   Yes. I believe I have found the children. I have arranged to have them brought here today. You can question them yourself.

MONT.   The unprincipled rogue. He has disgraced the name he bears. I have put up with him long enough. Send Miss Clark to me.

BROWN.   Don't tell her of the children till we are sure they are hers. [*Crosses to R.C.*]

MONT.   Oh, Brown.

BROWN.   Yes, sir.

MONT.   Have you sent for the plumber to look over the sanitary conditions of my bathroom? It annoys me.

BROWN.   Yes, sir. He should be here now. [*Exits R.C.*]

CHAR. [*Enters L.C.*]   Are you feeling well this morning?

MONT.   Well enough to talk business with you. Your bank account is overdrawn.

CHAR.   I know it. You keep me down to cases.

MONT.   I'll keep you down to day labor if you're not careful, young man. Where were you last night?

CHAR.   At the club.

MONT.   You're a liar.

CHAR.   Uncle, you forget yourself.

MONT.   Silence, sir. I want you to find Albert Cooper.

CHAR. [*Aside*]   My God, does he know? [*Aloud*] Albert Cooper is dead, uncle. I've told you that repeatedly. How could I have married his wife were he alive? He was shot down while escaping from prison, years ago. He died in the hospital and was buried in potters' field.

BROWN. [*Enters R.C.*] The plumber has sent his apprentice. He's a new man, shall I let him come in?

MONT. Yes, send him in. [*Albert, dressed in overalls, with plumber's tools, enters R.C. at signal from Brown*]

BROWN. Right this way, my man. [*Crosses to L.2., opens door. Charlie staggers down C., clutches edge of table, turning his back to Albert. Albert bows, crosses behind Charlie, exit L.2. and throws down tools off L.*]

BROWN. Miss Clark is waiting to see you, sir.

MONT. Let her come in. [*Brown exits R.C.*] Charlie, you may go; I will talk with you some other time. If Cooper is dead his children must be found and justice done them before I die. [*Charlie crosses rapidly to L.2., opens door a little, looks off*]

MONT. What are you doing there now?

CHAR. Watching your plumber. He looks like a sneak thief. Better get him out of here as soon as possible. [*Gertrude enters R.C., goes down C., bows head*]

MONT. Never mind him. Leave me, I have something to say to Miss Clark. [*Charlie turns, bows low to Gertrude and exits L.C.*]

GERT. You sent for me, sir?

MONT. Yes, come over here beside me where I can see your face. [*Gertrude sits on ottoman at Montgomery's feet. Removes her glasses and keeps them off throughout the scene*]

MONT. I'm good-natured now. The morphine is in my veins. I'm not going to scold you.

GERT. You never scold me, sir.

MONT. No, because you're kind to me; you know your business. Gertrude, you've been faithful to me; a loyal, patient nurse. I shall provide for you in my will.

GERT. I expected no reward, Mr. Montgomery.

MONT. I know that. I have learned that this woman he calls his wife is an adventuress. It was you, Albert Cooper's wife, whom I believed I was aiding all these years. I tried to avoid disgrace, and at the same time aid the family my nephew ruined. He told me Cooper was dead, that he had married his widow. I forgave him for that and searched for the children.

GERT. Yes, yes, my children, where are they? Oh, sir, I have suffered more than human heart can bear. When I got out of the hospital where he left me to die, my babies were gone, my health was gone. I had lost my hair; I was so changed no one knew me. Then they took me back as a nurse. That is how you came to get me, sir.

MONT. It must have been the Almighty who sent you, Gertrude, and if suffering can atone for sin, there may be light yet for both of us. I am stricken with death, have but a few days to live, but before I die I want to see the little family so cruelly separated by my nephew once more united.

BROWN. [*Enters R.C.*] The parties I spoke of are here, sir. Will I wheel you in the garden to see them, or shall I have them come in?

MONT. Gertrude, you go and see the maid keeps her eye on that fellow in the bathroom. I will send for you when I'm done with these people.

GERT. Oh, my heart seems to be bursting with joy, Mr. Montgomery; your kind words give me new life—new hopes. [*Places arm about old man's neck and kisses him. They are both in tears. She hastens to exit L.2., wiping her eyes with handkerchief. She screams offstage, reels back, clutching at her bosom and looking off L.*]

MONT. What's the matter, Gertrude?

GERT. That man, sir!

MONT. Didn't you know he was there?

GERT. [*Slowly shakes her head. Hammering upon metal heard off L., Gertrude pushes door slowly open again. Her lips move in a frightened whisper*] No, no, it can't be, it can't be!

MONT. What are you frightened about, Gertrude?

GERT. [*Crosses rapidly to Montgomery*] Oh, Mr. Montgomery, that man in your apartments! There is something about him reminds me of Albert.

MONT. Nothing but your nerves, my girl. He's only a poor, harmless plumber. Run on now and see that he doesn't charge me for anything he's not doing. [*Gertrude adjusts her glasses and exits L.2. Ned and Flossie enter R.C. in store clothes, badly worn but tidy. They enter hand in hand, and approach Montgomery, timidly looking all about. Mother Murphy follows them on R.C., wears green bonnet, plaid shawl, and stands C. Brown and Mike, in uniform, follow Mother on R.C. and stand in doorway*]

NED. This certainly is a swell joint, and that's no idle dream.

FLOS. Ned, look at the gold handle on the coal shovel.

NED. See the big pair of curling-irons beside 'em! [*Pointing to tongs and brass-handled shovel on the hearth*]

MOTH. I must be in one of those dreams people get after eating mince pie.

MONT. Are these the children, Brown?

BROWN. Yes, sir, and this is the good woman who has cared for them.

MOTH. Top of the mornin' to you, sir.

MONT. Is this Mrs. Murphy?

MOTH. It is. Mother Murphy, as I'm known on the Bowery, sir.

MONT. Don't you remember me?

MOTH. Seems to me I do, sir.

MONT. I used to be in business on Broome Street.

MOTH. Are you the old gentleman I used to scrub for?

MONT. I am, Mother. Are these the babies I left with you in 1890?

MOTH. The very same, sir, and the devil of a time I've had scratching for their living.

MONT. I sent you money to provide for them every month by my nephew, until you moved and he could find you no more.

MOTH. Devil a bit did I ever see of your nephew or any money, sir.

BROWN. The woman speaks the truth. This officer will vouch for her honesty.

MIKE. That I will, sir, and pardon me, but you might as well know all the truth while we are at it. One of the worst gamblers of the Tenderloin poses as your nephew and obtains money by using your name.

NED. Yes, and he insulted my sister last night.

MOTH. Don't mind him, sir, it was no insult. The young gentleman was kind to us.

MONT. Enough! Brown, you have convinced me. Take them away. I must have time to think. Oh, the shame, the disgrace of it all!

NED. We're not here to disgrace anybody. If you are ashamed of us we will go. I didn't want to come. It kept me from work.

MONT. Then you work, young man?

NED. Yes, sir.

MONT. What do you do?

NED. Sell papers.

MONT. Would you work just as hard if this mansion was yours?

NED. Yes, sir. I'd have to if I wished to keep it.

MONT. Leave the boy with me, Brown, he interests me. [*Brown motions to Mother, and exits R.C. with Mike*]

MOTH. Come, Floss. [*Crosses up R.C.*]

FLOS. Can't I stay, too? Oh, it's all so grand!

MONT. Let the girl remain if she wishes. I will see you before you leave, Mrs. Murphy, and give you a check for what I owe you.

MOTH. God bless you, sir! What will I do with all that money? [*Exits R.C.*]

MONT. Come to me, children, I'll not harm you. I'm only a poor, sick old man, with a broken heart, waiting patiently for the reaper.

FLOS. [*Sitting on ottoman before Montgomery*] What's a reaper?

NED. Don't ask foolish questions, Floss. He's the fellow that reaches out and takes in all the chips.

MONT. That's right. The fellow that rakes us all in some day. Do you remember your parents, children?

NED. No, sir, we weren't old enough.

FLOS. I do, I'm older than him. I remember mama, she was always crying.

MONT. Would you like to see her again?

FLOS. Yes, sir, very much.

NED. Would I like to see her? Say, I'd eat her up. [*Pounding heard on metal off L.*] What's going on in there? Is someone tapping the till? [*Peeping at keyhole, L.2.*]

FLOS. You must not peek, Ned, that's rude. I want to look at some of those books awful bad, but I wouldn't ask. [*Pointing to center table*]

MONT. You may look at them, my dear, while Ned and I go and investigate the noise in my apartments. [*Flossie crosses to center table, examining books*]

NED. Is that your room in there?

MONT. Yes. Do you think you are able to assist me to enter? [*Trying to rise*]

NED. Do I? Just try me. Lean on my shoulder hard as you want to. I'm strong. [*Assisting Montgomery to rise*]

MONT. [*Leaning on Ned and walking L.2. by aid of cane*] You would be a handy boy to keep around here. Wouldn't you rather work for me than sell papers?

NED. How much do you pay?

MONT. What salary do you want?

NED. All I can get.

MONT. We will talk it over. Easy now, don't let me fall. [*Ned pushes open L.2., exits with Montgomery*]

CHAR. [*Enters L.C. dressed in velvet jacket, riding boots. Crosses down R. Is about to open R.2. when he sees Flossie leaning with both elbows on table engrossed in book. Aside*] She here?

FLOS. [*Looking up and smiling*] Hello, Prince.

CHAR. Hello, what are you doing here?

FLOS. Reading a book.

CHAR. Did you drop from the sky?

FLOS. Do I look like an angel?

CHAR. Yes, and a very beautiful one. What brought you here?

FLOS. My feet. I don't have carriages like the one you promised to take me in.

CHAR. Did you come here to get the carriage ride I promised you?

FLOS. Certainly, and that ring my brother made me give back.

CHAR. Are you joshing me? How old are you, anyway?

FLOS. That's pretty hard to say, seeing I don't know who my mother is or when I was born; but I feel—oh, let me see, quite a young lady—about eighteen, I guess.

CHAR. You don't look sixteen, but you are sweet enough to kiss. Then you're not mad with me after what happened last night?

FLOS. No, why should I be? You treated me all right.

CHAR. Then here's the ring. [*Places ring on Flossie's finger and goes to embrace her*]

FLOR. [*In stylish riding-gown, hat and veil, enters R.2.*] What is that girl doing here?

CHAR. You'll have to ask her. I haven't found out yet.

FLOS. My, but ain't you swell. [*Circling about Flora*]

FLOR. Who are you?

FLOS. Flossie Murphy.

FLOR. Who brought you here?

FLOS. The old woman.

FLOR. Where is she now?

FLOS. Out in the garden. [*Crosses up to R.C.*]

CHAR. This is the girl I told you about, Flo. I gave her mother my address last night but I didn't think she'd bring her girl here. The old lady needs the money and I want the girl.

FLOR. Shame, she is only a child!

CHAR. No matter; so much the better. Now's the chance to get her. You take her down to the side entrance. [*Pointing R.2.*] I'll have the carriage sent round to you. I'm going horseback and will meet you in the park.

FLOR. Suppose she won't go?

CHAR. Yes, she will. Quick now or we will be discovered. [*Pushing open R.2.*] Come here, Butterfly, do you want to take that ride?

FLOS. Sure I do, if you ask the old woman.

CHAR. You go down to the carriage with this lady. I'll go and tell your mother.

FLOR. [*Crosses R.2.*] Come, my dear, we'll not be gone long. [*Stretches her hand forward to Flossie*]

FLOS. [*Advances slowly R. and gives her hand to Flora*] My, what beautiful diamonds. See, I have one on my hand also. It's not very big, but it's my engagement ring. [*Kisses ring and looks over her shoulder at Charlie and exits*]

FLORA. Charles Montgomery, hell has no fires hot enough for you. [*Smiling*]

CHAR. How about yourself?

FLOR. Oh [*Shrugs shoulders*], I'm resigned to my fate. I don't think about such things. It's unpleasant. [*Exits R.2., closes door. Riding master appears L.C.*]

CHAR. Send James around to the side entrance with the coupé. Hold my horse ready in the front drive. [*Master salutes and exits L.C. Montgomery and Ned enter L.2., Montgomery leaning on Ned*]

CHAR. Uncle, I am waiting for a check.

MONT. You'll have to keep on waiting. [*Sits L. of table by Ned's aid. Ned stands L.C.*]

CHAR. [*Leans on table*] Don't get it? Do you want the bank to pull me up and disgrace you?

MONT. Disgrace me, you low-lived dog. You've done nothing else during your whole life. Ned, is this the man who insulted your sister?

NED. Yes, sir.

CHAR. The boy lies. I never saw him before.

MONT. Silence, sir. Where's your sister, Ned? I want her evidence, also.

NED. She must have gone out. I'll get her. [*Exits R.C. on run*]

MONT. Charlie, I want you to take this woman of yours and get out.

CHAR. How dare you speak of my wife like that? Uncle, if you were a younger man I'd—[*Raising arm as if to strike Montgomery*]

MONT. [*Rising and clutching table*] You'd what? My God, has it come to this? Raise your arm to me, after all I've done—I'll cut you off, sir! You and your adventuress you call your wife. This excitement is killing me. My heart, Charlie—it's humming away like the tongue of a monster bell. Call my nurse, Gertrude, I'm dying—help—[*Falls insensible upon rug in front of table, center*]

ALB. [*With kit of tools and short section of lead pipe in his hand enters L.2., runs forward and tries to catch Montgomery as he falls. Kneels and, laying his pipe and tools down, raises Montgomery's head*] What are you standing there for, man? Run for help. [*Charlie R.C. bending over Montgomery. Ned, Brown, Mike, Mother, enter R.C. in order named—Gertrude, wearing glasses, enters L.2.*]

NED. See, the old man has been murdered.

CHAR. Yes, cruelly murdered, struck on the head by that man, who is an escaped convict. See, his weapon lays beside him.

GERT. [*Crosses C. in front of Montgomery's body*] You lie, Charles Montgomery. It is true this man is an escaped convict, but he would not be guilty of murder.

CHAR. How do you know?

GERT. [*Removing glasses*] Because he is my husband.

ALB. [*Catching Gertrude in his arms*] Flora, my wife.

GERT. [*Freeing herself*] Yes, Albert, your wife once and for all time, had it not been for that man. [*Pointing to Charlie. Kneeling*] Mr. Montgomery was not murdered. There is no sign of a blow upon his head. He was suffering from an aneurism, the most dangerous disease of the heart. Undue excitement caused it to burst. [*Arising*] This man died of a broken heart.

CHAR. Yes, and left me his sole heir to millions. I defy you all. I am master of this house now. There is no room here for escaped convicts and beggars. So get out. [*Lawyer, white hair and Prince Albert, with legal document, enters L.2., crosses to L. of table*]

NED. [*Climbing on table and bending down so he can pat Charlie on shoulder*] Hold on, Prince Charlie. I might have been a beggar once, but I ain't no more. The old man changed his mind just a few minutes before he died, sent for his lawyer, cut you off and left his money to me. Read that and then you get out. [*Takes legal paper from lawyer, hands it to Charlie. Charlie opens it, staggers back, looks up to lawyer, who nods*]

CURTAIN

		Mother		*Ned*		*Brown*	
Mike		*Montgomery*		*Lawyer*		*Gertrude*	*Albert*
	Charlie						

PICTURE FOR 2ND CURTAIN

Mother		*Brown*		*Charlie and Riding Master*
	Mike		*Lawyer*	

POSITIONS FOR 3RD CURTAIN

Ned   Gertrude   Albert

PICTURE

Albert, Gertrude, and Ned in group L.C. downstage. Albert has arm about Gertrude. Gertrude has hand on Ned's head. Ned is showing will to his father, Albert. Mike and lawyer stand facing upstage talking to Mother and Brown near conservatory R.C. Charles and Riding Master in heated conversation in hallway seen through L.C. door, Charlie pulling on his gloves. Montgomery's body lies in front of table C., head L., feet R.; Butler with folded arms and bowed head at feet. Little maid with white apron and cap, kneeling, crying at his head L.

Arrange for curtain call after second curtain. Positively do not let character who plays Montgomery take this call. Let the boy come last with father and mother. Do not let Flora or Flossie take this call. This is important to further interest in play.

ACT III.

SCENE 1: *One month later. Broadway after dark in front of Shanley's. Drop in 3.—painted to represent entrance to restaurant. Arch door R.C. with interior backing. Window L.C. with interior backing. Set piece representing rear of cab R.2. There can be profiles with backings so as to show drivers on the box in livery. Curtain discovers Mike, in uniform of Broadway police, hustling supers as newsboys and venders, beggars and so forth R. and L.— supers as ladies and gents enter and exit from R.C.*

BROWN. [*In business suit enters from R.*]   Hello! Mike, been transferred?

MIKE.   Yes, promoted to the Broadway Squad. Have you found Miss Flossie?

BROWN.   Not yet. Flora Bradley doesn't deny she took the girl to ride, but says she let her out in the park and she ran away.

MIKE.   A likely story. What does the coachman say?

BROWN.   Anything for money and they have lots of it.

MIKE.   Too bad the boy Ned can't get his own.

BROWN.   Yes. Prince Charlie's attorneys claim the old man was tricked into signing his property away. The codicil reads "To Cooper's boy to provide for the mother and help find the father."

MIKE.   Yes, and the mother signed as witness. What more do they want?

BROWN.   She signed as Gertrude Clark, the nurse. Now she can't prove she is Cooper's wife or that Ned is her boy. They won't take a convict's testimony in the case. If the girl could be found, she was old enough to remember her mother. Her identification would establish the boy's right to the property.

MIKE.   All the more reason for them keeping her hid. [*Calling R.*] Here, move on. Don't bump that lady, or I'll bump your head.

MOTH. [*Enter R.1., talking off R.*]   You have a foot on you like a rhinoceros. You popped my corn for me. Oh, me, oh, my. [*Hopping on one foot*] What's that? Here, officer, arrest that Welsh rabbit, he called me a cuckoo. [*Bumps into Brown*] Excuse me, sir.

MIKE.   Don't mind them, Mother.

MOTH.   Don't mind them, who—those loafers or me corns? Oh, it's you, is it?

BROWN.   What are you doing on Broadway, Mrs. Murphy?

MOTH.   Looking for me poor gal.

BROWN.   Where's Ned?

MOTH. Doing the selfsame thing and trying to support himself. My business has gone to the devil with all my trouble. The lawyers offered to advance Ned money, but he's so proud he refused it. I hear you're doing what you can, sir, and I'm much obliged to you. Hist, Mike, can I borrow your ear for a minute? [*Crosses L.*]

MIKE. You can if you don't whistle in it.

MOTH. Walk down the street. I need protection. Excuse us, Brown, he'll be back in a wink.

BROWN. Going to get a drink?

MOTH. No. no. I said in a wink—one of those things you get on Broadway after dark. [*Winks at Brown, exits after Mike, L.1. Gertrude, in plain street dress, with small parcel of dry goods, enters R.1.*]

BROWN. Hello, little woman, I was just speaking of you. I see the governor has pardoned your husband.

GERT. Yes, Brown, he was never guilty. I found out too late that Charles Montgomery forged the checks that sent Albert to jail and turned me against the father of my children.

BROWN. And I shall help you. [*Clasping her hand*]

GERT. I understand, Brown. I only hope my daughter is in the hands of an honest man like you.

BROWN. Would you know her if you met?

GERT. I suppose not, though my mother heart should tell me.

BROWN. Where is your husband?

GERT. Looking for employment. We all want work. I'm sewing, but it takes us from the search for Flossie.

BROWN. Let me help you. [*Reaching for money*] I have money saved and you are welcome.

GERT. No, Arthur, you have done enough.

BROWN. You look tired. Won't you come in and have supper?

GERT. In Shanley's? Oh, no. I'm not dressed well enough. Besides I have this work to deliver. Ned promised to meet me here. He will be around with his extras before long. I shall walk up and down and watch the people till he comes.

BROWN. If I find him, you shall both go to supper with me. [*Exit L.1.*]

GERT. All lights, music and bright faces. I wonder if there are any hearts in there as heavy as mine. What a beautiful girl in that cab. She's going to alight. [*Looks R.*]

FLOS. [*In stylish gown, with jewels and so forth, enters R.1., passes Gertrude*] Why couldn't that stupid driver let me out in front of the joint, instead of waltzing me round the corner into a dark street. Guess he don't know who I am. Shanley's, this is the place. I won't know how to act in that swell bakery. I feel so funny in all these new togs. I want to stay on the street and show off. Charlie don't want anyone to see me. He put me in the cab and told me to keep out of sight. I don't blame him, I must look out of sight. I guess he's afraid he'll lose me. He says if the old woman gets me, she'll put me back to washing dishes. [*To Gertrude*] Who you looking at? Didn't you ever see a lady before? [*Gertrude bows head, crosses L.C.*] My, but these common people are rude. I suppose she knows I'm going to be a bride. When Charlie bought me these clothes he told me they was my wedding *trousers.* He's getting awful fresh. I don't know whether I will marry him or not. [*Exits R.C. Waiter seen seating her at window L.C. Flossie ties napkin round neck—drinks out of water bottle—jokes with waiter, whispering to him from behind. Waiter throws his head back and is seen shaking himself with laughter*]

GERT.   Poor, wild, young thing. I wonder who she is. My, but she is beautiful. Her face seems to fascinate me. I will walk back this way on my return and see if she is still there. [*Starts L. but stops, watching Flossie as if fascinated. Charlie and Flora enter R.1. in evening dress without seeing Gertrude*]

FLOR.   Fool, you are taking a desperate chance.

CHAR.   She wouldn't stay cooped up any longer. She's so changed her mother wouldn't know her.

FLOR.   I should hope not. [*Gertrude bows head and slowly exits L.1. Charlie and Flora turn and watch her*]

CHAR.   Who's that?

FLOR.   Some hungry beggar. Why don't you take the girl and get out to Europe before they catch you up in the game?

CHAR.   She says I must marry her first.

FLOR.   And will you?

CHAR.   You know me. I shall make her think so. You must go on playing the sister gag. [*Exits R.C. Flora laughs and exits R.C. Drops chatelaine bag containing purse*]

ALB.   [*Plain, rough, but neat clothes, enters R.1.*]   I can't find employment. No one wants me. My mind is always on my lost child. Had I known her that night on the Bowery, when she gave me this rose, I might have saved all this suffering. [*Taking rose from inside vest and kissing it and replacing it; sees bag*] Hello, has my luck changed? [*Picks up bag*] A pocketbook, and filled with bills. Thank God, my prayer has been answered. This will relieve my wife and boy from want. Help us to find our Flossie. No, I can't keep this. It wouldn't be right. I'm under suspicion now. I must be careful.

FLOR. [*Enters R.C., with waiter, followed by Charlie*] There it is in that man's hands. He must have snatched it from me as I got out of my carriage.

ALB. I just picked it up, ma'am. [*Offering bag*]

FLOR. [*Snatching bag from Albert*] You were counting the money and placing it in your pocket. There is some missing.

ALB. A thief don't stop on Broadway to count stolen money. [*Mike enters L.1. Crowd gathers from R. and L.*]

CHAR. You seem familiar with their methods. Officer, this man has robbed my wife. I want him arrested.

MIKE. Cooper, what does this mean?

ALB. They are mistaken. I found the bag and returned it.

CHAR. Lock him up, officer. I know him to be a common thief.

MIKE. And I know him to be honest.

CHAR. If you refuse to arrest this man I shall prefer charges against you.

MIKE. Your word don't count for much at headquarters. You are not above suspicion yourself. Take that hand-painted fairy and go inside. [*Crosses up steps*]

CHAR. You are all witnesses that this officer has insulted me, and he refused to do his duty. That man is a thief.

ALB. Let me at him, Mike. [*Rushes at Charlie*]

MIKE. [*Catches Albert and pushes him back*] Hold on, Cooper.

ALB. I'll get you yet, Charles Montgomery. God help you when I do.

MIKE. Go on, go on, don't be a fool. [*Backs Cooper off R.1. Charlie and Flora seen standing inside beside Flossie. Charlie sits facing out, head close to Flossie's face, talking earnestly*]

GERT. [*Enter L.1.*] Yes, she's there still. [*Looking in window*] She has company. No wonder that man's talking to her. Where have I seen him before? I wish he would raise his head—my God, it is Charles Montgomery, and he has ensnared and will ruin her as he did me—as he has so many others. [*Staggers back, puts her hand to face*] If I could only warn her. Get her away from him some way.

MOTH. [*Enters L.1.*] What's this crying in the street, Mrs. Cooper? Have you gone daffy? Just as we are getting you straightened up of all your trouble.

GERT. Look, Mother Murphy, do you see that man?

MOTH. See that man? Faith, I'm not blind. I see two of them. One is making love, the other spilling soup down his back. [*Pointing to waiter who is just serving Charlie and Flossie*]

GERT. No, no, not the waiter. I mean the gentleman.

MOTH. Faith, there is no gentleman there, my dear. A man that would talk to a gal like that while she's trying to eat her victuals is no gentleman.

GERT. Don't you see who it is?

MOTH. Sure enough, it's Prince Charlie—and say, what the devil has come over my eyes?

GERT. What's the matter, Mrs. Murphy?

MOTH. The girl I'm lookin' at. Make the snakes crawl back in Ireland, but it's her.

GERT. It's who?

MOTH. That brazen huzzy in the silk petticoat. Look at her with the airs of a lady and the jewels of a Dutch heiress. Eatin' her soup with a fork. Look at her, woman. Don't you know who that is? [*Gertrude shakes her head*] That's Flossie Murphy Cooper. That's your own daughter, my dear. [*Gertrude gives a stifled scream and clutches Mother for support*] Be still now. Don't be a fool because your child is—brace up—brace up and be a man. [*Messenger boy in uniform of W.U.T.Co., about same size as Ned, enters R.1., exits R.C. Is seen again at table L.C. with Flossie and Charlie. Charlie seals and hands boy a message*]

GERT. My child, my little Flossie in the power of that man! Quick, Mrs. Murphy, we must do something to save her.

MOTH. Easy, now. Easy. We'll do that same thing but we will be diplomatic. That man is a smooth-tongued slippery cuss. You wait here and keep your eyes on him while I get a cop.

GERT. What is he giving that messenger boy?

MOTH. I suppose it's a date with another gal. He has a hundred but the divil will have him when I get back.

FLOR. [*Following messenger on R.C.*] Hurry now, catch that car and change at 34th Street. [*Messenger starts L.*]

GERT. Stop, boy, give me that message. [*Grabs message*]

FLOR. What do you mean, woman. Let that boy alone. [*Messenger dodges Gertrude and exits L.1.*]

MOTH. Here, give me that. Come back here, you little divil. I'll catch you. I'll turn you up and spank your—[*Exits L.1.*]

GERT. You adventuress, I have found you at last.

FLOR. So it's you, is it?

GERT. Yes, the nurse who foiled your plans to poison the dearest old man who ever lived. The mother of that little girl who you stole and are leading to ruin. Give her to me at once.

FLOR. Be still, woman, don't make a scene. You shall have her. See, you are attracting a crowd. [*To waiter*] Quick, Lewis, call Mr. Montgomery.

Tell him to bring the girl. [*Waiter exits. Charlie and Flossie seen to rise hurriedly and enter R.C.*]

FLOR. Quick into that carriage and get away—I will stay and have her locked up.

FLOS. Who is it? What does she want?

CHAR. Never mind. Come.

GERT. Flossie, Flossie, my child. Don't you know me? [*Stepping forth and reaching toward her*]

CHAR. Come. [*Pulls Flossie R.*]

FLOR. [*Stepping between Flossie and Gertrude*] Hands off. I will have you arrested.

FLOS. Stop. You hurt me. Let me see what she wants.

CHAR. Come on, I say. [*Jerks Flossie off R.1. by the arm*]

GERT. Oh, please, someone stop them. They are stealing my child. [*Ned with extras enters R.1.*] Ned, my boy—help—[*Starts toward Ned, staggers, fainting. Ned throws down papers. Catches Gertrude, lays her C., kneels behind her. Crowd gathers about in sympathy*]

FLOR. She's a rank imposter, deserving of no sympathy. Someone call the patrol.

NED. Stop. She is no imposter. She has fainted from worry and grief. This woman is my mother, and I am here to protect her. You are the one who should be arrested. [*Pointing to Flora*]

FLOR. Who will take your word. You're only a boy of the streets—a ragged beggar.

NED. Child of the streets, yes, but no beggar.

MOTH. [*Enters dragging messenger boy by ear*] Come on, sonny, or I'll twist your ear off. [*Sees Ned*] What's the matter? Have I come too late?

FLOR. Release that boy. I sent him on an errand. What are you doing with my message?

MOTH. Holding it for the police. Where the divil are they? When there is a fight they all run the other way.

NED. Here's the cop—it's Mike. We're all right now. [*Calling*] Mike, Mike.

MIKE. [*Enters R.1.*] Hello, Ned. What do you want?

NED. I want you to arrest that woman. [*Pointing to Flora*]

MIKE. What's the trouble?

NED. I don't know, but I am going to find out.

MOTH. That woman knows where your sister is, Ned. Flossie was in that restaurant a minute ago with Prince Charlie. They sent this boy away with

a message. Here it is. I can't read, but I can run like hell, can't I, boy?
[*Hands Ned the message*]

NED. [*Tearing open the envelope and reading, aside*] "Frank, meet me at
the Waldorf-Astoria, Room 604. I want you to perform a mock marriage.
Come quick." [*Crumbles message in his hand*] Not as quick as I will go.
Here, boy, I want to trade jobs with you. Lend me your coat and cap. I will
deliver this message. [*Pulls off his coat and hat. Throws them on top of his
bundle of papers, jerks coat and cap off of messenger boy and puts them on*]

MIKE.   What are you going to do?

NED.   Turn detective. Look after my mother, Mike, and don't let that
woman get away. Here, boy, you can sell those extras for me. When I get
back I'll have money enough to set you up in business. [*Hands messenger
boy his papers, hat and coat and exits R.1. on the run. Mother, who has
been kneeling by Gertrude during this scene, raises her to her feet, just as
Ned exits. Gertrude calls "Ned, Ned," stretching forth arms. Brown enters
L.1. Throws his arm about Gertrude and she starts to exit L.1. between
Mother and Brown. Mike has started to drag Flora off R.1. She puts up a
fight and Brown handcuffs her. Crowd laughs and taunts her—"oot, oot, oot,"
slap Lewis the waiter with their hats and drive him in restaurant*]

LEW. [*Pulls apron, tries to make a stand*]   You loafers, hoodlums. [*Shakes
fist, throws flower pots and exits. Sticks head out of window, shakes fist.
Lights out. Dark change*]

SCENE 2: *Same night. Room in the Waldorf-Astoria. Drop in 2. with windows
R.C. backed by house-tops. Railing and ladder of fire escape seen through
L.C. Arch door draped by heavy curtains R.2., supposed to lead into bed-
chamber. Red bunch off this entrance. Door opening off L.2. White off this
entrance. Table C. containing novels, fruit, candy, flowers and so forth. Over
table drop-light or standard lamp. Fancy chairs, R. and L. of table. Couch and
writing desk R. Couch well downstage R. Desk R. Chair before desk, pencils,
paper, pens, and so forth in desk. Fancy sofa pillow on couch. Newspaper,
cuspidors, rugs, wastebasket. Full mirror downstage L. Statue of Moorish
slave and flower set so as to reflect by mirror. Electric button for call bell in
practical circular molding to break away, on return piece L.*

FLOS. [*Discovered before mirror in evening dress, jewels on her hands and
at her throat. She is dressing her hair with flowers*] I wonder who my
mother was. As I remember her, she was very pretty. I wish she was with
me tonight. Charlie has gone for the minister. He's going to tie the knot
right in this room. Now it's come down to saying yes, I'm scared maybe I

ain't doing right. [*Crosses to couch*] I'd gone home and got Mother Murphy and Ned if they'd let me, but I'll make it all right when the job's done. I'll have money enough so they won't have to work no more. This is a bully book. It's by Laura Jean Libby. It tells about a poor girl just like me, who married and became a duchess. I don't believe I'd marry a Dutchman. [*Charlie enters L.2., closes door and listens. Flossie sitting up with book in lap*] Behold the bridegroom comes. What are you listening for, Prince? Are you scared your mother-in-law's coming upstairs?

CHAR. No, you see I have no business in the room. They are very strict at this hotel. I didn't dare to register you as my wife.

FLOS. Well, I should say not. Where's the preacher? The crimp is all coming out of my hair. [*Crosses to mirror*]

CHAR. [*Lighting cigaret*] See here, Flossie, if my friend doesn't come pretty soon we can't get married till we get over the pond.

FLOS. No, sir, you don't float me across no pond on promises.

CHAR. Now come, Flossie. Don't be obstinate. It will be only a matter of a few days.

FLOS. Yes, I know, but there's lots can happen in a few days. Suppose I get seasick, or the ship goes down?

CHAR. Then we will die in each other's arms and sink together.

FLOS. If we do the fishes will find my marriage certificate buttoned under my shirtwaist. I ain't putting myself up as any saint, Prince. I may not be as polite and soft-spoken as some girls. I use words that ain't writ down in the Bible, but I say my prayers when I don't forget about it, and when I do I ask God to keep me right for the man I'm going to call husband.

CHAR. Yes, you're a diamond in the rough, and, hang it all, I like you, Floss. I'll be truthful with you if nothing more.

FLOS. Haven't you always been?

CHAR. Not exactly. You see the fact of the matter is I can't marry anyone. [*Crosses L.*]

FLOS. Then what have you been foolin' around for all this time?

CHAR. Because I am madly in love with you.

FLOS. This book says, "Beware of him who speaks of love and not of marriage vows."

CHAR. Then you believe that book?

FLOS. Yes. It is a very good book.

CHAR. Hang what the good book says. Come over here and sit beside me. [*Seats himself on couch*]

FLOS. Promise me you'll not get fresh. That you won't start no lolly-gaggin'.

CHAR. I promise.

FLOS. Cross your heart.

CHAR. Cross my heart. [*Makes sign of cross on right side*]

FLOS. Get out. Your heart ain't on that side.

CHAR. No, but it will be when you sit down here. [*Making room on his left*]

FLOS. [*Sits down timidly and adjusts skirts; raises her eyes*] Why don't you tell me I look nice?

CHAR. You certainly are a swell looker for a kid.

FLOS. Get out. I ain't no kid. I'm most seventeen.

CHAR. Old enough to smoke. Have a cigaret?

FLOS. The old woman would beat hell out of me if she saw me smoke one of these. [*Taking cigaret*]

CHAR. But she won't see you. [*Putting his arm about her; his hand on her bare arm*]

FLOS. Take that cigaret-holder off my shoulder.

CHAR. A cigaret-holder?

FLOS. Yes, your hand. It's all stained from the smoke. [*Pushing Charlie's hand and moving down*]

CHAR. That's nicotine.

FLOS. What's nicotine?

CHAR. Nicotine comes from the cigaret. It's poison.

FLOS. Then why do you offer them to me? [*Looking at cigaret in her hand*]

CHAR. Oh, they won't hurt you.

FLOS. They won't do me no good. Let me see you make it come out of your nose.

CHAR. What?

FLOS. The smoke.

CHAR. Oh. [*Blows smoke through nose. Flossie laughs*] What are you laughing at?

FLOS. When you do that you look just like the Devil.

CHAR. [*Springing to his feet, crosses C.*] So I am, the Devil in the form of a man. God placed such bewitching creatures as you on this earth to make men what I am. Come, you have tempted me long enough. You must be mine. [*Starts forward and as Flossie springs up, clasps her in his arms*]

FLOS. Quit now. You hurt me. Let me go. What are you looking like that for, Charlie? You frighten me. [*Begins to sob and cry*]

CHAR. [*Releasing her*] Oh, if you are going to cry, I'll let you alone.

FLOS. [*Snuffling and smiling through her tears*] Then I'll keep on crying all the time. [*Sits on couch*] My, but you're roughhouse when you get started. Worse than the Chatham Square gang what took me to Coney Island.

CHAR. See here, Floss, why can't you look at this matter in the right light? I want you to go to Europe with me. I'll give you everything money can buy. Diamonds, fine clothes, horses, carriages, servants—nothing but a good time. Christmas every day in the year.

FLOS. You must want to work Santa Claus overtime.

CHAR. I'll be your Santa Claus, and I'll not kick at my job. Come, what do you say? Haven't I given you beautiful presents already? Have you no gratitude? What more do you want?

FLOS. A plain band of gold on that finger.

CHAR. You shall have it. Anything else?

FLOS. Yes, a man with a long face, who will tell you how to put it on.

CHAR. Rot. You'll have to cut out the man with the long face.

FLOS. Then you will have to fill up the pond before you'll get me to cross it.

CHAR. See here, do you think I'm going to be foiled by a strip of a girl like you? Are you aware I have you in my power? That I can do with you as I please?

FLOS. Maybe you can if you are good to me, but if you speak like that and get me mad, I'll tear something. [*Rips lace on sleeve*]

CHAR. Don't destroy that dress. It cost me a hundred dollars.

FLOS. [*Ripping lace on other sleeve*] I don't care if it cost a thousand. If you get me riled, I'll tear it off. [*Throws herself on couch in convulsion of sobs*]

CHAR. See here, my fine lady, if you are going to fight me like that, I'll place you back on the Bowery in rags.

FLOS. [*Springing up*] Send me back. There's where I belong. Give me my old garments and let me go back. Then such men as you may pass me by. My soul will feel more secure with my body clothed in rags. [*Crosses C.*] There's the flowers you gave me, your rings, your diamond necklace, your dirty old picture—all you gave me. I'll give you everything, everything but what you want. [*Tearing jewels, locket, and so forth, and throwing them at Charlie; then picking up skirts and jumping couch, exits behind curtain R.2. Charlie starts after her. Ned pounds on door off L.*]

CHAR. [*Pauses and looks over shoulder in frightened manner*] Who's there?

FLOS. [*Off R.*] The Devil come to claim his own. Take that, and that, and that. [*Throwing shoes, corset, stockings, petticoats, undergarments, one at a time, through curtain at Charlie, who dodges these missiles C. Ned keeps up a vigorous hammering at the door. Flossie off R.]* If you come in here, Charles Montgomery, I'll kill you. [*Throwing her high-heeled shoe and striking Charlie*]

CHAR. Oh, I'm not coming in, don't worry. [*Rubbing his arm*] Be still, Floss, there is someone at the door. [*Crosses and listens at door with back to window*] Who's there, I say. [*Aside*] Whoever it was, they have gone. [*Stands listening. Ned, as messenger boy, appears on fire escape, breaks window and springs into the room*]

CHAR. [*Staggers back and crosses down R.*] What is the meaning of this?

NED. I came to deliver a message, sir. [*Holding out book*]

CHAR. Is that any excuse for breaking in like a burglar?

NED. Yes, when the door is barred. My message is important.

CHAR. Well, sir, what is it?

NED. The Cooper family have elected me a committee of one to settle accounts with you and bring home my sister.

CHAR. Come, boy, get out of here or I will throw you out of the window.

NED. [*Pulling revolver and pointing at Charlie*] I don't think you will.

CHAR. Put that down. What are you going to do?

NED. Ask my sister a few little questions. If you have harmed her I'm going to kill you. [*Takes doorkey from door L.2., puts it in pocket*]

FLOS. [*Entering R. from behind curtains in her old dress and crosses, kneeling by Ned*] No, Ned, don't do that. See, I am ready to go home with you.

CHAR. Take that pistol away from him, girl. You can't tell what he may do. The boy's gone mad.

NED. Mad, you bet I am. Why didn't you come and take it away?

CHAR. If I could only get over and touch that bell.

NED. I'll let you touch it. The answer might not be just as you expect.

CHAR. On second thought, I guess I'll let it alone.

NED. Yes, I think you'd better.

FLOS. Ned, put up that pistol and take me home.

NED. Not if you've disgraced it.

FLOS. No, no, Ned. He tempted me. But see here are my old beads. The cross is still over my heart. You know my promise to Mother. No, no, Ned. I gave him back his clothes and jewels. I would not pay the price he asked.

NED. [*Putting up pistol in back pocket, raising Flossie to her feet and kissing her*] I believe you, my sister. See here in his own handwriting is a plan to ruin you. [*Hands Flossie message*]

FLOS. [*Reading*] A mock marriage. So you never meant fair by me from the first. [*Charlie springs forward and overpowers Ned. Takes pistol from him*]

NED. Quick, Flossie, touch the bell. [*Charlie strikes Ned on head with the pistol. Ned places hand to head and falls across couch unconscious*]

CHAR. [*Dashes to Flossie and pulls her from bell*] Come away from there.

FLOS. Too late, I have rung the bell.

CHAR. See, I've quieted your brother. If you give an alarm, I'll treat you the same way.

FLOS. Oh, Ned, Ned. [*Throwing her arm about Ned*] Speak to me, Ned. Coward, to strike a boy like that. [*Picks up flower urn and dumps out flowers and breaks it over Charlie's head. Charlie catches Flossie by throat and chokes her*]

FLOS. Help. Let me go. You are choking me. [*Charlie drops Flossie L. Bellboy pounds at door. Charlie picks up petticoat, binds it about Flossie's head, drags her off behind curtains R.2. Returns, takes key from Ned's pocket, opens door part way*]

BELL. Did you ring?

CHAR. Yes. You will find a well dressed Chinaman in the smoking-room waiting to see Charles Montgomery. Send him up.

BELL. Yes, sir. [*Charlie closes door and locks it. Ned rolls off couch and tries to rise. Charlie springs forward, turns Ned on his face and ties his hands behind him with strings. He takes strings from corset that lay on the floor*]

NED. You'll get all that's coming to you when I get away. Where's my sister?

CHAR. She's thinking over the folly of her ways.

NED. Do you ever think?

CHAR. No, I'm too busy to think.

NED. You'll have plenty of time to think in the place where I'm going to put you.

CHAR. Where's that? Over in Blackwell's?

NED. No, in the cell my father left vacant in Sing Sing. [*Bellboy knocking at door*]

CHAR. Now if you holler when that door opens, I'll use this on you. [*Shows pistol*]

NED. Oh, you'll find me game. I'll not squeal. I ain't found out all I want to yet. [*Charlie drags Ned up and throws him beneath window, pulls portieres about him and opens the door*]

BELL. [*Off L.*] Here's your Chinaman.

CHAR. Come in, Sam. [*Sam enters L.2. with long, blue canvas bag over shoulder. Charlie shuts door and locks it. Sam unshoulders his pack*] Sam, I can't do anything with that girl. We will have to take her away in that bag. Do you think you can carry her out without creating suspicion?

SAM. I am strong. If she is still, it will all go well.

CHAR. Oh, she'll be still all right. What have you in there?

SAM. Nothing but odds and ends. [*Showing lanterns, parasol, Chinese lace*]

CHAR. Good, you will find her in there. Hide the contents of your bag under the bed.

SAM. That's my business, always to hide something.

CHAR. It pays you well.

SAM. Maybe. I don't know. We will tell better in the end. [*Exits R.2., behind curtain. Bellboy knocks at door L.2. Charlie opens door L.2.*]

BELL. [*Off L.*] Here's your cord and wrapping paper, sir. [*Hands folded heavy paper and ball of cord to Charlie*]

CHAR. You're a good boy. Tell them at the desk not to have the maid bother us in the morning. We may sleep late.

BELL. [*Off L.*] Yes, sir.

CHAR. [*Shuts door*] Now, young man. I'll fix you so you can't walk in your sleep. You might fall out of a window. [*Pulls Ned to his feet, sets him in chair, and commences to bind him to chair, down C.*]

NED. Why don't you have the Chink put me in the bag?

CHAR. I'm afraid you'd kick.

NED. You bet I would. If I had a pair of spurs I'd ride his neck.

SAM. [*Enters R.2.*] What, one more fellow? I didn't bargain for two.

CHAR. Oh, this fellow don't count.

NED. Don't I? I can count Chinese all right. Yip son, yip soik, yip sa, that means I wouldn't give three cents for a pigtail.

SAM. Boy foolem all time. He no care.

CHAR. Have you a pill that will make him sleep?

NED. Yes, roll me a couple so I can dream I'm wealthy.

SAM. [*Producing two pills, taking one out between thumb and forefinger*] You take this you think you're Morgan.

NED. If I was, I'd scuttle every ship that carried Chinamen.

CHAR. Force it in his mouth while I hold his head. [*Sam tries to put pill in Ned's mouth. Ned bites his finger, spits out pill*]

SAM. Oh. [*Jumps about shaking his hand*] Muc j-er hy—pink-I-tye—muley-coy—wene—I—jar—we—fow—gemar.

CHAR. Did he bite you?

SAM. Yes, he bites like a mad dog.

CHAR. Did he swallow it?

NED. I swallowed something. I don't know whether it was the pill or the end of the Chink's finger. Whatever it was, I'm going to throw it up. Oh, Lord, ain't I sick. [*Coughing and gagging*]

CHAR. I'll just put this bell on the bum as an extra precaution. Give me that big knife of yours. [*Sam pulls big knife from up his sleeve. Charlie takes it, pushes blade behind button of bell, hits back of blade with butt of revolver and cuts off button and wire*] Is the girl ready? [*Handing knife to Sam*]

SAM. She all right.

CHAR. Bring her along then. The boy's all right. [*Sam exits R.2. Charlie unlocks door, puts key on outside, turns out electric lights. White light streams in from hall on Ned who hangs head as if asleep. Charlie ties handkerchief over his mouth, gives his head a couple of pushes*] That pill fixed him. All right, come on, Sam. [*Sam raises curtain R.2.; dull red gleam streams out. Sam lowers curtain, goes back. Lights seen to go out. Sam bowed with bag on his back filled with dummy to represent Flossie's length. Staggers out and exits L.2. in the ray of white light that streams in from L. Charlie shuts and locks door on outside. Lights very low, stage quite dark. Noise of cars and city bustle in the distance. Clock striking twelve*]

NED. [*Tumbles chair over and tumbles about floor. Gets handkerchief off his mouth by rubbing it on leg of table*] Help, help! If I could only get free. [*Pounding his forehead against desk*] If I could break this chair and find something to cut my hands loose. [*Working downstage and crushing legs of chair by pounding them on legs of table*] Help, help. [*Suddenly the light is turned on and Flossie is seen center with her hand on the student's lamp bending over table, looking down at Ned who lies panting on floor.*]

FLOS. Ned, Ned, my brother. Don't you know me? [*Kneeling by Ned*]

NED. Yes, Flossie. Where did you come from?

FLOS. That room. [*Pointing to R.2.*]

NED. I thought you was in the bag.

FLOS. I got out while they was giving you the pill. Where's your knife?

NED. In this pocket. Hurry, cut me free.

FLOS. [*Gets knife from pocket, starts to cut the cords that bind him*] Hold still now, or you'll hurt yourself.

NED. How did you fool them, Floss?

FLOS. I wrapped a heavy statue of Venus in the bed-clothes, put it in the bag and hid under the bed.

NED. [*Springing to his feet and trying door*] Brave girl, you've saved us both. The door's locked from the outside.

FLOS. Ring the bell.

NED. There's no bell to ring. Stay here. I'll give the alarm. [*Springs out of window*]

FLOS. Ned, Ned, don't leave me alone.

NED. I'll only be gone a minute. [*Goes down ladder. Charlie unlocking door outside L.2.*]

FLOS. What's that? [*Stops and listens*] Someone is unlocking the door, they are coming back. [*Key heard rattling in lock. Flossie starts to exit R.2.; Charlie enters, followed by Sam*]

CHAR. [*Throws door open, grabs Flossie*] Smart, ain't you. I've got you this time. [*Flossie screams; Charlie places hand over her mouth, throws her on couch*] Quick, Sam, the chloroform. That's the quickest. [*Sam throws down bag, produces bottle from folds of his frock and administers chloroform*] The boy has escaped. He has given the alarm. We are in a trap.

SAM. No, we go up, not down. Lock the door.

CHAR. [*Locks door*] What do you mean?

SAM. The roof. We are safe there; it is dark.

CHAR. I see! You mean the fire escape?

SAM. Yes.

CHAR. But the girl?

SAM. You go quick. I carry her. [*Ned and bellboy pounding on door L.2. Charlie exits, fire escape and up ladder. Sam picks up Flossie, throws her across his shoulder. Steps upon chair, from there through the window onto the fire escape and is seen ascending the ladder. Bellboy throws door open, working at pass-key. Ned enters followed by Brown and Mike. Crosses, throws open curtains R.2.*]

BROWN. Too late.

MIKE. Yes, the birds have flown.

NED. They have fooled me this time, but I'll find her if I have to search every den in Chinatown. Mike, you go down the elevator. Brown, go down the stairs. Boy, you go down the fire escape. I'm going on the roof. [*While he is speaking he has picked up the bag and opened it. Just as he finishes, he dumps out figure of Venus, from which bed-quilts fall, leaving the figure lying on the floor in the nude. Ned springs out the window and up the fire escape. Mike throws quilt over Venus and runs down stairs*]

SCENE 3: *Drop in 1.—Roof of the Waldorf-Astoria.*

CHAR. [*Enter R.1.—looks back*]   Come on, Sam. They are after us. Someone's coming up the ladder behind you. [*Crosses L.*]

SAM. [*Enter R.1. with Flossie on his shoulders; looks back*]   Damn, boy, he come up.

CHAR.   We are worse off than we were before. A mile in the air. No way to get down. That boy has alarmed the whole house. We are on top of a hornet's nest.

SAM.   We lay the girl down there. Hide behind chimney, catch boy, throw him off.

CHAR.   What will we do then?

SAM.   Go down same way as we come up. [*Exits L.1. with Flossie*]

CHAR.   Good. Hurry, here he comes. [*Hides behind tormentor R.*]

NED. [*Enters R.1.*]   I feel as if I was on Washington Monument. If that Chink went down with my sister he'll be caught. If he's up here, I'll find him. [*Charlie enters R. and creeps toward Ned on tiptoes*]

NED. [*Turns, pulls knife*]   Hold on there. Your Chinese friend dropped this on the fire escape. He must have known I'd need it. [*Brandishes Sam's big knife. Charlie reaches for pistol*]

NED.   Take your hand out of your pocket or I'll cut it off. [*Jumps forward and slashes at Charlie*] Throw 'em up.

CHAR. [*Throws up hands*]   You're losing time. The Chinaman is the man you want.

NED.   Not so bad as I want you. Show me where he is or I'll cut your buttons off. [*Slashes buttons off of Charlie's coat. Sam enters L.1.—creeps up behind Ned, pinions his arms behind him*]

CHAR. [*Takes knife from Ned*]   Good boy, Sam. Now we will throw him down an air shaft. [*Catches Ned by feet, swings around with his back L. Flossie enters L.1. Creeps up behind Charlie*]

NED.   Let me go. Help, help. [*Kicks vigorously*]

FLOS. [*Puts hand into Charlie's back pocket and gets his pistol, points it at Sam*]   Drop him.

CHAR. [*Looks over his shoulder*]   That's what we are going to do—over the edge of the roof.

FLOS.   Drop him or I'll shoot. [*Charlie and Sam drop Ned to a sitting position*]

NED.   Oh, what did you tell them to drop me for, Floss? They jarred all my teeth loose.

CHAR. [*Pointing L.*] There they come up through that sky light. Quick, Sam, we must fight. [*Flossie looks over her shoulder L.*]

CHAR. [*Grabs pistol from her, swings her into Sam's arms R.*] Take her down the ladder, Sam. I'll hold them off with this. Get my carriage. Don't wait for me. [*Sam exits R.1., dragging Flossie. Charlie crosses to R.1., keeps Ned off with pistol*]

NED. [*Crosses L. beckoning off*] Hurry, fellows! Here they are, quick or they'll get away. [*Charlie turns and exits R.1. Ned follows Charlie off R.1. on the run. Charlie shouts offstage R. Ned enters R.1., staggers C. clutching his arm*]

MIKE. [*Enters L.1.*] What's the matter, Ned? Are you shot?

NED. Yes, he winged me, but I still have a good pair of legs. Come on. [*Exits R.1. on the run. Mother Murphy enters L.1. with Venus in her arms upside down. Runs C. puffing and blowing*]

BROWN. [*Enters L.1. with pistol in his hand*] What did you bring that up here for?

MOTH. Faith, I don't know. Some one yelled "Fire" and I thought I'd save something.

BROWN. You have her upside down, Mother.

MOTH. So I have. All the blood will rush to her head. [*Turns Venus over and wraps her in her shawl. Brown exits R.1. on the run*]

BELL. [*Enters L.1., bare-headed, followed by police officer, with night-stick*] That's her, officer. She stole that out of Number 604.

MOTH. You're a liar. I live at Number 13 Billy-Goat Alley.

OFF. What have you in your arms?

MOTH. Me youngest child, sir.

OFF. How old is she? [*Sizing up the length of the bundle*]

MOTH. I don't know. I can't remember.

OFF. You can't remember?

MOTH. She is just getting her teeth, sir.

OFF. [*Taps Venus with night-stick*] My, but she must be a hard nut for her age.

MOTH. She has stiffening of the joints, sir.

OFF. Well, come on. I'll take you both to the lockup. [*Catches Mother and starts to pull her R. Brown shoots several shots in rapid succession in R.1. entrance*]

OFF. Owo—wo—wo. [*Dodging*] I guess we'll go this way. [*Exits L.1. on the run*]

MOTH. Come back here and help me down. [*Exits L.1. Dark change*]

SCENE 4: *Cellar in Chinatown. Drop in 3. painted like brick basement. Backed by eight-foot platform. Same as used in Act I. Hole 4'x4' cut in drop R.C., backed by prop. Bricks to break away. This hole is eight feet from floor opening onto platform. Door L.C. opening onto platform. Stairs coming down to stage. Return pieces R. and L. painted as wall of brick cellar. Holes representing dog kennels. Dogs chained to these kennels. Bulldog chained to bottom of stairs. Pile of straw up C. Barrel beside stairs, upside down with lighted candle on it. Scene quite dark. Curtain discovers Chinaman in blue trousers held up by belt; white undershirt and bare arms. He is whipping and driving dogs back into kennels with black snake whip.*

SAM. [*Enters from door at top of stairs, descends and picks up candle, holds it aloft and shades eyes with hand*] Prince Charlie, Prince Charlie! All right come down.

CHAR. [*Carrying Flossie in his arms, descends stairway; pauses part way down*] What an ugly brute. Will he bite?

SAM. All right, come on. I no tell him hurt you. He bite by and by. [*Charlie descends and stands Flossie on her feet L.C.*]

FLOS. [*Crying softly, crouches behind Charlie to get away from bulldog*] Don't let him bite me. Please don't. Keep him away.

CHAR. Oh, he's not the only dog here. Look about you. There are other dogs.

FLOS. [*Looking timidly about her as Sam holds candle aloft so she can penetrate the dark corners. She shudders and clings tightly to Charlie's arm*] Yes, I see them and you are the worst looking dog of them all. You, I mean. [*Pointing to Sam. Sam grins and shows teeth*]

CHAR. That's right. Show your teeth.

FLOS. So this is the end of my honeymoon. I would have never believed it. I expect every minute to wake up and find the past few hours a horrid dream.

CHAR. You can wake up if you only say the word. You said you preferred rags to my offer.

FLOS. And so I do. I hate you, Charles Montgomery.

CHAR. Then why do you cling to me?

FLOS. Because I am afraid of the other dogs.

CHAR. Still full of spunk. By my word, I hate to leave you here.

FLOS. You couldn't be so cruel? You wouldn't be as bad as that, would you, Charlie? [*Hands on his shoulder*]

CHAR. Do you know where you are? These dogs are mad. Their bite means a horrible death.

FLOS. I'm much safer with them than I am with you. Go.

CHAR. Come on, Sam. Bring the light. I guess a little of this will cause her to change her mind. [*Starts up stairs*]

FLOS. Please don't take the light. I'm afraid of the dark.

CHAR. Oh, it's not the dark that will hurt you. Are you going to tie her, Sam?

SAM. No. He no let her come up. [*Pointing to bulldog; mounts stairs. Chinaman whips dog back, follows Sam*]

FLOS. [*Clutches him by belt and pulls him back*] Don't go. Stay here. You have a whip, you can keep them away. [*Chinaman raises butt of whip to strike Flossie*]

CHAR. [*Pulls pistol and points at Chinaman*] Hold on, you yellow dog. Strike that girl and I'll blow your brains out. Put down that whip and come up here. [*Chinaman lowers whip, runs up stairs*]

SAM. [*Begins a string of cuss-words at other Chink*] Mucker hy—pink ky tie pepwo w-wow yip.

CHIN. Yip wow—wow yip—pink ky tie—no brow ky tie—mucker hy loo.

SAM. Mucker hy—loo—damn fool. [*Crosses Charlie on steps, followed by other Chinaman. Sam stands on the platform at top of steps and as other Chink passes, Sam kicks him, then stands at top of steps and holds candle for Charlie*]

FLOS. Why didn't you let him strike me. I'm better dead than left here. I shall die of fright.

CHAR. I don't want you to die. I didn't bring you here for that. I want to give you a chance to reflect and be a good girl.

FLOS. Be a bad girl, you mean. Do you think I could give myself to you after what you have done. No, I mean to kill myself.

CHAR. Oh, you wouldn't do that.

FLOS. Don't be too sure. [*Bows head on knees in prayer*]

CHAR. Good night. I said "Good night," Flossie. What are you doing? [*Flossie turns around and holds up the cross from the beads she is saying*]

CHAR. What's that, I can't see?

FLOS. The cross mother gave me the night she ran away.

CHAR. Bah. Cling to it. Lots of good it will do you. [*Turns, runs up stairs and slams door shut. Ray of white light shines under door and into Flossie's face as she remains kneeling and whispering her prayers. Soft music of sacred hymn. Ned heard tapping bricks of rear wall with iron bar on top of platform. Bricks fall to floor one at a time, but Flossie does not turn to see what causes the sound. Soon Ned is seen through the hole, sitting astride the sewer pipe and knocking out bricks. Mike holds a lantern down through a manhole just above him. Rope hangs from man-hole to platform. Ned takes the lantern from Mike and ties it to the end of rope and lowers it over wall into cellar*]

NED. Flossie, Flossie!

FLOS. [*Turning*] Ned, Ned, my brother. [*Falls fainting on the straw*]

NED. She's down there, Mike. When I tell you fellers to pull, hoist her up. [*Sam, followed by Chinaman, opens door and starts down stairs. Ned pelts them with bricks and holds them at bay until Mike pulls Flossie to safety. Chinaman whirling around center with bulldog fastened by his teeth to the seat of his trousers. Other Chinks around him pelting dog with bricks but hitting the Chink. They are kept busy dodging bricks which Ned throws from above*]

ACT IV.

A palace on the Hudson—one month later. Scene shows old Montgomery summer home. Big stone mansion, well off L. Broad stairway leading to verandah, open doorway off L.2., backed by curtain. Backdrop landscape showing the river. Stone wall covered with ivy, across in 3. Center gateway with large posts. Wood wings R. and L., foliage borders. Rustic table and chairs down L. Garden bench down R. Curtain discovers:

FLOR. [*In summer gown; on the table are flowers which she is sorting*] One whole month since I heard from Charles Montgomery. He has left me in sole possession of this beautiful estate. His infatuation for that doll-faced girl was a lucky thing for me. He will never dare come back to this country with a term in prison staring him in the face.

LEW. [*Lewis, same as character in Act III. Enters L.3.*] Your lunch, madam. Where shall I serve it?

FLOR. Out here, Lewis. The weather is too nice to go indoors. I expect my attorney. You may serve for two.

LEW. I've been wishing to speak to you in private, madam.

FLOR. What is it, Lewis?

LEW. I'm obliged for your bringing me here from the city and paying me big wages, but I must give my notice, madam.

FLOR. Tired of the country life, already?

LEW. Not that. The police watch this place. They make me nervous. I got what you call the Holy Dread. [*Shrugging shoulders*]

FLOR. They are looking for Prince Charlie. You've read the papers. You know what for. They'll not molest you nor I.

LEW. I am not so sure. I am not satisfied.

FLOR. Very well, sir, you may go.

LEW. Thank you.

FLOR. When your month is up.

LEW. What? When my month is up. Never. By then I will be in jail six months. [*Shaking head, exits L.2.*]

FLOR. Fool, he is easily scared like all the rest. Money will do anything. The police will never molest me. I was careful to cover my moves in the game. Now I am rich, powerful. In the position I have worked so hard to gain. [*Exits R.2. Sam, disguised as common laboring Chinaman in plain blouse, black slouch hat, and small package done up in red bandana handkerchief, enters C., crosses, looks in door without seeing Flora*]

FLOR. [*Reenters*] Here, fellow, what do you want? Get out or I'll set the dogs on you.

SAM. [*Turning and showing teeth in smile*] I no feared of dogs.

FLOR. Sam, I didn't know you. How dare you come here?

SAM. Prince Charlie, he told me, he afraid.

FLOR. Then he's in hiding here; didn't go to Europe?

SAM. Europe too far.

FLOR. What does he want?

SAM. Money.

FLOR. He won't get it.

SAM. I no know.

FLOR. I do know.

SAM. I think you got green eyes.

FLOR. I like your impudence.

SAM. You hate little girl with big mouth.

FLOR. What! Me jealous of that little beggar?

SAM. She no beg, she fight. Her bludder, the littey feller, he fight like hell. He bloken up my business. No good.

FLOR. [*Laughing*] Yes, I read in the paper your business had all gone to the dogs.

SAM. Yes, dogs all gone. By and by police catchey me, catchey you, catchey Prince Charlie. Catch whole damn business.

FLOR. Sit down, Sam. I won't let them catch you.

SAM. Me sit beside you? What I catch?

FLOR. Catch me, if you do what I ask you. I'll not hurt you. Sit down.

SAM. [*Sits cautiously on end of bench*] This like old times on Pell Street.

FLOR. I want you to give me some of that stuff that puts people to sleep.

SAM. What for? Old man dead. You got plenty money.

LEW. [*Enters L.2.*] I believe I'm standing on my head. I'm either crazy or I'm back in the Latin quarter in Paris and don't know it. [*Exits L.2. Mother*

Murphy, with an expressman bearing a small tin trunk tied up with rope on his shoulders enters C. Expressman lets trunk down with a thud. It breaks open and old shoes, petticoats, canned goods and so forth fall out. Flora springs up with a scream]

MOTH. Good morning.

FLOR. What are you doing here, woman?

MOTH. I've come to spend my summer vacation, but if you keep boarders with pigtails I'll look up another boarding house. Here, pick up those things. I'll sue you for damages. [*Expressman gets on knees and fires clothes back into trunk, pushing down with foot*]

FLOR. Here, man, take that rubbish out of my grounds; and you, woman, get out before I have you thrown out!

MOTH. Easy now, don't get excited. I was invited here by the gentleman who owns these grounds and I'll not get out.

FLOR. The gentleman who owns this estate is not in this country.

MOTH. Oh, yes, he is. I saw him this very morning.

FLOR. I don't believe you. I shall have you put out. Lewis, oh, Lewis, come here quick! [*Exits L.2. Sam takes bundle and starts for gate C.*]

MOTH. Here, Chineser, where you going?

SAM. I go buy bar of soap for my laundry.

MOTH. You'll have bars in the laundry where you're going and they won't be bars of soap either. Get hold of that trunk and help this man take it in the house or I'll run this umbrella through you. [*Poking Sam with umbrella*]

SAM. What for, you fool? I not got time. I'm busy. [*Starts up*]

MOTH. [*Catches Sam around neck with crook of her umbrella*] Come back here. I'll keep you busy. [*Sam grabs handle of trunk. Mother whacks Sam over back with umbrella and Sam and expressman exit L.2. with trunk, on the run*]

MOTH. I'll show them who's boss around here. This place belongs to me boy, and if he's not here yet I'll take possession in his name. They won't bamboozle Mother Murphy. [*Crash and bump off L.*] There goes me trunk. They let it fall downstairs. [*Picks up skirts and starts to exit up stairs*]

Ex. [*Enters L.2. wiping forehead with red handkerchief*] Fifty cents, please.

MOTH. Fifty cents for what?

Ex. The trunk.

MOTH. It didn't cost but forty. Look at it, look what's left of it. [*Pointing off L.*] Get out of this or I'll have you arrested for assault and battery. [*Throws expressman off of steps, chases him out of gate C., striking him over head with umbrella*] Fifty cents. I'll give him fifty cents with the bumbershoot. [*Exits L.2. Lewis enters L.2. as if thrown out. Falls down steps. Picks himself up and shakes fist off L.*]

MOTH. [*Off L.*]   Out, you pigtailed heathen, out I say. [*Sam stumbles out L.2. with head stuck through an oil painting, broken frame over his shoulders. Mother throws flower pot through door at him*]

FLOR. [*Enters L.2., screaming, with fingers in her ears. Crosses R. to Lewis and Sam, who are behind bench*]   See, she has ruined my beautiful oil painting of the battle of Santuary. [*Removes wreck of painting from Sam's neck*]

LEW.   I think it is the battle of "Who'll run," ma'am.

FLOR.   Why don't you protect me, Lewis? Why don't you put her out?

LEW.   Didn't you see me put her out?

SAM.   Come outside, Irish. [*Brandishing big knife. Mother throws a lamp at Sam through door. Sam jumps aside, Lewis catches lamp*]

FLOR.   Run, Lewis, run and get the police. The woman's crazy.

LEW.   We are going to be dispossessed. [*Looking at lamp and picking up wreck of frame, flower pot, and so forth*]

CHAR. [*Enters C. in excited manner. Wears long linen duster, driving gloves, cap, with carriage whip*]   Flora, Sam, quick. I'm followed. I must hide.

SAM.   Let us all hide.

LEW.   In the house? [*Pointing*] Not me!

CHAR.   What's the trouble here?

FLOR.   That Irish woman. She's gone mad, taken possession of the house.

CHAR.   I am still master here, though I am a refugee. They have me cornered and I must hide. This is the last place they will search. Follow me. We will take care of the Irish. [*Exits L.2. followed by Flora. Lewis falls upstairs, dropping bundle of wreckage, Sam has his knife out and is cautious and looking for a fight. He exits L.1.*]

MOTH. [*Enters, creeping about corner of house L.1. She has sleeves rolled up and an axe*]   Now, where the divil did they go? [*Carriage containing Ned, Flossie, and Gertrude, all in stylish clothes, drives up to gate C.*]

NED. [*Jumps out, assists Gertrude to alight*]   Come on, mother. [*Flossie jumps out by herself. Gertrude enters gate with arm about Flossie, who is R., and Ned, who is L. Carriage draws off R.*]

MOTH.   May your shadows never grow less, but that's a sight for my poor old eyes. The mother and her children united at last.

NED.   Don't cry. You shall be our mother still.

FLOS.   Yes, our grandmother.

MOTH.   What's that? A grandmother? I'll have you to understand I'm only four and twenty.

NED. Mother, we are rich. The lawyers tell me I've won my suit.

MOTH. Why didn't you win a swallow-tailed one while you were at it? You look like a Baxter dude; and Flossie, your heels are so high you'll break your neck.

NED. You don't understand, Mother. We have come to take the law on these people. This home is to be ours when the papers are served.

MOTH. Well, I've quit selling papers, but I've got possession here and that is nine points of the law.

GERT. My children would not wait. They were so eager to see this estate they have fought so hard to gain.

FLOS. Yes, I'm going to have Prince sent up for ten years. It would have been cheaper for him to marry me.

NED. You're a silly goose, Floss. Now you've got the money without the man.

FLOS. What is money to me without the man? [*Crosses L., looks off*]

GERT. [*Shaking head*] I believe she loves him still.

MOTH. She's a fool. A girl of her age will fall in love with anything that wears breeches.

NED. [*Sitting at table, pounding bell*] Let us have some refreshments. Is there no one at home? Sit down, Mother. Sit down, Floss.

MOTH. Hist, Ned, there's a hornet's nest around here somewhere. You don't want to stir it up.

NED. What are you doing with that axe?

MOTH. There is a monkey here with a tail as long as me arm. I'm going to amputate it.

LEW. [*Enter L.2.*] What did you ring for? This is no public garden.

NED. I rang because I was hungry. Bring out all you've got and be quick about it.

LEW. You're a loafer. I'm not here to serve you.

NED. Then I'll hire somebody that will. I'm proprietor of this joint. [*Crosses*] There's your first week's wages, including tips. Now get to work. [*Pulls out big roll of bills, hands Lewis several*]

LEW. Five, ten, fifteen, twenty-two, twenty-seven [*Throwing up both hands and thrusting money in pocket*], I haven't time to count it. Oh, Lewie, Lewie, you must be smoking! You are a gentleman, monsieur. I serve you for the rest of my life. Ladies, what is your pleasure?

FLOS. Bring me a cocktail with a cherry and some low-necked clams.

GERT. Floss, I'm surprised at you.

LEW. She shall have them, madam, if I dig them myself. One minute I will serve you with wine. [*Exits L.2.*]

NED. Hear that, ma, we're going to have wine. I tell you, girls, money is the thing that talks. [*Pulling a big handful of bills and commencing to shuffle them like cards*]

MOTH. If it could beat that waiter talking I wouldn't want that roll under me pillow. Me, oh my, that must be a million dollars. Think of all that talking to I need.

NED. Here, Mother, buy yourself a house and lot. [*Hands Mother several bills*]

MOTH. You're getting extravagant. You'll be broker in the morning and back to selling papers. How much is this? I can't read.

NED. Sixteen hundred dollars.

MOTH. [*Drops axe and places hand to her head, staggers over and falls on bench*] Do you want me to die of heart disease? [*Turns back to Ned, pulls up dress and stuffs money in her stocking. She has on old stockings, one red and white; the other light blue. Lewis enters in rush, L.2. Places tray with bottle of wine and glasses on table. Ned, throwing feet up on table and tilting chair back and peeling off bill from roll, which he hands Lewis. Lewis stumbles up stairs in his haste to exit, L.2.*] What's the matter with that fellow? He must have the blind staggers.

NED. He has the disease they all get when they see the long green.

MOTH. I'm going to look for that Chineser. [*Ascends steps L.*]

GERT. My children! You have just been restored to me. I don't wish to deny you any pleasure, but the wine cup will be your ruin. Promise me you will drink no more.

FLOS. I promise, mama. I thought it was the swell thing to do.

LEW. [*Enters L.2. with bottle of wine*] Pardon, monsieur, if I have kept you waiting. This is one hundred years old.

NED. No wonder you was a long time getting it. Take it into the house and drink it yourself.

LEW. We—we, Gates—[*Exit L.2.*]

NED. I'm a Gate this time, next time I'll be a door. I guess I'll introduce myself. [*Starts up steps*]

GERT. Where are you going, Ned?

NED. To look for trouble. You stay here.

GERT. Better wait till your attorney arrives.

NED. Tell them I've taken possession. [*Exits L.2.*]

CHAR. [*Enters L.1., doffs cap*] Ladies, this is a pleasure, I assure you.

GERT. Charles Montgomery, what are you doing here? [*Raising her arm and throwing it about Flossie*]

CHAR. If you will permit me to be so bold, I might ask you that same question.

GERT. We are here to claim our own. The courts have granted the estate to my son.

CHAR. Indeed, and what is to become of me?

GERT. That is for the courts to decide. If you are caught, you will likely go to the penitentiary, where such men as you belong.

CHAR. See here, woman, I'm desperate. I know I've wronged you, but you've had revenge enough. I'm ruined. You have all the money and property which is rightfully mine, I am at your mercy. These grounds are surrounded by officers of the law. Your damned husband and boy have run me into a trap. My only chance to escape is that you will aid me. Come, what do you say?

GERT. No! After the disgrace, the sorrows you have brought into my life, I have no feeling for you but contempt. I shall be glad to see you punished.

CHAR. Then you refuse?

GERT. Yes.

CHAR. And will tell them you have seen me here?

GERT. Yes.

FLOS. I won't, Charlie. I'll cut my tongue out first. Please, mama, let him go.

GERT. I'm not stopping him. Look into my face. Do you love this man, Flossie? [*Flossie bows head, begins to cry*] Look, Charles Montgomery; see what your lying tongue has done for this poor child! Robbed her of an affection that should have been bestowed upon someone more worthy. A love so pure and strong it would shield you now. For her sake, go, and our lips shall remain sealed.

CHAR. I love the girl and would make her my wife. Give her to me and I will try and atone for the past.

GERT. Too late. I would rather see her dead. You are a criminal. You have nothing but disgrace to offer her.

CHAR. You're right, I'm a lost soul. There's not a ray of light or hope before me.

FLOS. [*Advancing and giving him her hand*] I shall pray for you every night, Charlie, just as long as I live.

CHAR. Good-by. I shall never be taken alive, but if I escape, your kind words and the knowledge of the love I once cast aside will help me to be a better man. Good-by. [*Bends and kisses Flossie's hand, crosses up to gate. Flossie puts handkerchief to eyes, crosses down L. to Gertrude who puts arm about her*]

ALB. [*Enters C. in neat business suit*]   Hold on. I have something to say to you before you go.

CHAR.   Albert Cooper, what the hell do you want?

ALB.   Satisfaction for the long days and nights I lay in a cell and grieved for a wife and children you stole from me, and then left to die of starvation and hunger.

CHAR.   Can't you forgive me? Your wife and daughter have done so.

GERT.   It is false. I did not forgive you; neither has my daughter. We were only sorry to see you fall so low.

ALB.   There are some wrongs you can't ask a man to forgive. Come, Charles Montgomery, you must give me satisfaction. [*Throws off coat. Flora enters L.2. Stands at top of steps*]

CHAR.   If it is. any satisfaction to see me die, look with all your eyes. [*Pulls pistol, attempts to shoot himself in heart*]

ALB. [*Springs forward and wrestles with him*]   Kill yourself? Not if I know it! [*Pistol is discharged between them*]

FLOR. [*Places hand to her breast*]   Charlie, Charlie, you've shot me! [*Falls to porch and rolls down the steps. Albert and Charlie separate, Albert L. with pistol, Charlie R. Lewis enters to top of steps*]

CHAR.   Cooper, that is your work. You have killed that woman.

ALB. [*Kneels by Flora, places hand on heart*]   Her heart beats. She's not dead. Quick, someone, get a doctor. We will take her in the house. [*Mike and Brown enter C. Mike crosses L. to Albert. Charlie starts up C.*]

BROWN.   Stop. Where are you going?

CHAR.   To get a doctor. That woman has been shot.

BROWN.   Who shot her?

CHAR.   That man with the pistol.

FLOR. [*Raising herself and clinging to steps*]   Help, I want water. Charlie, I'm dying. Why did you shoot me?

BROWN.   She says you shot her.

CHAR.   She don't know what she is saying. It was an accident.

BROWN.   Oh, then this man didn't shoot her?

CHAR.   No, we struggled for the weapon. I meant that bullet for myself. [*Gertrude kneels by Flora. Lewis enters L.2. with glass of water; hands to Gertrude, who places it to Flora's lips. The water turns red as she drinks*]

FLOS.   Oh, why doesn't someone run for a doctor?

GERT.   It would do no good. The woman is dying.

CHAR.   I wish it was me instead of you, partner. We've played a losing game.

FLOR. I got what I deserved. I made you what you are, Charlie. It was all my cursed love for gold. Lots of good it will do you beggars. [*Staggering to her feet*] Take me inside the house, Lewis, away from these. Don't look at me with pity. I don't want it. If you gain possession here, it will be over my dead body. I hate and defy you all. [*Lewis, supporting Flora, leads her off L.2.*]

CHAR. Let me go to her. [*Starts L.*]

MIKE. No, you must come with me. I have a warrant for your arrest. [*Produces handcuffs*]

FLOS. [*Crosses C.*] Let him see her, Mike, just a few minutes, for my sake.

CHAR. I'll not run away or do myself any harm. I promise you that.

FLOS. Please, Mike. [*On her knees*]

MIKE. All right, go ahead.

LEW. [*Enters L.2.*] Quick, sir, the madam wants you. She is dying. [*Charlie exits L.2. followed by Lewis and Mike. Flossie bows head crying*]

ALB. [*Throwing arms about her*] Don't cry, daughter. He's not worth it.

FLOS. Father, have you that rose I gave you the first night we met?

ALB. Yes. It's been over my heart every hour since then. [*Hands Flossie rose from inside pocket*]

FLOS. It shall remain on mine till the judgment-day.

MOTH. [*Enters L.1. leading Sam with a rope about his neck, his hands tied behind his back, and Ned hanging back on his cue*] Come along here, you son of Pekin.

NED. Here he is. This is the man you want. Go 'long, Sam. Get a bag, Floss, and we'll throw him in the river. [*Brown takes rope from Mother and pulls Sam over R. Handcuffs him*]

NED. Hello, father, what's the news?

ALB. I've the deeds for your property, my son. [*Handing legal papers*] We have received justice at last. My little family is united. We will begin a new life from today. [*Messenger boy enters gate followed by newsboys and characters from the Bowery*]

NED. Father, this is the gang from Chatham Square. I've invited them up to dinner.

THE END

NO MOTHER TO GUIDE HER

By Lillian Mortimer

SCENE PLOT

ACT I

Landscape drop in full stage. A set house on the left side of stage. Porch with raised platform if convenient. A fence with gate center, up stage in front of drop. There is a garden bench or chair down R. If desired there is a tree center. Other furniture to dress stage as a farmer's home.

ACT II

Should be a dense woods, with a gypsy camp in foreground. There should be a tree over left. Or left center. A tripod with fire effect under kettle is right. There may be the back of an old wagon showing, if available and desired. Stumps or kegs to represent same about the stage. And a small tent up stage.

ACT III

Livingstone's room, as described in Act.

ACT IV

A wood, or rocky pass, or almost anything of this type will suffice. Or same set or same exterior used in former act will do. Except there is a cabin on stage left.

PROPERTY PLOT

ACT I

Small kitchen table, and cover. Two chairs. Two books. Double-barrelled shotgun. Newspapers. Rocking chair. Sofa. Market basket. Suitcase. Bundle of sticks.

ACT II

Four grass mats if available. Three stumps, or kegs. Bass drum for thunder.

ACT III

Telephone. Fancy chairs and rocker. Dresser, if available. Carpet and rugs. Center table and cover. Fire log, andirons and tongs. Small clock. Glass for crash off stage. Soap box. Step ladder. Hassock. Rope.

ACT IV

Table. Stumps, etc. Drum—bass. Kitchen chair.

CAST OF CHARACTERS

JOHN LIVINGSTONE, *a bank robber*

RALPH CARLTON, *in love with Rose*

SILAS WATERBURY, *the town constable*

JAKE JORDAN, *an escaped convict*

FARMER DAY, *Rose's father*

ROSE DAY, *secretly married to Ralph*

LINDY JANE SMITHERS, *in love with Silas*

BESS SINCLAIR, *a shop girl*

MOTHER TAGGER, *a tool of Livingstone*

BUNCO, *comedy soubrette*

HARRY PATENT
TOMMY FISCHER
WALTER PERKINS } *the sweet-singing gypsies (off stage)*
FRANK CALDWELL
PARSON THOMAS

OFFICER KEOUGH
POLICEMAN TODD } *officers*
CAPTAIN HENNESSY

TIME: PRESENT.

PLACE: NEW YORK STATE.

SYNOPSIS OF SCENES

ACT I: HOME OF ROSE DAY. THE MURDER.

ACT II: THE GYPSY CAMP. TORNADO.

ACT III: IN THE BIG CITY. THE BANK ROBBERY.

ACT IV: OLD HUT IN THE HILLS. THE WAGES OF SIN.

ACT I.

AT RISE: *Lively music. Lights, sunshine. Strong yellow lights. Farmer Day discovered seated on rocker on porch L. reading paper. Lindy standing at gate shading her eyes. Has sunbonnet on.*

DAY. See anything of Rose, Lindy?

LINDY. No, and it's nigh about time she was comin' home. Three weeks is a long enough visit fer any gal. There comes that city feller. I don't like him. I think he's set on makin' love to Rose.

DAY. Well Lindy, he seems like a pretty good feller.

LINDY. Good? Shucks I wouldn't trust him as fur as I can see with my eyes shut. If I was a gal I'd ruther have that other feller. He's lookin' mighty calf-like at our Rose too. Oh but I'll be glad when both of 'em is gone. I don't like keepin' summer boarders nohow. [*Livingstone enters gate up C.*]

LIV. Ah, Miss Lindy, how well you are looking. [*Lindy business. Crosses R.C. and sits*] Reading the evening paper, Mr. Day? What's the news? [*Livingstone standing R.; business with shotgun*]

DAY. Hain't read none yet. Got a job?

LIV. No, but Farmer Bailey wants someone to oversee his farm next month. I can have that if I want it.

DAY. That's a good job—better take it.

LIV. I think I shall. I've got some money put away but I don't want to use it till I get married, to buy a little home.

LINDY. [*Sitting under tree, C.*] And how much do you happen to have, young feller?

LIV. Oh, about ten thousand.

LINDY. Make it yerself?

LIV. No, my grandmother left it to me.

LINDY. More fool she.

LIV. Well I'm not a fellow to beat around the bush Mr. Day. I'm in love with your daughter.

LINDY. There now, what did I tell you?

LIV. I'd like to marry her—buy a little home and settle down.

LINDY. Well, ef Rose was my gal—

DAY. Hush, Lindy. Wall—I'm in no hurry fer my gal to marry, Mr. Livingstone, but whoever wins her heart kin have her—I'll not stand in her way.

And when I'm gone there'll be a tidy sum for her too, so she won't be beholdin' to her husband.

LIV. Oh, you have some money in the bank here? [*Crosses down below steps L.*]

DAY. No siree. I don't trust no banks with my money. I·keep it right here in the house.

LINDY. Yes, and a bigger fool I never see. Some morning you'll wake up with yer throat cut from ear to ear.

DAY. I'm not afraid, Lindy. [*Silas enters, glasses on and newspaper open*]

SILAS. Gosh—see the paper?

LINDY. What's up?

SILAS. Stebbin's bank broke into and robbed at three o'clock this morning.

DAY. You don't say? [*Looks at his paper*]

SILAS. Yes siree. Found the watchman tied hand and foot.

DAY. Get much?

SILAS. Five hundred dollars.

LINDY. Land sakes. [*Looking over Si's shoulder at paper*]

SILAS. Town constables are lookin' up the records of all strangers in town. [*Looks at Livingstone*]

LIV. [*Laughs*] Lucky I can give a clear account of myself—I was in bed by ten o'clock last night.

DAY. That's what ye were, Mr. Livingstone, but yer pardner wasn't in last night, was he? [*Rises*]

LIV. [*Crosses R.*] No, he hasn't come back from the city yet. I expect him tonight. [*Silas busy C. following Livingstone*]

DAY. I guess I was right about the banks, eh Lindy? [*Exits in house*]

LINDY. Oh, I don't know. [*Crosses to house*]

SILAS. Oh—that reminds me—

LINDY. Comin' inside, Si?

SILAS. Don't mind ef I do. Got something to say to you, confidential. He, he.

LINDY. Oh you get aout. [*Exits in house*]

SILAS. Wait for me Lindy. [*Trips on stairs*] Dern them steps. [*Exits after Lindy*]

LIV. [*Crosses to house*] Well, I suppose the safest thing for me to do would be to light out. That was the neatest job I've done in some time, and if I wasn't so in love with that girl Rose—[*Mother T. enters gate from C.L., looks round, sees Livingstone*]

MOTH. T. St. John. [*Weird music*]

Liv. Mother! What are you doing here? Anything wrong with the money?

Moth. T. That's safe enough but I'm afraid we had better move on. They'll be sure to suspect us.

Liv. Well they can't prove a thing. I want you to hang around for a day or two—I may have work for you. But don't come here again unless I give you the signal. You shouldn't leave the camp.

Moth. T. But I must have a leetle whiskey, my boy—a leetle drop of whiskey. I can't send anybody—[*Close to him*]

Liv. Whiskey? Why you're stupid with whiskey now. [*Crosses to R.*]

Moth. T. Cruel boy—I haven't had a drop today. [*Follows him R.*]

Liv. Bah!

Moth. T. It's the beautiful truth, I swear.

Liv. Shut up. Here. [*Gives her flask*] Now be careful. Don't get drunk and blab.

Moth. T. Trust me, darling. Whiskey makes Mother Tagger's brain work. Without it, it would stop. [*Drinks, puts bottle in apron pocket*]

Liv. Well, be careful.

Moth. T. I have some news for you. Fine news—he, he, he.

Liv. Well, stop your cackling and tell me.

Moth. T. The child is dead.

Liv. [*Crosses L.—then back to her*] Sh-hh—How did you manage it?

Moth. T. With those hands. Choked the life out of it. Ah—it's so easy to wring their little white necks. I love to hear them sputter and choke—He, he, he.

Liv. [*Crosses L.*] You make my blood run cold. Where is the body?

Moth. T. Buried in the wood darling. Buried where the beautiful violets grow. Ha, ha, ha. [*Music stops*]

Liv. Well, the kid's done for and if the girl causes me any more trouble she'll go the same way.

Moth. T. Where is she now?

Liv. I left her in New York—the fool.

Moth. T. Ah—young blood—young blood—he, he, he. [*Drinks*]

Liv. [*Crosses to R.*] Beats the deuce how the women love me. I can't help it.

Moth. T. And now there's another one, eh? The girl with the pretty face. [*Points to house L. Lights change to red sunset*]

Liv. Yes, but she doesn't seem to be in love with me. I can't understand it. But if she'll have me I'll settle down and be honest. If she won't—well there'll be another job for you, mother. She'll love me. They always do.

Мотн. T. Oh, you wicked boy. He, he, he.

Liv. You'd better go now.

Мотн. T. Oh you wicked boy—he-he, he. [*Exits gate C. to L.*]

Liv. [*Pause, crosses to gate*] Useful old devil. Well I'll go and jolly the old man, and find out where he keeps his money, then if the girl marries me, all well and good. If not I'll take her by force. Once in the Gypsy camp in Mother Tagger's clutches, she'll do as I say. [*Exits into house*]

Rose. [*Runs on from R. with Ralph; runs up steps on porch laughing*] Oh, how good it seems to be home again. Now don't look so blue, Ralph dear —it will all come out right, I know.

Ralph. [*C.*] I'm afraid it was a wild thing to do, dear. I ought to have asked your father's consent.

Rose. Oh but it's so much nicer to have a secret all to ourselves. Won't they all be surprised when I tell them we've been married for three long weeks. [*Laughs*]

Ralph. You are so happy dear. May you never have cause to regret it.

Rose. Regret it? Why should I Ralph?

Ralph. Well I've been rather wild, I'm afraid.

Rose. Oh, Ralph—

Ralph. Yes, dear.

Rose. Come here and sit down and tell me truly—[*Pushes Ralph to tree seat, sits L. of him*] Mind now—not even a little white fib. Did you—did you —ever love any other girl?

Ralph. Well, sweetheart, I'll tell you truly if you'll also speak truly. Did you ever love any other man?

Rose. Why Ralph—I—[*Crosses quickly to steps*]

Ralph. [*Laughs cheerfully*] Never mind dear, you needn't. I know you love me best of all. You are my wife and I am going to make you happy. But I have been wild. [*Crosses to Rose*]

Rose. But you have sown your wild oats now dear.

Ralph. Yes, yes, but if you should hear that I have done something. [*Takes hand*]

Rose. Oh hush—you couldn't do anything so bad—if you had—

Ralph. Well—?

Rose. You are my husband and I shall stand by you as a wife should.

Ralph. God bless you, dear. [*Kisses her hand*] I'll try to be worthy of your love, and if in the future you should hear stories of me, remember how dearly I love you. My mother died when I was a boy. [*Crosses to R.*] Had she lived —But there—I have you to love me now. Let me tell your father tonight.

Rose. No, no—I shall tell him myself. I'm going in now. Oh, what a sensation I shall create. Come in presently. [*Livingstone enters from house*] Oh good evening, Mr. Livingstone. [*Ralph sits C.*]

Liv. Good evening, Miss Rose. Your visit has done you good. You look charming. [*Takes her hand*]

Rose. Thank you. [*Exits into house*]

Liv. Hello, Ralph. [*Crosses to him*] I just got in. Lucky you were not at home last night. The bank was robbed and all strangers are under suspicion.

Ralph. [*Rises in alarm*] You don't mean—

Liv. Yes I do. Made a good job of it too. [*Crosses to L.*] Say what are you hanging around Rose for. You let her alone. I've made up my mind to marry her.

Ralph. What?

Liv. You heard what I said, and if you bust in, I'll make it damned hot for you. Understand? [*Close to Ralph*]

Ralph. Don't try to intimidate me, Livingstone. I know you are capable of anything but you can't frighten me.

Liv. Have you forgotten the Camden case?

Ralph. I was innocent of that crime.

Liv. Yes, but the evidence was all against you and we had to jump out. Now I've stood by you and if you don't stand pat, I'll send you to Sing Sing. Nothing could save you. [*Laughs and takes out cigar*] Have a cigar? [*Ralph ignores him*] Oh, take a cigar, and let's take a walk and talk this matter over. I don't mean you any harm. [*Takes Ralph's arm; they go to gate*] But don't interfere in my game, that's all. [*They exit C. to L.*]

Bunco. [*Enters C. from R. Looks around*] Well, dis place looks kinder respectable. Guess I'll have to hang out here tonight. Bess can't go no furder. Well here goes to tackle de landlady. Gee me feet is so heavy dey feels like hams. [*Knocks at door*]

Lindy. [*Calls loudly from within*] Who's there?

Bunco. [*Jumps back to C.*] Gee—me heart's bumpin' a hole in me ribs. [*Lindy opens door*] Howdy.

Lindy. Heavens on earth, child.

Bunco. Is it? First I'd heard of it.

Lindy. Where did you come from?

Bunco. Aw say, lady—don't look at me like dat. I haven't got me Sunday clothes on cause I was afraid de walkin' might spoil em. Me automobile broke down and me and Bess had ter tramp from New York.

Lindy. New York? Child alive, ye ain't walked from New York?

Bunco. Dat's right.

LINDY. Where's yer father and mother?

BUNCO. Dead.

LINDY. Both of 'em?

BUNCO. Yep—poor things.

LINDY. How did they die?

BUNCO. Cut their throats eating peas with a knife.

LINDY. Good Lord. An' ain't ye afraid to be tramping the country all alone?

BUNCO. Nope—I always carries dis. [*Shows revolver*]

LINDY. [*Screams*] Oh—Good Lord—[*Pushes it away*]

BUNCO. Don't be afraid, lady—it ain't loaded.

LINDY. [*Sits on steps*] Well I never—What are you wearin' them there clothes this hot weather fur?

BUNCO. Dese?

LINDY. Yes.

BUNCO. Well ye see, lady, dese is de only chilly weather clothes I got. I have to wear 'em—[*Shows bundle*] cause me trunk is full. Oh say now, lady, I don't care for myself, but poor Bess is so hungry, and sick and tired. If you could take her in tonight and give her something to eat, I'd work for it. I don't know much about farmin' but you bet your life I could learn.

LINDY. And who is Bess?

BUNCO. A poor girl what's seen lots of trouble. We worked in de factory togedder—then a smooth-tongued feller comes along, and won poor Miss Bess—den—den left her wid her little baby.

LINDY. A baby? I can't take her in. [*Rises and goes up steps*]

BUNCO. Oh, don't say dat, lady. Don't be too hard on poor Bess. You see she's an orphan and ain't got no mother to guide her. She was just planning dying, so I thought if I could get her to the country, de beautiful trees, de green grass and flowers would do her good. [*Pleading*] Bess loves de flowers, she does.

LINDY. Where is she now?

BUNCO. Out there. [*Points R.*] Settin' under a tree, waitin' till I come back. Say, take her in, won't you an' I'll work like de devil to pay you back.

LINDY. You go fetch her right in.

BUNCO. Say, you'se de real article—you'se are. I'll work fer you as dough you was my husband. [*Exits gate C. to R.*]

LINDY. Well I never. That's a strange child.

SILAS. [*Enters from house*] I say, Lindy—

LINDY. Was you a speakin' to me, Silas Waterbury?

SILAS. [*L.*] Yes, I was a sayin'—

LINDY. Well say it again, and remember to call me Miss Smithers.

SILAS. Now what's the use of bein' mad, Lindy.

LINDY. *Miss Smithers!* [*Turns*]

SILAS. Lindy, ain't ye ever goin' to change it to Mrs.?

LINDY. Mebby I be—mebby I been't. When I see a man as *is* a man.

SILAS. Gol dern it, Lindy—what am I?

LINDY. The biggest fool I ever saw.

SILAS. Oh you get out. [*Sits on steps*] Lindy I'm as tired as Tom Turner is busy.

LINDY. What? Lazy Tom Turner.

SILAS. He ain't lazy no more.

LINDY. No?

SILAS. Nope. He's the busiest man in town.

LINDY. Dew tell?

SILAS. [*Crosses to her*] Yep—he's got the seven year itch and a Waterbury watch, and when he ain't scratchin' he's windin' his Waterbury.

LINDY. [*Crosses up stage*] You git out.

SILAS. And that reminds me, when I was up to New York State last fall— [*Crosses up to gate*] Jake Tod said to me, sez he—Jumpin' Crocodiles—look at that.

LINDY. Shut yer head—[*Turns to Bess and Bunco who have entered*] Come here, you pore young 'un.

BUNCO. [*Crosses to C.*] Dere now, Bess—don't get skeered. Old Spinach won't hurt ye.

SILAS. That gal's makin' fun of my whiskers.

LINDY. Ye pore critter—how white ye look. There now—don't be afeared —and fer the land's sake don't cry. Si Waterbury—what are ye standin' there for like a bump on a log. Go tell Miss Rose to come here. Step lively.

SILAS. I'm a steppin'. [*Trips upstairs*] Dern them stairs.

LINDY. That's right—break yer neck. [*Bunco leads Bess C. to bench*]

SILAS. Not yet, by Ginger. [*Exits into house*]

LINDY. Now you see here a minute. [*Kneels beside Bess*]

BESS. Oh you are very kind. I have not been well. I—I—

LINDY. Heaven's on earth—don't flop. [*Rises*]

BUNCO. Hully gee, Bess—brace up. You see, lady, she ain't had nothin' to eat since yesterday. [*On knees beside Bess, R.*]

LINDY. Lord love us—nothing to eat since yesterday. You come right inside. [*Rose enters from house*]

ROSE. What is it, Lindy?

LINDY. Land sakes, this poor critter ain't had nothin' to eat since yesterday.

ROSE. Oh, you poor child. [*Crosses to Bess*]

BESS. I'll be better soon.

ROSE. Come right in. [*Helps her up steps*] You poor child. [*Exits with Bess into house*]

LINDY. [*L. of Bess*] Yes come right in. We'll get you something to eat. [*Exits with others into house*]

BUNCO. [*Crosses to house*] We're goin' to get somethin' to eat. I can feel it in my bones. Gee—dis must be a dream. [*Exits into house after others*]

JAKE. [*Enters gate C. from R.*] Dis must be de place all right. Looks as dough de Gov'ner struck it rich. He had a finger in de bank robbery you can bet, and de pretty girl dat lives in here is his game or I'm a gentleman. [*Sits C.*] Wonder where he left de poor shopgirl he took a fancy to when he was in New York. Well dat's none of my business—I'm broke and he's got to give me some coin. [*Starts for house*] Here comes de young lady. [*Exits quickly gate C. to R.*]

ROSE. [*Enters, speaking to Aunt Lindy in house*] All right, Aunt Lindy. [*Enters with basket*]

LINDY. [*Calls from inside*] Rose—Rose—

ROSE. Yes.

LINDY. Get two pounds—don't forget.

ROSE. Yes—two pounds of granulated sugar—is that all?

LINDY. Yes. [*Rose goes to gate singing*]

LIV. [*Enters gate L.*] How happy you are, Miss Rose.

ROSE. Of course.

LIV. Can you spare me a moment? I have something to say to you.

ROSE. No, no—not now. I must run to the store. Aunt Lindy has taken a couple in; poor things are half starved. I am going to the grocery store to get some things.

LIV. Let me have a few words with you tonight?

ROSE. No—no—not tonight. [*Exits laughing, gate C. to R.*]

LIV. She is not indifferent to me. I'll win her yet. She shall be my wife before the month is over. [*Up C. outside gate looking after Rose. Enter Bunco with pan of potatoes and knife*]

BUNCO. Hully gee—look at de swell guy. Do you belong to dis house?

LIV. [*Crossing down fiercely*] What's that to you?

BUNCO. [*Backing away*] 'Cause if you do I'm goin' to move. I don't like de cut of yer lip, see?

LIV. Get out, you tramp. Don't talk to me or I'll—

BUNCO. [*Points knife at him*] Look out—don't run up against dis—you might get a puncture.

LIV. [*Laughs*] Say, you're not half bad. I like you.

BUNCO. Well—like me furder off. [*Points knife again*]

LIV. Well, you are a character.

BUNCO. You're annoder.

LIV. I'll see you later. [*Crosses up C. to gate*]

BUNCO. Yes—you will.

LIV. Au revoir, fair lady.

BUNCO. Over the river—you big bluff. [*Livingstone exits gate C. to R., laughing. Bunco crosses to R., sits thinking*] Gee, I wonder who he is? I hope he don't own dis house. [*Bess enters from house*] Oh, Bess, come here and sit under de tree and see me peel potatoes. We're goin' to have dem for supper. Don't yer stomach feel just grand? I never was so full in my life.

BESS. [*Crosses and sits L.*] It's just heavenly, Bunco. I'd be so happy if my heart didn't hurt so.

BUNCO. Oh, now, Bess—don't say that.

BESS. Oh, Bunco, I want my baby—[*Cries*] My little baby.

BUNCO. Now don't worry and de first baby I see layin' around loose, I'll swipe fer you. I will—honest.

BESS. But that wouldn't be my baby, Bunco.

BUNCO. Gee—that's right. Well, all kids look alike to me.

ROSE. [*Enters gate C. from R.*] Here you are. Do you feel better? So Aunt Lindy has put you to work has she, Bunco?

BUNCO. Yes'm. She's going to keep Bess here till she's strong and well again.

ROSE. I'm so glad. [*Crosses to L.*] There—I've forgotten the sugar.

BUNCO. Oh, gee. [*Laughs*] Let me go and get it for you. [*Pan on seat R.*]

ROSE. I left it on the counter of the little store on the corner.

BUNCO. [*Crosses up C.*] De little store over dere on de corner? [*Points R.*]

ROSE. Yes—straight ahead, Bunco.

BUNCO. All right, miss, I'll be right back. [*Exits gate C. to R.*]

ROSE. Would you like a book to read, Bessie?

BESS. No, thank you, miss.

ROSE. Perhaps you would like to come in and lie down.

BESS. I'll stay here if you don't mind, miss.

ROSE. Why, certainly I don't. There now, you mustn't worry. No doubt the future has much happiness in store for you.

BESS. God grant it. But it looks very dark, miss.

Rose. You must be brave. I'll be back in a little while to keep you company. [*Crosses to house*]

Bess. Thank you, miss. [*Rose exits house*]

Bunco. [*Enters gate C. from R., singing. Carries sugar and a bunch of flowers*] Say, Bess, you ought to see de guy what keeps de store down on de corner. [*Laughs*] He's a peach. Say, you can buy anything in dat store from a paper of pins to a beefsteak. Ain't dese sweet? Dey are fer you. [*Gives Bess flowers*]

Bess. Oh, thank you, Bunco.

Bunco. I found dem growing right by de roadside. Oh, say, Bess, yer eyes is all wet. You've been crying again. Oh, gee. [*Crosses down, gets pan*] Just wait till I get dese in de house—den I'll come out and tell you a funny story. [*Laughs*] Oh, brace up. [*Exits house*]

Bess. Dear little flowers, I love you—I love you.

Liv. [*Enters gate C. from L., sees Bess*] By Jove—there she is. Now's my chance. [*Crosses to tree*]

Bess. [*Startled, recognizing him*] John!

Liv. Bess!

Bess. [*Into his arms*] Oh, John, I've found you at last!

Liv. [*Annoyed*] Now how did you get here?

Bess. I have been so ill, John. Our baby has been stolen, but you'll find it for me, won't you, John? And now we'll be married, won't we? You promised, you know, and I knew when you didn't come you were ill and in trouble.

Liv. [*Nervous*] Yes—

Bess. They discharged me from the shop. The girls wouldn't speak to me—all but Bunco. She brought me here.

Liv. Sh-h—don't talk so loud. Listen, you must come with me at once.

Bess. Where?

Liv. To be married. [*Bunco enters, listens*]

Bess. Oh, you are glad to see me, aren't you, John?

Liv. Yes, yes, of course. [*Tenderly*] Come, dear—come with me. [*Crosses up C.*]

Bunco. Where are you going, Bessie?

Liv. [*In a rage*] Stand out of the way.

Bunco. Well, I guess not. Bess, don't go with that guy. He means you harm.

Liv. Come, Bessie.

Bunco. She shan't. [*Stops Bess, takes gun out of boot*] Come and take her. Come in the house, Bessie.

BESS. [*Pleadingly, to Bunco*] Oh, Bunco.

BUNCO. Go in, kind lady. [*Bess exits R. Bunco crosses to him*] Say, I know you now. Listen, don't you come foolin' around Bess again or I'll put a bullet through your sky-piece. [*Crosses up steps*] Dat's straight. [*Exits house*]

LIV. [*Extreme R., starts for her as she exits*] Well, I'm in a devil of a hole if that girl blabs. I must go and see old Mother Tagger at once. [*Starts for gate*]

ROSE. [*Enters, apron on, fanning herself*] Supper will soon be ready.

LIV. [*Taking her hand*] Rose, will you be my wife?

ROSE. Oh, Mr. Livingstone, I'm so sorry you said this.

LIV. Why?

ROSE. Because I am already a wife.

LIV. What?

ROSE. I like you so much and want you for a friend, but I have been married for three weeks.

LIV. To whom?

ROSE. To Ralph Carlton.

LIV. [*In a rage*] Ralph Carlton! God! [*Staggers*]

ROSE. [*Cross R.*] I am so sorry.

LIV. [*Shakes hands*] I wish you every happiness.

ROSE. Let us always be friends.

LIV. Thank you, Rose.

ROSE. [*As she crosses to house*] You'll be in to supper?

LIV. [*Sadly*] Not tonight.

ROSE. I am sorry. [*Exits into house*]

LIV. [*Crosses to house in a rage*] So Ralph Carlton, you have come between me and the woman I love. Well, you'll have a short honeymoon, my lady! Ha, ha—you'd look well in widow's weeds. [*Turn at gate. Ralph enters C. from L.; slowly down R. Savagely*] Congratulations!

RALPH. What do you mean?

LIV. [*Angrily*] Oh, you know what I mean. Your wife has told me all. Married for three weeks, eh? Nice way to treat an old pal. Why didn't you tell me before? You knew I loved Rose.

RALPH. [*C.*] She didn't love you. [*Livingstone crosses L.*] Now, Livingstone, I'll admit I've been weak, but I swear from tonight on I intend to be a man, and make Rose proud of me.

LIV. [*Crosses to Ralph*] And I swear that you shall go to Sing Sing.

RALPH. For God's sake, Livingstone, you wouldn't do such a fiendish thing. What about Rose—it will only break her heart. [*Sinks into seat C.*]

Liv. Listen. The money I got from the bank last night I sent away. I'm going to jump out to 'Frisco and I'll need money. Now the old man has got money in the house. Tonight I want you to stand guard while I get it, then I'll go. We may as well part friends. Will you do it?

Ralph. No!

Liv. What? Then it's war?

Ralph. [*Rises*] Yes—if it must be.

Liv. [*Crossing L.*] Do you dare defy me?

Ralph. We may as well understand each other now. I am innocent. Why should I fear you? But I believe I know the true murderer. [*Jake enters gate C. from L.*]

Liv. What do you mean?

Ralph. I mean that I think you killed the old banker.

Liv. [*Draws knife, starts for Ralph*] So—you suspect *me?*

Jake. [*Comes between them*] Hold on, pardner.

Liv. [*Amazed*] Jake Jordan.

Jake. Glad to see me, eh? [*Business with Livingstone; knife. Then with revolver*] Hold on—dat's no way to treat an old pal. Give me dat knife.

Liv. What?

Jake. Give me dat knife. [*Does so*] Dat's a nice boy. [*Ralph exits gate C. to R.*]

Liv. [*Crosses to L.*] What do you want?

Jake. Just a little expense money, gov'nor.

Liv. I haven't any.

Jake. What? And de bank robbed last night, too?

Liv. Sh-h-h—how much do you want?

Jake. Dat's business. A twenty-dollar bill will do, gov'nor.

Liv. How long do you intend to bleed me?

Jake. Jest as long as I need de money. But if ye get tired, ye can make a test wid a rope around yer neck, fer I'll squeal as soon as the money stops.

Liv. [*Starts for him*] What?

Jake. Hold on! Give me de dough.

Liv. Here—[*Gives him money*]

Jake. Don't try to throw me over, gov'nor. I've got ye—and I'm goin' to keep ye. Good-night. [*Exits gate, L.*]

Liv. Damn him—if I could only get a hold on him, I'd—[*Ralph enters gate. Has a complete change of manner toward him*] Oh, Ralph—let's be friends. I was too hasty. Help me tonight—it will be the last time—then I'll go away. It's the easiest way to get rid of me.

Ralph. Let me think.

Liv. All right—meet me in the orchard at ten. [*Exits gate, C. to L.*]

Ralph. [*Sits under tree*] What shall I do? I'd give ten years of my life to dig up the wild oats I've sown.

Rose. [*Enters*] Is that you, Ralph?

Ralph. [*Trying to appear happy*] Yes, yes.

Rose. [*Crosses to him*] What is it? What's the matter?

Ralph. Nothing, dear, nothing.

Rose. I thought I heard you heave such a dreadful sigh. Supper is ready—come in. [*Hesitates*] You might ask me to kiss you before we go in.

Ralph. [*Kisses her*] Rose—God bless you.

Rose. I'm so happy, Ralph.

Ralph. May you always be happy, dear. [*Exits with arm about her*]

Liv. [*Enters gate, C. from L., followed by Mother Tagger*] Hang around for a half an hour or so. The girl from New York is here. Take her to your camp—dope her with whiskey—and keep her hid till we are ready to leave. [*Mother Tagger nods*]

Moth. T. Yes, yes.

Liv. Can we depend upon Jordan?

Moth. T. Yes, yes.

Liv. Good. Go now.

Moth. T. He, he, he—oh, you wicked, wicked boy. [*Exits C. to L.*]

Bess. [*Enters from house*] Oh, my heart aches so. I couldn't breathe in there. [*Crosses and sits at tree*]

Liv. My luck is with me. [*Crosses to her*] Sweetheart. [*Very tenderly*]

Bess. [*Rises in fear*] John!

Liv. Come with me, dear—we'll be married at once.

Bess. [*Retreating*] No, no—I won't.

Liv. You won't?

Bess. No, I can't trust you, John.

Liv. [*Quickly*] You won't come, eh? [*Catches her*] Then I must force you. Come. [*Bunco enters from house*]

Bess. [*Screams*] No!

Liv. [*Hand over her mouth*] Shut up! You'll trouble me no more. [*Forces her up stage as Mother Tagger enters C. Jake enters following Mother Tagger*]

Bunco. [*C. Takes gun from boot*] Let her go. [*Mother Tagger hits Bunco on head—she is unconscious*]

Liv. Good. Come, come! Hurry! You brought the horse and wagon, Jake. Help us put her in. [*Exit Bess, Livingstone, Mother Tagger and Jake C. to L.*]

BUNCO. [*On floor, coming to*] Ouch! I was knocked out, eh? [*Gets gun*] Now look out fer me, Mr. Bluff, 'cos dis time I'm goin' to shoot. [*Exits gate, C. to L. Silas and Lindy enter*]

SILAS. It's goin' to be a right smert night tonight, Lindy. That reminds me. One beautiful moonlight night in the summer old Doc Brown fell down a well and was instantly killed.

LINDY. Land sakes! What was the coroner's verdict?

SILAS. He said he should have attended the sick and let the well alone.

LINDY. [*Looking around*] Si Waterbury, I wonder where them gals is gone. [*Crosses to gate, C.*]

SILAS. [*At gate*] I'm afraid you've got a white elephant on yer hands, Lindy Jane. And that reminds me—

LINDY. Shet yer head. Somethin' always reminds ye of somethin' else. [*Crosses down C.*]

SILAS. [*Follows her*] Everything always reminds me of you, Lindy. Say, Lindy, when are ye goin' to say yes? This sweetheartin' fer ten years is gettin' monotonous.

LINDY. Oh, it is? Then quit it. [*Goes to gate, C.*]

SILAS. I can't. It's a habit now.

LINDY. Well, dern yer buttons. [*Crosses to him*]

SILAS. [*Sweetly*] See the stars up there?

LINDY. What stars?

SILAS. That reminds me—[*Kisses her*]

LINDY. Si Waterbury—ef you do that agin, I'll scream.

SILAS. I never heerd ye scream, Lindy. [*Kisses her again*]

LINDY. Oo—ooo, Si Waterbury. [*Crosses down L.*]

SILAS. Did ye see stars, Lindy? [*Laughs*] Good-night, Lindy. [*Exits gate, C. to R.*]

LINDY. [*Angry*] Well, I never see sich a man. [*Giggles*] But he do kiss the sweetest. [*Crosses to gate, sits C., sighs softly*]

DAY. [*Enters from house*] That you, Lindy?

LINDY. [*Fans herself with apron*] Yes, it is, sir.

DAY. It seems to me yer gettin' too old to be larkin' round this time o' night. [*Crosses and sits R.*]

LINDY. Oh, shet yer head. [*Exits into house*]

LIV. [*Enters gate*] Lovely night. I'm tired—I guess I'll go to bed. Good-night. [*Exits into house*]

DAY. Nice young man. [*Rises and cross up*]

LINDY. [*Enters and crosses to gate*] I can't understand where them two gals be.

DAY. Guess they've gone, Lindy. You took them in—gave them something to eat, and now they're on the tramp agin.

LINDY. Land sakes, I never would have believed that. Well, I'm goin' to bed. Good-night. [*Exits in house. Rose and Ralph enter from house*]

ROSE. Let's go out on the porch. Oh, is that you, father?

DAY. Yes.

ROSE. Isn't it a lovely night?

RALPH. I'm going for a little stroll. I've got a headache.

DAY. You won't be long?

RALPH. [*At gate*] Oh, no. [*Exits C. to R.*]

ROSE. Father, I have something to tell you.

DAY. Not tonight, daughter—I'm too tired. I know it's a love affair. He has spoken to me.

ROSE. He? Who?

DAY. Mr. Livingstone.

ROSE. Oh!

DAY. Good-night, daughter.

ROSE. But, father—

DAY. See that the doors are locked. Lots of robberies lately.

ROSE. I'm not afraid with my little revolver under my pillow.

DAY. [*Laughs*] You'd be afraid to use it.

ROSE. Would I? Don't you believe it.

DAY. Well, good-night, daughter.

ROSE. Good-night, daddy. [*Kisses him. Day exits to house*] I wonder where Ralph went. [*Runs up to gate*] Oh, there he is—I'm going for a little stroll with him. [*Exits gate, C. to R.*]

LIV. [*Sneaks on from behind house*] I must meet Ralph. He'll do as I say tonight. [*Looking off*] Hello—there he is and Rose is with him. [*Hides behind tree, C. Ralph and Rose enter gate*]

ROSE. Yes, both girls have disappeared. I suppose we'll never see them again. I wouldn't have believed they could have been so ungrateful. Well, I'll go in now. Good-night, dear husband.

RALPH. Good-night, dear wife. [*Kisses her*]

ROSE. Good-night. [*Exits, house*]

RALPH. Poor little woman—I'm afraid I've wrecked your happiness. Whichever way I turn, ruin seems to stare me in the face. But prison or no prison, I've sworn to lead a new life and I'll keep my word. Now to find Livingstone. [*Turns up, exits gate C. to L.*]

Liv. [*Comes from behind tree*] Yes, and tomorrow shall see you in custody, if my plan succeeds. His dear wife! I could kill him myself, with pleasure. [*Exits gate, C. to L.*]

Bunco. [*Enters C. from L.*]   Gee, I'm tired. [*Crosses to R.*] I followed the horse and buggy until we came to the gypsy camp where they took poor Bess. I can't do nothing tonight, but tomorrow I'll tell Miss Rose everything. I wonder if dey'll take my word against his. [*At gate*] Gee, whiz! Here he comes back. Me out of sight! [*Hides behind tree. Ralph and Livingstone enter gate, L.*]

Ralph.   I tell you I won't, Livingstone.

Liv.   Don't be a fool. It's easy enough and no danger. Just wait in the hall and watch. If you hear a noise—give me the signal. [*Crosses L.*]

Ralph.   But think what it means to me. My God, Livingstone, is there nothing I can do instead of this?

Liv.   Nothing. Come on—cover your face up. [*Takes out revolver*]

Ralph.   You are not going to use that?

Liv.   If I have to. Come! [*Exits into house*]

Ralph. [*Aloud*] Yes, John Livingstone, I will stand by the door and watch, but I'll give the alarm and put you behind the bars where you would send me. [*Exits into house*]

Bunco.   Christopher Columbus! Burglars! I thought dere was somethin' crooked about dat guy. De oder one didn't want to do it. Hully gee—what'll I do? Guess I'll have to take my trusty and go after dem. Dey're comin' back. [*Hides again*]

Lindy. [*Off stage, screams*]   Help, help! Rose, Rose! [*Ralph fires three shots inside. Rose rushes on*]

Rose.   What was that? Burglars? My revolver.

Bunco.   Miss Rose—dey're comin' out. [*Ralph enters from house, runs to gate, Rose shoots*]

Ralph. [*Staggers—falls*]   Oh, my God!

Bunco.   She's killed him.

Silas. [*Enters gate*]   What's the matter?

Lindy. [*Enters from house*]   Rose's father has been murdered.

Silas.   Burglars?

Lindy.   Yes.

Liv. [*Enters from house in bathrobe*]   Did you get him?

Rose. [*Enters from house*]   Have I killed him?

Lindy.   Look! Look!

Rose. [*Staggers*]   Oh, my God!

Liv.   He's killed your father.

Rose. No! No!

Liv. It's true as Heaven.

Bunco. [*Coming from behind tree*] *You lie like hell!*

ACT II.

At Rise: *Gypsy camp. Mother Tagger sits by the fire. Bess is in a stupor L. by tree. Jake looking at Bess.*

Jake. Say, dat gal looks mighty bad. What's de gov'nor going ter do wid her, eh?

Moth. T. That's his business, dearie.

Jake. I'm all right when it's face to face with a man, but when it comes to frighten women, hah, I'll leave dat to de white-livered dogs dat sticks a man in de back. [*Crosses down right*]

Moth. T. Don't speak like dat, dearie, he might hear you.

Jake. Who?

Moth. T. Your master.

Jake. Livingstone?

Moth. T. Yes, yes.

Jake. [*Laughs and crosses to L.*] My master? Why if I wanted to squeal the electric chair would have his black heart forever.

Moth. T. But think of yourself, dearie.

Jake. Oh, I'm not afraid of de prison bars, and dat's de worst dey could do with me. Say, why don't you put that gal in there so she can lie on the mattress?

Moth. T. No, I like to hear her groan, and see her white face turned up to de stars, he, he, he.

Jake. Well, if dere's a hell, there's a hot place waiting for you. [*Crosses to C.*]

Moth. T. He, he, he, burn higher, and higher. How I love to see you dance and play, throwing your fiery arms around each other. He, he, he. [*Looking above*] It's going to storm, eh? Well, let the wind blow. [*Sings*]

"Blow, blow, winds
While the pot bubbles, oh.
We're wrapped in warmth
And care not for trouble, oh. [*Thunder heard in the distance. Drinks whiskey and puts bottle away on floor*]

Liv. [*Enters C. and slaps Mother Tagger on back*] What the devil are you doing there?

MOTH. T. [*Rises and screams*] How you do frighten a body, creeping around like a snake. [*Crosses to fire*]

LIV. Guilty conscience, eh? [*Laughs*] Always croaking and drinking. You make my blood run cold. [*He shivers and warms his hands by the fire. Sits*]

MOTH. T. Then warm up, darling. Drink, he, he, he. [*Points to bottle*]

LIV. Shut up that cackle. [*Drinks from bottle*]

MOTH. T. What news, eh?

LIV. Rose is going to marry me tonight. [*Rises and crosses to C.*]

MOTH. T. What?

LIV. Yes. I've persuaded her it would be so romantic to be married by moonlight in the gypsy camp.

MOTH. T. He, he, he, and the boy, her husband—has she forgotten him?

LIV. No, she believes him dead, as I told her.

MOTH. T. Yes, yes.

LIV. And for three months while she had the fever, I was devotion itself. She believes me to be her best friend, and to save her good name, she has consented to be my wife. [*Laughs*] And she will marry me to give the *child* a name. [*Bess begins to come to*]

MOTH. T. How you must love her.

LIV. Love her? Yes, I am determined to call her mine. Perhaps it will be for a week, a month, but I shall make her my wife.

BESS. [*Rises to her knees weakly*] You shan't do it, y' shan't do it, I'll tell her all.

MOTH. T. [*Starts back*] What?

LIV. What the devil! I thought you had her out of the way.

BESS. I am your wife in the sight of Heaven, you shan't ruin her life too.

LIV. Shut up, or I'll choke you. [*Has crossed to her and chokes her*]

MOTH. T. Be careful, my darling, and don't squeeze too hard. It's a thin little throat, he, he, he. [*Goes up behind Livingstone*]

LIV. You keep your mouth shut if you're wise, or I may be tempted to put you out of the way altogether. Give me the drugged whiskey. I told you to keep her under the influence, why haven't you done so?

BESS. [*On knees*] Oh please, please, don't make me take that dreadful stuff. I'll be quiet. Oh, let me go away from here. I won't trouble you any more. But don't torture me like this. [*Mother Tagger takes drugged whiskey from stocking leg*]

LIV. No, I can't trust your blabbing tongue. You must stay with Mother Tagger until we leave the village.

BESS. But she is so cruel to me. Why can't I die.

Liv. It's a devilish pity you can't. I'd help you if I dared. [*Throws her on stage and takes bottle*] Here, drink this.

Bess. No, no, I'll be quiet, I'll be quiet.

Liv. Drink it, I say. [*Bess holds it to her mouth*] There, that will keep her quiet until the wedding is over. [*Bess spits it out as he turns away*]

Moth. T. He, he, he.

Liv. Let's put her in the tent mother, here take care of this. [*Gives her the bottle. They put Bess in tent. Mother Tagger puts bottle back in her stocking—as Livingstone looks at his watch*] Now I'm going, I'll be back soon. Keep the girl in the tent and don't you dare get drunk. [*Exits R.*]

Moth. T. Don't get drunk, eh? [*Screams*] Leave you to have all the fun, while Mother Tagger does all the work, no, no, no, my pet, my pretty pet. [*Takes out bottle, drinks*] Oh, oh, it's the drugged whiskey, oh, Lord! I'm poisoned, I've drunk the drugged whiskey, what will I do? It may kill me. Oh, oh, I must go to the apothecary shop. Oh, I'm poisoned, I'm poisoned. [*Does funny business and exits R.*]

Bunco. [*Enters R. Looks around*] Dere's no one here, I'll just call Mr. Ralph and let him rubberneck. [*Calls off*] Mr. Ralph, oho, oho—[*Ralph enters R.*] Oh, I say now Mr. Ralph, don't ye go looking fer trouble, yer too weak.

Ralph. Don't be afraid, little girl, I'm stronger then you think.

Bunco. But dere's three to one. I'll do all I kin to help ye, but what's a girl in a bunch like dis?

Ralph. Well, you've got a heart that's too big for your little body. [*Sits L.*]

Bunco. Oh, my heart's all right, all right. And I've worked in de factory and I kin hold my own where dere is people dat's honest. But when you're bumped about de outside world ans have shuffeled fer yourself, you soon learns to tell a good man from a bad one. Say, you're all right. [*Puts out her hand*]

Ralph. Thank you, Bunco. [*They shake hands*]

Bunco. But say, don't stay here now Mr. Ralph, there's danger.

Ralph. You mean well, little girl, but you don't understand. When a man through his own folly has tangled the threads of his own life, there's nothing left for him to do but to untangle them again. I must see this man Livingstone, tonight. [*Crosses up stage*]

Bunco. He's de guy, the spider that will tangle you in his web again. Mr. Ralph, I tell you he is de devil.

Ralph. [*Crosses to Bunco*] But I have you by my side, and you are my little guardian angel.

Bunco. Yes, but I've lost my wings.

RALPH. [*Sits by fire*] Oh, Bunco, you're the only friend I have in the world. When everything looked dark you stood bravely by me. [*Rises*] Oh, little woman, your start in life was not too brilliant, but you have it in your power to grow up to be a noble woman. And Bunco never do anything that you'll regret all your life.

BUNCO. Well, I'll regret it if I stay here in this gypsy camp. I'll show you a short cut to the next town through the fields. If you stay here, they will pinch you sure. [*Crosses to tent R.*]

RALPH. [*Hands up to fire*] No—I'll wait. Come now, tell me about Rose.

BUNCO. Say, I never saw a man so stuck—

RALPH. I'm going to walk by the old farm house, perhaps I'll catch a glimpse of Rose. [*Exits L.*]

BUNCO. Gee—he's de grandest man I ever seed. I wonder where Bess is. She *must* be here somewhere.

BESS. [*Comes out of tent*] Bunco!

·BUNCO. Bess, Bess. [*They embrace. Bess staggers*] What's the matter, honey, is ye faint? What have dey done to ye?

BESS. Oh, Bunco, I feel so ill, I believe I am going to faint.

BUNCO. Hully Gee, don't faint. Dere, we'll go far away from here where no one will find us. [*Bess starts to sink to floor. Bunco tries to help her up*]

BESS. [*Cries*] Oh, I can't, Bunco, I can't walk. I'm so weak, my head swims.

BUNCO. Dere, dere, dearie. Try again, Bessie, try again, dat's de way. [*Helps her*]

BESS. I can't, Bunco. [*Falls*] You go, Bunco, don't let him get you. Go, leave me here to die.

BUNCO. Well, I guess not. Try again. Put your arms around my neck. So, dat's right! Don't be afraid honey, I'll take care of ye.

BESS. [*Trying hard*] Oh, we'll get away, won't we?

BUNCO. You bet. [*They start up R.*]

MOTH. T. [*Enters R.*] Ho, ho, what's dis? So, so, and where do you think you are going, eh?

BUNCO. Oh, you get out.

BESS. [*Bess drops to her knees*] Oh, Bunco!

BUNCO. Don't be afraid, Bess. [*Takes gun from her boot Livingstone enters R., sneaks down behind Bunco*] Don't you be afraid, Bess. I got my old trusty and if dey lay a hand on ye, de devil will have two new angels to shovel coal for him.

LIV. [*Grabs Bunco*] Mother Tagger, take the girl. [*Mother Tagger drags Bess to tent R.*]

BUNCO. [*Struggling with Livingstone*] You let her go!

LIV. Ha, ha, ha, you little devil, I'm glad to get my hands on you.

BUNCO. Oh, you great big coward, if I was a man I'd beat ye tell ye had to walk on crutches for the rest of your life.

LIV. Oh, you would eh? Give me the chloroform bottle, mother. [*Mother Tagger exits*]

BUNCO. No, no, I won't be chloroformed. [*Tries to get away*]

LIV. You *would* come into the lion's den, eh?

BUNCO. Lion? You're only a measly yellow pup.

MOTH. T. [*Enters with handkerchief*] Here, dearie. [*Gives him handkerchief*]

LIV. [*Struggles with Bunco, gives her chloroform*] I guess you'll keep quiet now. Mother, get me one of those sacks, hurry up. I'll just tie her into it, and after dark, put her in an empty boxcar and ship her where she'll never come back.

MOTH. T. He, he, he. [*Gets sack. Drags Bunco to L. Silas and Lindy heard off R.*]

LINDY. I tell you nothing on earth could make me do such a fool thing. [*They enter from R. and come down R.*]

LIV. [*Bows*] How do you do? I'm just arranging for the marriage.

LINDY. [*Sees Bunco*] Good land!

LIV. Yes, they are a very bad lot. They're very wild. I fear this one is quite intoxicated.

LINDY. Oh, the wicked child. [*Crosses to L.*]

SILAS. [*Crosses to L.*] Don't look intoxicated to me.

LINDY. What do you know about 'toxication?

SILAS. Well—er—not much.

MOTH. T. [*Looking at Bunco*] Oh dear, these gals will break my poor heart. When their father died he left me to take keer of them, but they're a bad lot. Take after their father who was an awful one for them 'toxication liquors.

SILAS. Smells as if the old gal likes 'em pretty tolerable. [*Crosses in front of Livingstone*]

LIV. I'll put her inside for you.

MOTH. T. Thank you, my good kind gentleman. [*Quickly puts Bunco in tent and goes up stage*] Can I do anything for you, dearie? [*She speaks to Silas*]

SILAS. Yes, I wanter have my fortune told.

MOTH. T. Well, I'll do my best. I must get in communication with the spirits. [*Sits L. Drunk*]

SILAS. If she communes much more with the spirits, I'm afraid she won't be able to commune at all.

MOTH. T. Give me your hand. He, he, he.

SILAS. Hi, hi, hi. [*Crosses to her*]

MOTH. T. [*Looking at his hand*] I kin see yer a great favorite with the ladies.

SILAS. Hear that, Lindy? [*Proudly*]

MOTH. T. You have many sweethearts.

SILAS. You said it.

MOTH. T. The gals all love you.

LINDY. Well, I never!

MOTH. T. But there is one you'll marry.

SILAS. Humph, I guess not.

MOTH. T. [*Looking closely at his hand*] She loves you and you love her.

SILAS. Bet your gollushes I do.

LINDY. Humph!

MOTH. T. I kin see her now. [*Looks up into the air*]

SILAS. She's on to you Lindy.

LINDY. Guess I ain't up in the air.

SILAS. Yes, sir, most of the time.

MOTH. T. It's a little woman with black hair.

SILAS. Black hair?

MOTH. T. Yes, black hair.

SILAS. That lets you out, Lindy. I wonder if it's Sally Tomkins?

MOTH. T. Yes, yes, that's her. Sally Tomkins, she loves ye, darling.

SILAS. I'll be darned. Guess that's about all I wanted to know. [*Turns to Lindy*] Going to have your fortune told, Lindy?

LINDY. Well, I reckon not. I don't believe in such foolish truck.

SILAS. [*Reaching into his pocket*] How much, mother?

MOTH. T. One dollar, darling.

SILAS. Here ye air. That's cheap enough to find out that Sally Tomkins loves me, eh Lindy? [*Crosses up to R.*]

LINDY. Si Waterbury.

SILAS. Ma'am?

LINDY. You've been flirting with Sally Tomkins.

SILAS. Get out. Well now, Lindy, I've been a courtin' you fer the last twenty years, and I can't wait twenty more for I git a wife.

LINDY. Then ask Sally Tomkins to marry you.

SILAS. [*At door R.*] I will by thunder.

LINDY. [*Following Silas*] Silas Waterbury—

SILAS. By the great tadpoles, she'll jump at me, you don't want me. [*Turns to go*]

LINDY. Yes, I do.

SILAS. What?

LINDY. [*Falls into his arms*] Oh Si—[*Enter Livingstone*]

SILAS. She's mine. By Hickory she's mine. I say Mr. Livingstone, ye kin fix up a double wedding tonight. [*With his arm around Lindy they exit R.*]

LIV. [*Laughs*] Quick, mother, get the bag, hurry up, there is no time to lose. [*Mother Tagger gets bag as Livingstone drags Bunco out*] There, now, over her head, give me a cord. [*They put her in bag and tie it shut*] There, now, my wise little shopgirl, I guess when you wake up, you'll wonder what it is all about, and what all happened. [*Mother Tagger exits into tent, drags Bunco to side of tent*]

RALPH. [*Enters L.*] John Livingstone.

LIV. Ralph Carlton, well, well, where did you drop from. [*Advances to tent, R.*]

RALPH. You know well enough, you scoundrel. From the hospital. I knew that as soon as I was well enough I'd be carried away to jail, so I took advantage of my first walk into the grounds, to get away and see you once more, my good kind friend. [*Advances toward him*]

LIV. Now don't be sarcastic, Ralph. I am your friend and will do all I can to help you. [*Crosses to Ralph*]

RALPH. How very noble! And my wife, you'll help her too won't you? I hear her father did not die.

LIV. Now see here, Ralph, I can't help if our plans turned out so devilish bad.

RALPH. Good you mean, for you. I'm going to see Rose and tell her all. [*Starts*]

LIV. She wouldn't believe you. You're very foolish old fellow to expose yourself. Better get out of the country.

RALPH. And leave Rose to you? No, I'll tell her; she will believe me. I'll tell her it was you who tried to kill her father.

LIV. Hush, you fool. Better get out of the country while you have a chance. [*Jake enters L. and remains up C. Then advances on Ralph*]

RALPH. I'll stay and face my accusers. And if I go to jail you shall go with me.

LIV. Seize him, Jake. [*Jake grabs Ralph, they struggle. Mother Tagger enters, as Ralph's revolver explodes. Livingstone hits Ralph with a billy, Ralph falls, and Jake drops on knee behind him. Livingstone draws knife and offers it to Jake*] Good, the fool! Here, Jake, kill him.

JAKE. Why don't you do it yourself, governor? [*Rises*]

LIV. [*Picking up Ralph's revolver*] I will, and while I am about it I'll just settle my account with you, Jake Jordan.

JAKE. What do you mean, Livingstone?

LIV. I mean my opportunity to get rid of you with no danger to me. You have hounded me long enough, Jake Jordan.

JAKE. Would you kill a man without giving him a chance?

LIV. Yes.

JAKE. You do. [*Crosses to him. Jake makes rush for Livingstone, who shoots Jake and he falls. Then drops the revolver near Ralph, then picks up Jake's knife. Mother Tagger looks down at him*]

MOTH. T. Is he dead?

LIV. Well, if he ain't he soon will be.

MOTH. T. You wicked, wicked boy. He's moving.

LIV. Shut up. [*Livingstone lifts Ralph to his feet*] There, there old pard, brace up, this is a bad business.

RALPH. [*Rousing himself*] What is it, what is the matter?

LIV. [*R.*] He's dead.

RALPH. Dead; who's dead? [*Sees Jake*]

LIV. [*Crosses to L.*] It's too bad, but luck seems against you. Of course it wasn't in cold blood, but in the tussle.

RALPH. I shot him?

LIV. Yes.

RALPH. I don't believe it.

LIV. I tell you you killed him. Look at your revolver.

RALPH. [*Crosses to Jake, picks up revolver*] Well, I'll go. The odds are against me just now. They may send me to prison, John Livingstone, but some day I'll meet you again, and God shall judge between us. [*Exits L. Jake has been coming to during this speech*]

LIV. [*Looking after him, then turns and crosses up to Mother Tagger*] He's gone and he will never come back. Come quick, we'll put this fellow in the wagon, he can stay there until after the wedding, and then I'll drive him to the river and throw him in. If the body is found it will be easy to fasten the crime on Carlton. Look, Mother Hag.

JAKE. [*Has risen*] You dog. [*Rushes at Livingstone who knocks him down, drags him to door of tent R.*] Now I'll put the police on Carlton's track. Don't you leave here until I return. [*Exits R.*]

MOTH. T. Don't leave here? Why darling I must have something to steady my nerves. [*Looks in tent, and following him*] She's all right. A murder and a wedding in one night. [*Kicks Bunco who is still in bag*] Everything looks safe. Now I'll get just one little drop. [*Exits L.*]

BUNCO. [*Rolling down C. and trying to get out of bag*] Help, help!

BESS. [*Enters from tent*] She's gone.

BUNCO. Help, help!

BESS. Oh Lord, what's that?

BUNCO. Bess, Bess. [*Bess runs up stage calling her, then crosses to upper L.*] Here in the sack, Bess.

BESS. [*Going to her*] Is it you, Bunco?

BUNCO. I guess so—what's left of me. Hully Gee—let's get out quick.

BESS. Oh, Bunco, my hands tremble so I can't untie it. There. [*Opens bag. Bunco jumps out*]

BUNCO. Gee, I'd like to live in that sack.

BESS. Did they put you in there?

BUNCO. Gee, I feel pale. My head's just swimming.

BESS. [*Starting up*] Come, Bunco, let's go. If they find us they'll kill us.

BUNCO. No, Bess, I can't leave now—I've got business here. [*Goes up and sees Jake*] Try to get a little air, pardner. Quick—some water Bess, quick. Is dat better? [*Getting Jake out and trying to revive him*]

BESS. [*Getting bottle of water*] Here, Bunco. [*Hands her bottle of whiskey*]

BUNCO. [*Starts to give Jake a drink, stops*] No, that may be drugged stuff.

BESS. No it ain't, Bunco.

BUNCO. Are you sure?

BESS. Yes, Bunco.

BUNCO. Here pardner, drink this. [*Jake takes drink*] Are you much hurt?

JAKE. The bullet just grazed my head. [*Partly rising*] You're a brick, kid. I'm all right now. [*Sits up. Mother Tagger laughs off L.*]

BESS. [*Frightened. Runs in tent as she speaks*] She's coming back. [*Sound of horses' hoofs approaching*]

BUNCO. Duck, pardner—quick. [*Bunco and Jake exit R. quickly*]

MOTHER T. [*Enter laughing from L.*] Ha-a, I feel better now. Ah—they are coming. [*Looks into tent*] Ha, the girl's asleep yet. [*Goes down R. Livingstone enters R. followed by Rose. They go down R. Si enters with Lindy, followed by Parson. Si and Lindy go down L. Parson down C. Lindy speaks as she enters; she goes down L.*]

LINDY. Oh, Si, I feel so nervous.

SILAS. What for?

LINDY. I never was married before.

SILAS. Well, you'll get used to it.

LIV. [*Has been talking to Rose, aside*] There cheer up, Rose. You look as if you were going to a funeral.

ROSE. I can't help it John, I have a horrible feeling of fear. If I could turn back now. A vision of Ralph arises before me as a warning. I have seen him in my fancy several times today. Oh, John, are you quite sure he is dead?

LIV. *You* saw the certificate. He died while you were quite ill. I buried him myself, poor boy.

ROSE. You are very kind, John. I'll try and be a good wife to you so you'll never forget your great love for me.

LIV. My one wish is for your happiness, Rose. Come, dear—you will soon be my wife. Come smile—I want to remember this as the happiest day of my life. Come, Parson. [*Parson goes C.*]

LINDY. Oh, Si, I've changed my mind.

SILAS. All right, I'll get Sally Tomkins. [*Starts; she catches his coat-tails*]

LINDY. [*As Parson prepares for the ceremony*] Oh, Si, I shall faint—I know I shall. [*Growing dark*]

PAR. [*Parson is C. Rose and Livingstone R. Silas and Lindy L.*] Are you ready? [*All bow, Lindy and Rose in dread*] If there be anyone here who sees a reason why these people should not be joined in the holy bonds of matrimony, let him speak now [*Loud thunder*] or forever hold his peace, and be silent.

BESS. [*Enters at tent*] I *do!*

ALL. Bess!

BESS. [*Coming down*] I should be in her place. He has promised.

ROSE. Bess—why are you here.

LIV. She is the old woman's grandchild and is insane. [*Mother Tagger comes down and grabs her*]

BESS. No, no—Miss Rose—don't marry him.

MOTH. T. Come, my poor crazy child. Come, dearie, come. [*Pushes her into tent. Parson goes up and talks to Mother Tagger. Silas and Lindy talk aside L.*]

LIV. Come, dear.

ROSE. Oh, John—I can't—I can't.

LIV. Sweetheart, will you allow the ravings of a poor demented creature to affect you?

ROSE. Oh, I'm afraid, John.

LIV. Come dear, come. You're nervous. You'll soon be my dear little wife. Go on, Parson.

PAR. [*Coming down C.*] Do you, Rose Day, and Lindy Jane Smithers, take these men, John Livingstone and Silas Waterbury to be your lawfully wedded husbands, to love honor and *obey* until death do you part?

ROSE and LINDY. [*At the same time—meekly*] We do.

LINDY. Oh, Silas!

SILAS. You're mine, Lindy—you're mine—at last. [*Starts to embrace her. There is a big roar of thunder and they jump*]

PAR. Then I pronounce you man and wife, and whom God has joined together, let no man put asunder. [*Rose swoons and faints*]

LIV. She's fainted.

LINDY. [*Crossing to her*] Rose—my poor Rose.

SILAS. The kerridge is waiting. [*Lifting her up*]

LIV. Yes, you take her home. I will follow you. Go at once before the storm overtakes you. I'll settle with this good woman.

SILAS. We'll wait for you.

LIV. No, no—go at once. [*Pushing them off R. As they all exit, the fury of the storm increases, with wind, thunder and lightning*] Now, mother—quick—[*Looks for Bess*] By Heaven—she's gone!

MOTH. T. Gone?

LIV. [*Looking for Jake*] Is he still here? [*Jake appears at door of wagon*]

JAKE. [*As he appears*] Yes, and ready to settle with you.

LIV. We'll see. [*Pulls knife. They fight. Livingstone gets the better of the knife fight—stabs Jake and throws him off. Livingstone starts for Jake again with knife, to give him another thrust, and as he does so, Bunco enters from R., shoots him; he staggers. During all this action there is a terrible storm raging*]

ACT III.

The scene is a room in which the Livingstones are living. It is supposed to be a room where there is a bed but a cot may be substituted if a bed is not available. There are doors R. and L.U., and there is a window in center at back. There is a dresser up stage against the wall. Fireplace down L. in front of which is a chair. The bed is down R. There is a house screen up L. There is a large closet against the wall up R. or, if desired, a door leading into a supposed closet up there. A table R., and a couple of plain chairs. One to be placed R.C. At rise, Rose sitting in front of fireplace.

LIV. [*At dresser tying his tie, preparing to go*] I may be in at ten.

ROSE. Can't you stay in tonight, John?

LIV. [*Irritated*] No—*No!* I say. I have business to attend to.

ROSE. What business?

LIV. [*Still busy with tie*] Oh, I can't explain it to you.

ROSE. And why not? The baby is not well and I may have to send for a doctor. I don't like to be left alone.

LIV. Oh, I can't help it. It's not my kid.

ROSE. [*Rising*] John! [*Crosses to bed, puts baby down*]

LIV. [*Laughs*] What's the matter?

ROSE. [*With spirit*] Oh, I won't bear it any longer—I won't—I won't. Business! What business keeps you out night after night and until all hours in the morning. We have been married a year and in all that time you have scarcely spent a night at home. What business is it that must be done tonight, while all day you never leave the house?

LIV. See here, Rose, don't pry into my affairs or you'll be sorry. [*Going to her*] What I want you to know I'll tell you—and if you don't like it—well you know what you can do. [*Exits abruptly R.U.*]

ROSE. Oh, what a fool I've been—what a fool. I didn't love him when I married him and now I hate him. But it serves me right—I am a coward. Afraid to face the world with my baby. [*Picks up baby from bed*] Because your father was a criminal I dared not claim him. Well he has given you a name so we must be content, I suppose. [*Lays baby down again*]

BUNCO. [*Calls off stage R.*] Hey—Rose! Who-hoo—Rose—can I come in?

ROSE. [*Comes down to L.C.*] Yes—Come on in.

BUNCO. [*Enter R.U.*] I saw old Pain-in-the-Face go out so I thought I'd slip in. Is the kid asleep? [*Goes to baby*]

ROSE. Yes. Be careful and don't wake him.

BUNCO. I wonder if dis kid's goin' to look like its father.

ROSE. I hope so.

LIV. [*From outside off R.*] All right—wait a few moments.

BUNCO. [*Running up and looking off*] Gee—it's old Pain-in-the-Face—I'll duck. [*Runs behind screen up L. Livingstone enters door R.U., goes quickly to dresser, takes out jewelry*]

ROSE. [*Comes toward him*] What are you doing?

LIV. I'm in trouble. I want money.

ROSE. Don't take those. They belonged to my mother. Here—take this. It's all I have—but leave those. [*Offers purse or moneybag*]

LIV. [*Takes money*] I'll need it.

ROSE. No! I've changed my mind. You shan't have it. [*Resisting him*]

LIV. Let go, you fool—[*Jerks money from her*] Now give me those rings —[*In desperate tone*] Quick—hurry! [*Rose, frightened, gives rings*] Now give me the other.

Rose. My wedding ring?

Liv. Yes. Hurry up, I tell you. I'm in trouble.

Rose. Well—take it, but give me back the others. [*Takes ring, looks at it*]

Liv. Ralph's ring, eh?

Rose. Yes. Now give me back the others.

Liv. I guess not. I need them all. [*Puts them in his pocket*]

Bunco. [*Has slipped from behind screen and down back of him. Takes jewelry and money from his pocket*] And so do I. [*Bunco exits L.*]

Rose. Oh, John—John.

Liv. Let go. [*Throws her off*] Shall I tell you why my business takes me out at night? It's because I'm a thief—a housebreaker. Now will you hold your tongue? I'm in hard luck tonight, but tomorrow we may have plenty. So cheer up, Rose—Cheer up! [*Laughs and exits door R.U. Bunco enters L.*]

Rose. Good Heavens, Bunco, did you hear what he said?

Bunco. You bet I did and it's true—every word of it.

Rose. Bunco, do you know what you are saying?

Bunco. Yes I do. He's a devil, he's a thief, a bankrobber and worser.

Rose. A *worser?*

Bunco. Yes—a *worser*—a murderer.

Rose. *Bunco!*

Bunco. Why I believe it was he who tried to kill your father.

Rose. My God!

Bunco. Den he ruined poor Bessie's life, and tried to kill dat poor feller Jake in dat gypsy camp, and den made poor Ralph think he done it.

Rose. [*Crossing to L.*] Stop—Please, Bunco. For God's sake do you know what you are talking about?

Bunco. Yes, I'm talkin' about old Pain-in-the-Face.

Rose. You say you saw Ralph at the gypsy camp?

Bunco. Well, I didn't exactly see him, 'cause I couldn't see. But I heard his voice and I know it was him.

Rose. Can it be that Ralph—my Ralph—is alive and innocent. Oh, I begin to see it all now. [*Sink in chair L.*]

Bunco. [*Holding out money she took from Livingstone's pocket*] Here —you may need dis. And if I was you I'd put on Mr. Ralph's ring again. [*Rose takes ring*] Say, Miss Rose, did you marry him?

Rose. Yes—yes—and if he is alive I shall go mad.

Bunco. [*Picks baby up, upside down—funny business*] De baby's wakin'.

Rose. [*Screams*] Oh, Bunco! [*Lindy and Silas knock on R.U. door*]

Lindy. [*Outside*] Air ye home, Rose?

Rose. [*Holding the baby*] Open the door, Bunco.

BUNCO. [*Opening door*] Howdy! [*Dances C. to music. Lindy and Silas enter L.*]

LINDY. Where on airth did you come from?

BUNCO. Oh, I've got a good job taking keer of two kids in the flat next door.

LINDY. Well, I never. We've been to the opery, Rose. [*Crosses C.*]

SILAS. Drammer, Lindy.

LINDY. Opery! It was at the Opery House.

ROSE. Did you enjoy it?

SILAS. Yep. We had two good seats.

LINDY. [*Crossing to him confidentially*] Preserved seats.

SILAS. Yep. They were good ones anyway and you oughter see Lindy blubber.

LINDY. Hersh yer head. I guess you blubbered too when the poor gal was druv out by her hard-hearted paw. Yes—and the villain—say ye oughter see him Rose—he was a bad 'un. I'll foller her to the end of the airth, by Gum.

SILAS. [*Funny business with Lindy*] An' when the villain crep' up behind her with a big bowie knife—before he could jab him the hero pulled out his gun and *bang*—[*Shot heard outside*]

LINDY. Good Lord—what's that? [*Crosses to Silas, R.*]

BUNCO. [*At window*] Hully Chee—two coppers runnin' across the yard—and oh—oo a man is climbing up the balcony.

LINDY. Oh, Lord save me.

SILAS. Me too, oh, Lord. [*Both business of ad lib under the bed*]

BUNCO. Hully Gee! I'm pinched. [*Goes to closet R. Ralph enters through window in prison clothes*]

ROSE. Merciful Heavens!

RALPH. Lady—for God's sake, hide me.

ROSE. Ralph!

RALPH. Rose! [*Embrace*] My Darling!

BUNCO. [*Enters, sees Ralph*] Hully Gee! [*Exits in closet*]

ROSE. You are in danger.

RALPH. Yes, the police are after me.

ROSE. What shall I do?

BUNCO. [*Enters*] Get under the bed. [*Shot outside*]

ROSE. Quick—quick— [*Shot*] Here. [*Turns down cover. Ralph gets into bed*]

BUNCO. Now sleep like the devil. [*Rose C. turns down lights. Knock at R.U. door. Gets baby. Officers knock*] Hully Chee—dere's de cops. [*Crosses to chair, L.*] We ain't in. [*Funny business*]

Rose. Open the door, Bunco.

Bunco. [*Opens door*] Sh—hh—You'll wake the baby.

Off. We must come in. [*They enter*]

Bunco. My master is awful sick.

Off. [*L.C.*] Stand aside.

Rose. What is it sir? Why were those shots fired?

Off. We must search the house, lady. We are after an escaped convict. He was seen to climb the balcony. I can't say whether he came here or the flat above. But we must search.

Bunco. A convict. Oh, Gee! [*Crosses L.*]

Rose. Mercy, he isn't here, sir. You may search but please be as quiet as possible. My husband is very ill and has just fallen asleep.

Off. [*Quietly*] Sorry to trouble you, lady—[*Searches closet and under bed*] Hello—come out here—[*Pulls Silas out shaking; funny business*]

Bunco. Oh, Gee—isn't that funny!

Lindy. Oh, please, Mr. Policeman, don't take us to jail.

Silas. Shut up, Lindy—nothin' to be afraid of. We don't know nothin'.

Off. I can see that. What were you doing under that bed?

Silas. I was under there to bring Lindy out.

Rose. The shots frightened them, officer—sh-h-, dear. [*To Ralph*] It's nothing.

Off. Come. [*To policeman*] We must go through the other rooms. [*Exit L.*]

Lindy. My teeth is jest a chatterin'.

Silas. This ain't no place for a constable. I'm goin' home. [*Exits R.U.*]

Lindy. Silas Waterbury, wait for me. [*Exits U.*]

Rose. God protect you, dear. Have courage. Sit here, Bunco—quick. [*Bunco sits beside Ralph, Rose walks floor with baby*] There, there, dearie—sh—sh-h.

Bunco. Gee, ain't this excitin'? [*Crosses right to bed*]

Off. [*They enter*] Sorry we had to trouble you, missus. He's not there. We must go upstairs. Good-night. [*Crosses to C.*]

Rose. Good-night, officer. I hope you find him. It makes me nervous to think of a criminal at large.

Off. Oh, we'll get him. [*They exit R.U.*]

Bunco. Yes—you will. [*Puts key in door*]

Rose. Quick, quick, Ralph, put on this suit of clothes in the closet. [*Ralph goes to closet, puts on suit, hat, etc.*] Bunco, watch. Oh, God help me to get him away.

Bunco. Hully Gee, Miss Rose—don't flop—[*Runs to window*] Don't be afraid, Miss Rose—God will help him, *you bet.*

Rose. Don't leave the window, Bunco. Watch—watch. [*Bunco does fancy business, back to window*]

Ralph. [*Enters*] Rose—why are you here? And the *child*—

Rose. Our child, Ralph.

Ralph. My God!

Rose. He told me you were dead. I married him.

Ralph. Livingstone?

Rose. Yes.

Ralph. Oh, God! Where is he?

Rose. No, no—for my sake, Ralph, you must get away. I have proof against him. This girl heard it all—that night at the gypsy camp. But first you must get away.

Bunco. Old Pain-in-the-Face is coming back.

Rose. Too late.

Ralph. I'll meet him.

Rose. No, it would be madness. See, the child is ill. You are the doctor—do you understand?

Ralph. Yes.

Bunco. [*Gets chair for him*] Sit here, Mr. Ralph, de baby is sick and you are de doctor. Hully Chee—now he's a doctor. [*Livingstone sings drunken song off R.*] Hully Chee—if I'm discovered I shall be found. [*Bunco makes funny exit into closet*]

Liv. [*Enters R.U.*] How's the girl, eh? Miss her hubby? [*To Ralph*] Who the devil are you?

Rose. Oh, John—the doctor. The baby is ill.

Liv. Too bad, hic—[*Laughs*] Let it die, doc—it's better off. [*Crosses L.*]

Rose. John! [*Livingstone laughs*] This way, doctor. You will call again in the morning?

Liv. [*Faces Ralph*] What ails the kid, doc? [*Faces him*] By Heaven, I know you. [*Snatches off Ralph's hat*] Ralph Carlton!

Ralph. Yes, John Livingstone—I said we'd meet again. [*He rushes at Livingstone. Rose screams. During the struggle Livingstone hits Ralph on the head with butt of revolver, catches him as he struggles, throws him in closet*]

Rose. You've killed him.

Liv. Shut up, you fool. [*Throws her C.*] I'll fix your Ralph Carlton—I'll call the police. [*Goes to phone. As he locked closet door Rose has gotten scissors and cut phone wire*] What have you done? Oh, I see—you want to save him, eh? [*Struggles with her*]

Rose. Yes.

Liv. Drop those scissors.

Rose. I won't.

Liv. [*Shakes them to the floor, strikes Rose; she falls C.*] Try to save him! I'll fix you, eh. [*Gets rope at window*]

Rose. [*Rises, runs to closet*] Ralph—Ralph—[*Livingstone catches her, drags her to bed*] Oh, you devil—you murderer.

Liv. I am, eh? [*Chokes her with handkerchief, throws her on floor, cuts rope line and ties her to bed*] There—I guess you'll be quiet now. There's another telephone downstairs, I'll use *it*. I'll lock the door and keep the key in my pocket until I come back. [*Exits R.U.*]

Bunco. [*Crawls over transom, unlocks closet door*] I'll be with you in a minute, Mr. Ralph.

Ralph. [*Enters*] My darling, are you hurt? Bunco, get some water, quick!

Bunco. I'll turn up the lights. [*Does so, cuts rope*] Some water. Yes, sir. Hully Gee, dis door is locked. [*Tries closet key*]

Rose. I'm all right now, dear. Get away through the window before he gets back.

Ralph. Not without you. Will you come with me?

Rose. Yes.

Bunco. Come on—de door's open. I'll get de kid. [*Goes L. of bed for child. Ralph and Rose start for door. Livingstone opens it*]

Liv. The devil!

Bunco. [*On bed, with revolver in hand*] Throw up your hands. Hurry up! That's right. Now, Mr. Ralph, give him a knock on the coco.

Ralph. Take off your coat.

Bunco. Take off your coat.

Liv. Ah-h! [*Not taking coat off*]

Bunco. [*Crosses to him, poking revolver in his stomach*] There! Take off your coat or I'll puncture you. [*Livingstone crosses L. and takes off coat*] Dat's right.

Ralph. Now put on these.

Liv. Huh?

Bunco. [*Has gotten convict's clothes from closet*] Put 'em on! [*Covers him with gun*] Hurry up! [*Livingstone does so. Bunco jumps up and down on bed*] He won't put them on. Oh, no!

Ralph. Now the coat—[*Livingstone starts for Ralph*]

BUNCO. Oh, Gee, ain't we got fun—[*Pokes Livingstone in back with pistol*] Hurry up. [*Livingstone starts toward bed*]

RALPH. [*Ties him*] I guess the police will be as glad to get you as to get me, John Livingstone. [*Gags him, speaks to Rose*] Now we are going. I have a long account to settle with you. The end is not yet.

ROSE. Bring the baby, Bunco.

BUNCO. Yes, ma'am. [*Jumps off bed. Livingstone starts to move bed and all*] Whoa, Bill. [*Takes baby. Funny business across room with gun. Rose and Ralph exit R.U.*] How do you feel now, old Pain-in-the-Face? [*Kicks him*] I'll see you when the robins bloom in the spring, tra la. [*Exits after others*]

LIV. [*Struggles, works gag out of mouth*] Help—help—

MOTH. T. [*Enters at window*] Is that you, darling?

LIV. Mother Tagger—what luck! Come here and cut these ropes.

MOTH. T. How did you get into this, darling? I've been hanging around to tell you that Jake Jordan is free.

LIV. Jake Jordan free? The devil he is.

MOTH. T. True as Heaven, darling. [*Crash, scream outside*] What's that?

LIV. I'm off. [*Officers at door, R.U. Livingstone crosses and gets revolver from dresser drawer. One policeman jumps through window, other R. Jake enters R.U.*]

OFF. [*At window*] Here's our man. [*Livingstone shoots at officer at window. Jumps out. Others follow him. Officer falls to floor wounded, then rises and crosses to window. Jake shoots out of window*]

MOTH. T. [*On knees, starts praying*] Oh, oh, it's all over now! It's all over now.

ACT IV.

Over run from up L. Lindy enters L., skirt caught up, very tired. Sunrise, red and blue lights. Silas follows Lindy on; has shoes in hand and an open umbrella over his head.

LINDY. For land's sake, will you hurry? I never seed such a man in my life. Here's a tent—we can ask the way. And the next time I let you take the lead and follow you, you can lam me good. And as fer show theaters I'll never go again, 'less I'm sure we can ketch the last car home. My feet is so swelled and tired, I could jest lay down and die. Do you spect we're any nearer than when we started?

SILAS. Durned ef I know. We've walked about five thousand miles now I reckon.

LINDY. What?

SILAS. Five hundred miles.

LINDY. How fur?

SILAS. Five miles, I said. [*Wilting at her each time*]

LINDY. What on earth are you doing with your shoes in your hands?

SILAS. Ain't goin' to wear 'em out, by cracky. Paid a dollar and twenty cents fer them shoes.

LINDY. Why don't you take off your socks too? Paid ten cents fer 'em, ye everlastin' idiot. Well, air you goin' to the tent and ask where we air?

SILAS. Reckon I might. [*Goes to tent, looks in*] Jumpin' catfish! [*Jumps back, frightened*] The Devil must live here.

LINDY. The Devil must live here? What air you talkin' about?

SILAS. There was somethin' sittin' over the fire noddin' her head and laughin' and in the corner on some straw was a poor, wild-lookin' critter moanin' and groanin'.

LINDY. Let's go, Silas—we'll be murdered yet.

SILAS. If you had stayed and spent the night with Rose as ye was goin' to—

LINDY. What? And her with a convict hidin' in the bed? I guess not. Come on. Oh, Lord—my feet! [*Limps*]

SILAS. Gosh all hemlock—

LINDY. What's the matter?

SILAS. Stepped on a splinter. [*Picks splinter out of foot*]

LINDY. Then put on your shoes.

SILAS. Not for fifty splinters, by tar. [*Exits R. with Lindy*]

BUNCO. [*Enters up L. and runs down. Looks around*] Wonder what time it is. Must be six o'clock. I feel like breakfast. Oh, dere's a tent. Maybe we can all get a cup of coffee. [*Calls off stage*] Hoo-oo, hoo! Come on, yes, all right. [*Crosses back as Ralph and Rose enter up L.*] Give me de baby. Dere, dere—you poor child, is you cold?

RALPH. [*Down run*] Be careful, dear—be careful.

BUNCO. Shall I go to the tent and ask for some breakfast?

ROSE. No, no—don't do that, Bunco. I'm so afraid, dear, that we might meet someone who would know us and betray us to the police.

RALPH. Sit here, dear. Now listen. We can't wander around as we have done all night. I'll give myself up, dear.

ROSE. No, no, Ralph.

RALPH. It's the only thing to do now. I am innocent. Bunco there can prove that.

BUNCO. You just bet I can. [*Crosses up stage, back to audience*]

RALPH. Don't look so downhearted, Rose. Our sun will shine again. Already my heart feels light.

ROSE. Oh, Ralph, you inspire me with confidence. I couldn't bear to lose you again, dear.

RALPH. We must be brave and try to face with cheerful hearts whatever the future has in store for us. I feel sure that in the end all will come out right.

ROSE. But what shall we do with John Livingstone?

BUNCO. Put him in a cage and throw sugar at him. [*Crosses to tent*] Hully Gee. Sneak!

ROSE. What's the matter!

BUNCO. We're up against it. De old gypsy hag is in dat tent.

ROSE. Oh, what shall we do?

BUNCO. Come on dis way.

RALPH. Don't be so frightened, dear. Be brave.

ROSE. For your sake, I'll try.

RALPH. My brave little woman. [*All exit up L.*]

MOTH. T. [*At door of tent*] No sign of him yet, and I heard bloodhounds a-bayin'. I'm afeared they'll get him, the poor darlin', and if he should squeal, then my poor neck would be stretched. Oh, this is a sad, sad world. [*Drinks out of bottle. Bess appears at door*] Here, you come out—do you hear? [*Bess comes out*] Go to the spring and get the bucket filled. Hurry up, you lazy hussy. Hurry, I say. [*Pushes her*]

BESS. Oh, I can't—[*Falls*] I can't go so far and carry that heavy bucket. I'm so weak and sick and I've had nothing to eat today.

MOTH. T. Well, I've been away on business. He, he, he. [*Coughs and crosses to R.*] D'ye hear? Haven't had time to go to town for groceries. One day's starving won't hurt you. Ye ought to be used to it by now.

BESS. Yes, if one can get used to starving. I've been hungry often enough. Oh, why don't you let me die at once and not kill me by inches?

MOTH. T. It's safer by inches, darling. Then there's no danger. Oh, I'd have strangled you long ago if I'd dared. Get up! [*Kicks her*] Get the water before I beat you again.

BESS. I won't. [*Rises and faces her*] You may beat me till I die. I won't. I won't be your slave any longer.

MOTH. T. What? He, he, he. We'll see, my fine lady—[*Drinks*] We'll see. [*Crosses into tent*]

BESS. [*Falls on knees, sobbing*] Oh, dear God, let me die, let me die. Perhaps somewhere in Heaven I may have a *mother to guide me*. I'm so terribly alone here—so terribly alone.

Moth. T. [*Enters with whip*] So you'll stand out against me, eh? Get up —do you hear? [*Crosses to L.*]

Bess. I wont'—I won't!

Moth. T. [*Strikes her with whip*] Then take that, you lazy whelp. I'll teach you to mind. [*Raises whip again*]

Jake. [*Enters L.U., catches whip*] You she devil! If ye wasn't so old, I'd cut ye in pieces and leave yer bones fer the crows to pick.

Moth. T. Jake Jordan!

Jake. Yes. Thought I was in jail, eh? Well I've served my time. Ye've forgotten that, eh? Git up, sis. [*Helps Bess up*] Ye'll get no more beatin's.

Bess. God bless you, sir. [*Sits R.C. on stone*]

Moth. T. [*Screams*] What do you mean?

Jake. Jest this. I've made a full confession. If the cops land Livingstone tonight, he'll take his last rest at the end of a rope.

Moth. T. Would you squeal on a pal?

Jake. Pal? Has he been square with me? Tried to murder me in cold blood and you helped him—you dried-up old mummy. But I'll leave the Devil to settle wid ye.

Moth. T. Oh, don't talk that way, darlin', ye make my bones rattle. [*Crosses L., drinks. Dog barks*]

Jake. De hounds. Dey is on de trail again.

Moth. T. Oh, Lord. Oh, Lord—[*Starts to go*]

Jake. Stay where you are—de cops'll need you. Get into dat tent.

Moth. T. Oh, oh, darlin'—my sweet boy.

Jake. Don't darlin' me—you old crow. Get in there. [*Pushes her into tent*]

Bess. Oh, sir, will they catch John Livingstone?

Jake. Yes—unless he is sharper than those bloodhounds that are after him.

Bess. What's that? Oh, it's Bunco—it's Bunco! [*Bunco singing old song off stage, "When the Robins Nest Again"*]

Bunco. [*Enters L.*] Hully Gee—does me lamps deceive me? Bess! [*Embraces her*] And me old college chum—shake, Jake. [*They shake hands*]

Jake. You bet. Well, kid—you're all right.

Bunco. Well, say, where did you two drop from? I feel as if I'd found my family. Oh, Gee. Say, I helped you once, old pal—now you must help me. I know I kin trust you. De dearest friend I have in de world is in trouble. Will you stand by me?

Jake. Till death, kid.

Bunco. [*Shakes hands with Jake*] De same. Well he's just escaped from de pen and found his wife. Hully Gee—she's got two husbands now.

Jake. She married Livingstone, didn't she?

BUNCO. Yes. Livingstone's de guy dat sent him to de pen. Dey are in de woods hidin'. De cops have turned de bloodhounds loose.

JAKE. I know somethin' about his case.

BUNCO. You do?

JAKE. Yes. Bring them here.

BUNCO. You bet. [*Exits down R. Sunlight till curtain. Bess sways and faints*]

JAKE. Dat kid's all right. Sit down, sis. Dere—don't tremble so. You're safe. De cops will run Livingstone down, den de sun will shine brighter fer you. I've had a few ups and downs myself, but now I'm goin' to be honest. We're all lookin' fer happiness in dis life and it's wisest to be getting it by being straight, than by being crooked. [*Goes to stump, R.*]

BESS. Oh, it is, is it?

JAKE. Dere now—you've got a friend in me, sis, and don't you forget it.

BUNCO. [*Outside*] Come on, Mr. Ralph—here's de guy.

JAKE. Hello—dey're comin'. [*Ralph, Rose and baby enter L. Bunco runs to Bess*]

RALPH. Mr. Jordan! [*Holds out hand*]

JAKE. Jake, pardner.

RALPH. You'll help me out of this?

JAKE. You bet—and I kin do it too. I know you're innocent.

ROSE. [*Crosses to L.*] Bessie—if you had only known!

BESS. Oh, Miss Rose, will you let me see your baby?

ROSE. Don't wake him, Bessie.

BESS. Oh, baby—baby—[*Sobs*]

ROSE. There, there, you shall come home with me and have him as long as you like.

MOTH. T. Oh, oh, let me out. Good, kind gentlemen—let me out.

JAKE. Here comes a cop. [*Rose, Bess and Bunco cross up stage C.*]

MOTH. T. Oh, Lord. [*Officers enter with dog up R.*]

OFF. Hello, Jake—is that you?

JAKE. Yes, gov'ner—see any sign of him?

OFF. Dogs seem to have lost the trail. Who's that?

JAKE. A friend of mine, gov'ner. I say, ye might question de old hag in dere. She's de old hag who has done Livingstone's dirty work for years. I've got her in there. Question her.

RALPH. [*Crosses to C.*] One moment, Officer. I'm Ralph Carlton, escaped from Sing Sing. I want to give myself up until you have evidence of my innocence, and that will be soon.

OFF. Yes, we have the confession of Jake Jordan here, which looks well for you. However, I'll have to put the bracelets on you just as a matter of form. I believe you are an innocent man. [*To police*] See if the dogs can find the scent again. I have business here. Start for the caves, men. [*Other officers have their dogs*] Hallowell and Cane, have their dogs on the trail to the west. [*Police exit L.U. over run with dogs*] Now I'll see the old woman. [*Opens door to tent*] Come out, madam.

BUNCO. [*Down stage*] Oh, Gee— now mudder is goin' to get it.

MOTH. T. [*Enters from hut*] Oh, oh, oh, I'm an innocent woman, darlin'. Oh, oh, oh!

OFF. Innocent, are you? Well, Livingstone says not.

MOTH. T. What—have they got him? [*L.C.*]

OFF. Yes, and he will be condemned for murder.

MOTH. T. Oh, the wicked, wicked boy.

OFF. And it looks as if you'd die with him, my woman.

MOTH. T. Me? Oh, good Lord. Darlin'—what for?

OFF. Well, Livingstone has confessed that you were implicated in the Cosden robbery and the murder as well.

MOTH. T. He lies—he lies! The dog. He did it himself.

OFF. Also the attempted murder of the young lady's father.

MOTH. T. Oh, the hound. I was at the camp at the time. He did it himself.

OFF. Then how did you know he did it?

MOTH. T. He told me himself.

OFF. [*Making notes*] Ah, very good. I think I shall have to borrow your bracelets, Mr. Carlton. [*Does so. Mother Tagger starts to run*]

BUNCO. Hold on, mudder—[*Catches her*] We need you.

OFF. [*Puts bracelets on Mother Tagger*] Allow me.

MOTH. T. Oh, oh, darlin'!

BUNCO. How do you feel? Kinder natural, mudder?

MOTH. T. Wait till I get out.

BUNCO. Oh, I'll wait.

OFF. Oh, I'll take care of you. [*Exit L.U. Hounds bay*]

JAKE. The hounds are on the scent again. Sounds as if they were over by the falls. [*Goes up and exits, L.2.*]

ROSE. [*Crosses to Ralph*] Oh, Ralph, I'm so afraid.

RALPH. Go into the tent, dear. I'll be right back. [*Goes up and exits, L.*]

BUNCO. Where are you goin', Mr. Ralph? Hully Gee, I wish I was on the police force. [*Livingstone fires revolver off R.2. Rose exits into tent*]

BUNCO. [*Off stage*] Oh, look—*look*—he's coming.

LIV. [*Enters R.2.*] Stand out of my way. [*Throws Bunco R. Shots are heard outside. Livingstone covered with blood, revolver in hand. Ladies scream, dogs bark. Bess is R. Crosses to L. Rose R.*]

SILAS. As the constable of this county I order you to surrender.

LIV. I'll see you in hell first. [*Snaps revolver at him. He is out of shells*] Damnation! [*Up on run*]

SILAS. Surrender, or I'll fire.

LIV. Fire, and be damned. [*Runs to L.2. Jake comes out on run, meets him, knife in hand*] Jake Jordan!

JAKE. Yes.

LIV. I have no knife.

JAKE. [*Throws knife away*] Neither have I. The best man wins. [*Fight. Livingstone hits Jake on head, starts to exit L.U. Meets Ralph*]

RALPH. John Livingstone, I said we'd meet again. Fate has made me the instrument of justice. [*Backs Livingstone down run*] For years you have made me suffer. Now you shall pay for it to the last penny.

LIV. Have mercy!

RALPH. What mercy did you show me?

BESS. Ralph—for my sake. [*Grabs his arms. Ralph turns a second to Rose. Livingstone starts for him with knife. All scream. Jake shoots. Silas catches Livingstone*]

JAKE. Livingstone, old pal, you've planned your last crime. [*Officers enter*]

SILAS. We've got your man. He's dying. Take him away.

LIV. Jake Jordan, I'll meet you in Hell.

JAKE. No, guv'ner—I ain't goin' that way. [*Officers exit with Livingstone. Bess crosses to entrance. Bunco puts arm around her*]

RALPH. Rose!

ROSE. Ralph!

SILAS. *Lindy*, come into *camp*!

CURTAIN

BILLY THE KID

By Walter Woods

DESCRIPTION OF CHARACTERS

WRIGHT, *a man of sixty. White hair, long white moustache.*

MARY, *a woman of thirty-five.*

BILL, *fifteen at opening of play.*

BRADLEY, *a military looking man of sixty-five. Moustache and chin whiskers.*

NELLIE, *about Bill's age.*

DENVER, *a well preserved man of forty; looks younger.*

CON, *Denver's age and looks older.*

MOSE, *a clean-shaven old man.*

PEANUT, *black moustache and beard, low forehead, long hair.*

BUD, *a tough-looking character, stubby moustache.*

COSTUMES

BILL: *Act I: Ballet shirt, knee pants, soft hat. End of act, long coat, mask.*
  Act II: Black velvet coat, wide-necked shirt, light riding breeches, top boots, light sombrero.
  Act III: Leather breeches, blue shirt, red handkerchief about neck, cartridge belt with revolvers.
  Act IV: Same as Act II, with addition of long gray rain coat.

DENVER: *Act I: Traveling suit.*
  Act II: Black suit, outing shirt, slouch hat.
  Act III: Same, soiled and torn.
  Act IV: Same, more soiled and torn.

COLONEL: *G.A.R. uniform.*

MOSE: *Same.*

CON: *Act I: Overalls and jumper.*
  Act II: Cowboy outfit.
  Act III: "   "
  Act IV: "   "

WRIGHT: *Act I: Plantation suit of light crash.*

PEANUT: *Mexican suit. Last act, cloak.*

MONROE: *Cowboy.*

MOLLY: *Flashy dress.*

JENNIE: *Act I: Flashy dress.*
  Act III: Plain maid's dress.
  Act IV: Same, with wrap.

NELLIE: *Act I: Light summer dress.*
  Act II: Western riding habit, short skirt, shirt waist, sombrero.
  Act III: Neat house dress.
  Act IV: Walking suit with wrap.

(Three sets of scenery are necessary. Last act is the same as Act I, with the addition of a transparent return to house)

CHARACTERS

IN ACT ONE

STEPHEN WRIGHT, *a ranch owner.*	*(Old man)*
MARY, *his wife.*	*(Juvenile)*
WILL, *Mary's son.*	*(Lead)*
COLONEL WAYNE BRADLEY, *a retired army officer.*	*(Character)*
BOYD DENVERS, *an Eastern gentleman.*	*(Heavy)*
CON HANLEY, *a hand.*	*(Comedy)*
MOSES MOORE, *an ex-orderly.*	*(Character comedy)*
MAID	*(Utility)*
NELLIE	

IN ACT TWO

BILLY, THE KID, *a Western desperado.*	*(Lead)*
CON HANLEY, *his lieutenant.*	*(Comedy)*
BOYD DENVER, *owner of the Broken Heart Saloon.*	*(Heavy)*
"PEANUT" GIVANNI, *manager of Broken Heart Saloon.*	*(Character heavy)*
BUD MONROE, *a bad man.*	*(Character)*
HANK, *bartender.*	*(Utility)*
COLONEL WAYNE BRADLEY, *still retired.*	
MOSES MOORE, *still an "ex."*	
MOLLY ⎫ *women of the Broken Heart.* JENNIE ⎰	
NELLIE BRADLEY	*(Lead)*
MINERS, DEPUTY SHERIFFS, ETC.	

NOTE: Cast can be doubled to seven men, three women.

SYNOPSIS

ACT I. EXTERIOR OF WRIGHT'S COTTAGE
"THE OATH OF VENGEANCE"

ACT II. THE BROKEN HEART SALOON (THREE YEARS LATER)
"YOU SHALL FOLLOW ME"

ACT III. COLONEL BRADLEY'S DINING ROOM (ONE WEEK LATER)
"POLLY HAS ARMS OF HER OWN"

ACT IV. SAME AS ACT I
"VENGEANCE IS MINE"

ACT I.

SCENE: *Landscape in 5. Picket fence at back. Large Southern home with porch L. Canary in cage hanging from porch. Well curbing, foot and a half high, up L. Table and chair R.* DISCOVERED: *Con seated on well curb, smoking. Enter Maid from house, with bottles and glasses. Puts them on table. Enter Wright R.U.E. followed by Denver.*

WRI. Con! [*Con jumps up and gets busy*]

CON. Yis, sor.

WRI. Have the niggers bring up a few loads of gravel and fill that old well. [*Goes to table, sits L; Denver sits R.*]

CON. Well, well. All's well that ends well.

WRI. What's that, suh?

CON. I said, very well, sor. That would end the well, sor. [*Exit L.*]

WRI. [*Pouring drinks*] Somebody will fall in there yet. It's a nuisance. It's thirty feet deep and dry as a bone. We get all our water from the artesian well, yonder.

DEN. Thirty feet deep? A dangerous hole.

WRI. Yes, suh. Why a person could fall in there and no one would ever know what became of him.

DEN. [*Half to himself*] Excellent.

WRI. What's that, suh?

DEN. The—ah—whiskey is excellent.

WRI. You're a gentleman, suh. Any man who is a judge of whiskey is a friend of mine. [*They shake hands*]

DEN. I'd often heard of your Southern hospitality, and rather doubted its existence myself; but during my short stay here you have converted me for life.

WRI. Tut, tut, tut, suh! You have only received the treatment that any gentleman may expect. Have another drink. And remember, until you are ready to leave this—rather dismal landscape, you are my honored guest.

DEN. It's a beautiful spot—beautiful. And you have a charming wife and a wonderful son. No wonder you are contented.

WRI. Contented? Contented is not the word, suh. Happy, suh, downright happy!

DEN. [*Slight sneer*] Indeed?

Wri. Yes, suh. Why hang it, I'd like to see the man who could *help* but be happy with Mary for a wife. A lady, suh—one of your sort from up North. How she ever came to care for an old codger like me, is more than I can guess.

Den. You underrate yourself.

Wri. Not a bit of it. My youth is far behind. I'm rough in my ways, and I never took a prize in a beauty show. [*Denver laughs*] Although I am well fixed financially—

Den. [*Still laughing*] Well, there, there! That last remark doubtless—

Wri. Hold on, my friend. I was going to say that although I am well fixed financially, Mary would never wed for money, and if any man was to hint at such a thing, I believe I would kill him. [*Denver suddenly ceases laughing; he looks at Wright*]

Den. [*Intense*] I believe you would.

Wri. [*Light*] You and she must become great friends, suh. Perhaps—perhaps she sometimes feels sort of lonesome, way out here in the West, and you two can talk over New York until this ranch will seem like a suburb of the great city.

Den. I am sure Mrs. Wright and myself will become great friends but I hardly think we will discuss the East. During our short interview this morning, I could see that her whole interest lies with her home, husband and boy.

Wri. [*Huskily*] That's kind of you to say that, suh. Yes, suh—[*Fills glass to hide his emotion, spills liquor*] Yes, suh.

Con. [*Enters L.U.E.*] For the love of Hiven, don't spill it.

Wri. What the devil is the matter with you, Con?

Con. If I hadn't arrived just when I did, you would have poured it all on the ground.

Wri. Thanks for getting here in time. [*He talks to Denver*]

Con. [*Aside*] Thanks is it? That's a mighty dry reward for saving a man's whiskey. [*Aloud*] I've told 'em, sor.

Wri. Eh? Told who? Told what?

Con. Well, well, well, how forgetful ye are. I've told the niggers.

Wri. Oh, yes. About filling the well.

Con. That well and me, sor, are alike in one respect; and then again we differ with the advantage all on the side of the well.

Wri. How is that, Con?

Con. Well—we're both as dry as a bone. [*Wright and Denver laugh*]

Den. Very good, Con.

Con. But the well is going to be filled up.

WRI. [*Rises, crosses to Con, C., laughing*] So are you, Con. Help yourself, but go light on it. [*Goes up L. Con crosses to table, takes bottle and glass, all the time watching Wright. Seeing his back turned, is about to drink from bottle when he turns and sees Denver watching him*]

CON. Turn yer head, can't ye? What do ye want to be watching a man drink for? [*Growling*] Old Tom the peeper! My, my, but it's a beautiful pair of eyes ye have in your head. I love to look at 'em. [*Pours glass full and drinks*] Well, how did ye like the way I did it?

DEN. You seem to have taken a dislike to me, Con.

CON. I have not. I wouldn't take the trouble.

DEN. [*Low*] One word to Wright of your insolence to me today and he would kick you off the place.

CON. One word to him about the little talk I overheard ye having wid his wife this morning and ye would never leave the place alive.

DEN. [*Rises, uneasy*] What did you hear?

CON. That's none of your dom business. Turn yer head, will ye? I want another drink. [*Denver turns, agitated. Con drinks from bottle*]

DEN. Have another, Con?

CON. What's the use? The more I drink the less I talk.

DEN. [*Hurriedly*] Before you tell Wright anything I wish to see you alone.

CON. No, I'm not going to tell him. That seems to relieve ye, don't it? No, I wouldn't spoil his happiness for the world. But I'll keep me eye on you, my laddy buck, while ye stay here—which had better not be long.

DEN. Meet me here, in an hour—alone.

CON. All right. In the meantime, me and the well will proceed to get full together. [*Goes up stage*]

DEN. [*Aside*] And you, my friend, will be at the bottom of it.

WRI. [*As Con joins him*] Will the niggers start on the well at once? [*Con shakes his head*] No, suh? Why not, suh?

CON. Billy is using 'em for cattle, sor. He's learning to be a roper, sor.

WRI. I'll rope him. Tell him I want him. Tell him—*tell him*.

CON. T'ell with him.

WRI. What?

CON. I said I'd tell him, sor—[*Exit L.U.E. Wright laughs*]

DEN. The servant seems on excellent terms with the master.

WRI. [*Comes down*] Servants? Haven't a one on the place; they are all my friends. Master? There is but one Master—above. [*Crosses to table*]

DEN. [*Up L.*] And one servant who never fails us—below. [*Looks in well*] A dangerous hole, dark and deep. [*Con enters L.U.E. behind Denver and overhears his last remark. Wright is busy mixing a julep and does not hear the following*]

Con.   Nice place to pitch a man, eh?

Den.   [*Starts*] Damn you! [*Shows anger; Con stares at him insolently*]

Con.   Look at the purty eyes on him!

Den.   [*Recovers himself and laughs*] You possess the true Irish wit, Con. I see you are trying to have fun at my expense by making me angry, but I refuse to be a victim. You and I shall be friends. [*He holds out hand*]

Con.   [*Takes hand*] Whenever I meet you, I shall always be glad to hold your hand like this.

Den.   Thank you, Con.

Con.   So ye can't stick a knife in me. [*Denver, in anger, attempts to snatch hand away; Con holds it*]

Den.   Let go of my hand, you Irish cur, you are hurting me. Let go I say!

Con.   I'll let go when I get through wid it. You gave it to me. I didn't ask for it. [*Pinches his hand at every chance. Denver shows signs of pain*] There. [*Throws hand*] I'm through with that hand—forever.

Den.   I'll make you smart for this!

Con.   What's the use? I'm smart already. You said I had the true Irish wit. [*Laughs and crosses down to Wright*]

Wri.   [*Enters R.3.*] Hello, Con. Did you tell Billy? Is he coming?

Con.   Yes, sor. No, sor.

Wri.   Yes, suh—no, suh! What do you mean?

Con.   Yes, sor, I told him. No, sor, he ain't coming.

Wri.   Why not?

Con.   He's practising wid his revolver. He wants to be a crack shot.

Wri.   I'll crack him when I see him, confound him.

Con.   Yes, confound him, but Con couldn't bring him wid a yoke of oxen. [*Exit L.U.E.*]

Den.   [*Crosses to table*] That boy of yours, Billy, seems full of mischief.

Wri.   Full of life, love and kindness, sir. A better boy never lived. A little wild perhaps but that will wear off in time. Brave and reckless as any cowpuncher on the ranch; a hard rider, a good roper and a sure shot. But he ain't mine, more's the pity. You see, Mary was a widow when I married her. Had a little boy baby. But he's grown up just like mine and will never know the difference.

Den.   [*Surprised*] She had a child when she married you?

Wri.   Yes, poor thing. She had married a cur, a sneak who deserted her. Then he died, which I reckon was the only decent thing he ever did in his whole life.

DEN. [*Aside*] She had a child.

WRI. Mary is only half my age, suh. But our love is as young as a honey-moon. There's only one mar to my happiness. I'm sorry the scoundrel who caused her such unhappiness is dead. I should like the pleasure of killing him. [*Crosses to house*]

DEN. [*Aside*] A dangerous fool. I must be careful.

MAID. [*Enters on porch*] Supper's ready, sir. [*Exits*]

WRI. Supper! That's welcome news to a couple of hungry men, come in, suh. Come right in. [*"Marching Through Georgia." Exit house*]

DEN. [*Following*] She had a child. [*Exit house*]

COL. BRADLEY. [*Outside*] Column right, march! [*Enter R.U.E. in single file, Colonel, Mose and Nellie. They march down C.*] Halt. [*They do so*] On left into line. March! [*They line up. Nellie L., Mose C., Colonel R.*] Now we'll call the roll.

MOSE. No, sir.

COL. Never, sir. Damme, sir.

MOSE. Never, sir.

COL. When I have to swear, I can do it myself, can't I?

MOSE. I—should—say—you—could.

COL. Where's that girl? [*Calls*] Nellie—I mean, Sergeant, come here.

WRI. [*Enters from house*] Hello, Colonel. Glad to see you. [*They shake hands*] You are just in time. Drop the tactics and we'll go in and have a julep before supper. Mose, you are a deacon so I mustn't tempt you. Just make yourself comfortable.

MOSE. Thank you, sir. [*He drops military air and goes up, filling his pipe*]

COL. That's it. The army is demoralized by the accursed drink.

WRI. Why, I thought you would like a little something after your long ride. [*Calls in house*] Sam, never mind the juleps.

COL. Hold on there, never countermand an order. Besides, I didn't say *I* didn't want one. I said it demoralized the army. I am an officer. [*Exit both, laughing, arm in arm*]

MOSE. Wish this army had a little demoralizing. Deacon, eh! Only on Sundays. [*Sees bottle on table*] Attention! Forward march! [*Goes to table, salutes and picks up bottle*]

CON. [*Enters*] Heave to! [*He throws shovel of sand in well*]

MOSE. Heave two? I haven't had one yet.

CON. What are ye doing wid that whiskey?

MOSE. Whiskey? What—me a deacon? This ain't whiskey.

CON. The saints protect me. I've lost me taste. What is it?

MOSE. It's a—a—nerve tonic.

Con. Well, me nerves are all on edge. Give me a taste.

Mose. [*Filling glasses*] Mind this is only medicine.

Con. I know it. Make mine a big one. [*Mose takes glasses. Hands one to Con*] Well, here's looking at you. [*Con C. Mose R. of C. Enter Bill, R.U.E. He comes down between them*]

Mose. Happy days. [*Both drink. Bill slaps them on back and both spit out liquor*]

Con. Heave two.

Mose. One's enough for me.

Bill. At it again, eh? Mose, I'm ashamed of you, a deacon.

Mose. Only on Sundays, Billy.

Bill. Con, I thought you signed the pledge.

Con. I did not. I only swore off. There's nothing to prevent a man swearing *on* again, is there?

Bill. [*Laughing*] You are a pair of frauds.

Con. Supper's waiting for ye, Billy.

Bill. Well, I'll wait till you go, to keep you out of temptation. Besides, I want to tell you how well I'm getting on with my shooting. I hit the bull's eye ten times hand running.

Con. Ye did?

Bill. And I roped seven niggers out of eight.

Con. Billy boy!

Moses. Better study your schooling. All them things won't do you no good.

Bill. Won't eh? Oh, yes, it will 'cause I'm going to be a pirate.

Mose and Con. A what?

Bill. A pirate on the high seas. I'm going to hold up trains and stages.

Mose. What? On the high seas?

Bill. No-o. I'm mixed. The book I've been reading last was about a knight of the road, not a pirate.

Mose. Leave them books alone, son. They'll fill your head with trash.

Bill. No trash about this. I'm going to be one of 'em and Con is going to be my lieutenant. Ain't you, Con?

Con. [*Winking at Mose*] Sure thing, Billy.

Bill. No fooling now.

Con. Divil a bit.

Bill. Put her there. [*Holds out hand*]

Con. [*Wiping his hand on his pants*] Wait a bit, Billy; I shook wid a blackguard a while ago. [*He shakes his hand*]

Mose. Now, Con, don't go putting that boy up to any foolishness.

BILL. This ain't foolishness, Mose. We're going to hold up only the rich people and carry them off to our cave for ransom.

CON. What is a ransom, Billy?

BILL. I don't know.

CON. Well, how in blazes are ye going to hold 'em for it if you don't know what it is?

BILL. Oh, it means—death; hold 'em until they die, see?

CON. Well I think that will be a heap of trouble. Why not take a gun and ransom 'em as soon as we capture 'em?

MOSE. Con, stop teasing the boy.

BILL. Then we'll capture Nellie and I'll marry her.

CON. Oh, ho! Nellie is it? Sure yer stuck on her.

BILL. Never you mind, Con. She's going to be my wife some day.

MOSE. Great guns. What notions—Pirates, ransoms and matrimony.

COL. [*Inside*] Forward march!

BILL. Here she comes now.

MOSE. And here comes the Colonel. [*Stands at attention. The Colonel enters from house, followed by Nellie*]

COL. Halt! Where's the rest of the army?

NELL. Billy! [*Rushes to him*]

BILL. Nellie! [*They shake hands and retire up stage*]

COL. Attention! About face—*Halt*, do you hear? [*Bill and Nellie pay no attention. Con rushes down beside Mose, and presents arms with a spade*]

CON. Prisent.

COL. What are you doing here?

CON. I am a sub-sti-tchute.

COL. Get out, both of you. [*Con goes L. Mose does not move*] Well! What are you waiting for?

MOSE. The proper command, sir.

COL. Left face, forward march! [*Mose exits in house, followed by Con imitating his manner. Colonel crosses to table*] Now then, you young rapscallions. [*Sits*] I say, you—[*Bill and Nellie walk toward house, talking*] I'll have you on the—a—hip, sir. On the hip—hip—

CON. [*Enters at door*] Hurray! [*Exits. Colonel fumes; turns to bottle*]

BILL. When I'm a man, Nellie—

NELL. When you are a man. [*They kiss. Nellie exits in house*]

COL. [*Turns*] Eh? What's that?

BILL. What's what?

COL. That noise. Sounded like—[*Smacks lips like a kiss*]

BILL. O-oh—that? Why that was the little bird. Birdy chirped. [*Smacks lips at the bird*] Didn't you hear birdy chirp?

COL. Yes, but hang it, I never heard her chirp like that before.

BILL. [*Still making noise at bird*] Birdy wants her chickweed.

COL. I think birdy *got* her chickweed.

BILL. Say, Colonel, I want to whisper something to you.

COL. [*Rises, goes C.*] Well, what is it?

BILL. [*Whispering*] I love Nellie.

COL. Eh?

BILL. [*Louder*] I love Nellie.

COL. What's that?

BILL. [*Yells*] I love your niece, Nellie.

COL. Ouch! Well, you needn't take my head off. I'm not deaf. Say, Bill, I want to whisper something in your ear.

BILL. Go ahead.

COL. [*Whispers*] So do I.

BILL. Soda what?

COL. [*Louder*] So do I.

BILL. What kind of soda?

COL. SO—DO—I.

BILL. Ow! All right, Colonel, but I've won her and we're going to be married when I'm a man.

COL. [*Mocking Bill*] When you are a man, Billy. [*Smacks lips. Both exit, laughing, L.1.E. Enter Denver from house, followed by Mary Wright*]

MARY. You wish to speak to me alone? Speak quickly, I can grant you but a moment.

DEN. Indeed? [*C. Looks at her*] What a change. How—happy you must be.

MARY. Why—why did you come here. To torture me?

DEN. Bosh! I torture? I am going to take you away from this life of monotony to one of pleasure.

MARY. I am happy with my husband.

DEN. Your husband? You flatter me. You were never divorced to my knowledge. I still bear that title.

MARY. [*Putting hand to head*] Oh, I had forgotten. I fear I shall go mad —I thought you dead. This morning when you came like a black cloud from the wretched past, my heart stopped beating. I would gladly have died. After a little, rather than cause my—the man whose name I bear—the sorrow that your real identity would bring him, I decided to remain silent. But do not torture me more with your presence. My patience has a limit, and rather than endure your sneers and insinuations, I will tell Mr. Wright all.

DEN. [*Frightened*] You would tell him? Have you forgotten the love you once bore me?

MARY. [*Sits on steps*] Yes. As completely as you did when you so cruelly deserted me. Oh, my struggles for an honorable living were bitter but I bore them, until an honest love crept into my barren life and showed me true happiness. [*Wearily*] And now—it is all over.

DEN. Nonsense. I don't want you to leave him—that is, not yet.

MARY. And do you suppose I would pass another day under his roof knowing that I am not his wife?

DEN. Why not? He has certain deeds that I must get. You can help me in this. Then we will clear out forever.

MARY. Shame! When will your evil heart grasp the fact that I am not your tool?

DEN. Sh-h! [*Wright appears at door*] As you say, your husband is a prince among men. I do not wonder you are proud of him. [*Wright, thinking he has been unobserved, quietly exits, house*]

MARY. What treachery!

DEN. [*Smiling*] Diplomacy, my dear.

MARY. One word from me to the man you are so basely deceiving, and he would kill you.

DEN. Yes. I am aware of his bloodthirsty tendencies, therefore I have no thought of allowing you to tell him. Suppose I took to supplying him with past history. For instance, you spoke of your virtuous struggles from the time I left you until you married Wright, but I learned today that when you came to him you had a child.

MARY. Why that child is—

DEN. There, there. I don't care for explanations; they are tiresome. Enough that I know you—and you know me. At present I am in something of a hole—shady transaction back East. I had to leave suddenly. Wright has the very deeds I was supposed to have forged. By hook or crook I must have them. I came here, never dreaming of finding my charming consort of sixteen years ago. Fortune favors me. You will be of great assistance.

MARY. [*Rises*] Enough. I will at once inform my husband. [*Starts*]

DEN. He is not your husband. You are a bigamist. One word from me will land you in jail.

MARY. Do you think I care for that? I will tell the truth, take the consequences—and let you do the same.

DEN. But the boy—he has a home, a *name*. What would he think of you if he knew.

MARY. My boy!

DEN. Be reasonable—for his sake.

MARY. I will keep your secret today. Tonight I will take my boy and leave this place forever.

DEN. You'll help me get the papers and go with me, eh?

MARY. You contemptible cur—*No, I* would rather die.

DEN. Curse your tongue. Take care or I'll—[*Raises hand to strike*]

MARY. Oh, no, you won't. You are too cowardly to strike me. You know there are those who would call you to a swift account for assaulting me. You will vent your spite on the woman you have so cruelly wronged, in a more cowardly fashion and at a time when there will be no one to aid her.

DEN. You're right, I will. [*Mary exits*] Oh, I'll get even. I'll touch her heart. She's soft on her boy. Mothers always are. [*Laughs*] I'll lead that boy to a life of dissipation—crime, if I can manage it. Oh, I'll touch her to the quick. I'll shrivel her heart up like the blackened embers of a discarded camp fire. How I hate her brat. I could kill him by inches. I'd like to tear his heart out! I'd like to—[*His hand is raised above his head. Enter Bill L.1.E. Denver changes manner*]—to take you by the hand, my dear boy. I've heard so much of you. [*They shake hands*]

BILL. From Con?

DEN. Why—ah—yes, from Con.

BILL. Well, don't believe anything he tells you. He's the biggest liar in the state.

DEN. [*Laughs*] I don't believe he exaggerated in your case.

BILL. Well, if he didn't, it was an accident but he means it for the best. He's my pal.

DEN. Considerable difference in your ages, for pals, don't you think?

BILL. Oh, that don't make any difference. You see I never had any boys to associate with. I have been brought up with men. [*Crosses to table*]

DEN. Con said you were as much of a man as any of them. What do you intend to become—a scout?

BILL. A pirate.

DEN. [*Laughs*] A pirate?

BILL. That's what Con and I play we are going to be. [*Laughs*] It's only in fun, sir.

DEN. But you are too big and brave a lad to play at adventure, why not have a real one? Let's have a drink?

BILL. No, sir, I never—

DEN. What! You don't mean to say that a man like you never—? Oh I see, don't want the old folks to know, eh? Well, you can trust me. Here, take a drink.

BILL. [*Flattered, takes bottle*] Guess I can stand a pull. [*Drinks*]

DEN. The people around here don't appreciate you, not even your father. I hear you are a fine shot.

BILL. Oh, I can shoot some, sir.

DEN. I'll wager you can. What sort of a gun do you use?

BILL. This one. [*Shows Colt*]

DEN. [*Takes it*] Oh, a Colt. An old out-of-date pattern, too. [*Tosses it on table*] Let me show you something modern. [*Takes pistol from pocket*] See; a double-acting, self-cocking, shell-extracting revolver. [*Hands it to Bill*]

BILL. Gee! What a beauty!

DEN. It shall be yours if you are the lad of spirit I take you to be. [*Takes pistol, puts it in pocket*] Now let's play a little joke on your father, just to show him the stuff you are made of.

BILL. [*Drinks. Shows a recklessness from the effects*] I'm your man— what is it?

DEN. You know he keeps his private papers in the—ah—

BILL. Little safe in his bedroom.

DEN. That's it. Of course you don't know the combination—

BILL. Oh, but I do though.

DEN. All the better. Now here's the plan. Your father has boasted there is not a man in the state who would dare hold him up for anything. And as for cracksmen, he defies the cream of them to get anything from his safe. Now, if you will get all his papers—don't touch the money, that would be stealing—but just the papers, and bring them to me, I will tell your father there is one man in the state that was a match for him and show him the papers to support my statement. He, of course, will be thunderstruck, and when he asks who this wonderful fellow is, I will introduce, Billy, the Prince of the Road. [*Laughs*] What do you think of it?

BILL. [*Laughs*] That would be a fine joke, wouldn't it? I believe I'll try it.

DEN. Of course you'll try it. You couldn't let such an opportunity slip.

BILL. When shall we do it?

DEN. Tonight. They will all leave the house in a few moments to see the Colonel start for home. That is our opportunity. Get a piece of black cloth and make yourself a mask. Saddle your horse and tie him yonder. After the folks leave the house, you slip in the back way. Now go.

BILL. [*Starts*] Won't Con be surprised? My, but that stuff makes you dizzy, don't it?—and Mose laughed at me. I'll make them all proud of me yet. [*Exits L.U.E.*]

DEN. Fool! When I get the papers, I'll set the officers on his track. Two birds with one stone—the papers, and the mother's heart broken over a worthless boy.

CON. [*Enters from house*] Well, what divilment are ye hatching out now?

DEN. Con, you are hard on me. Let us forget the difference between us for the time. Here is ten dollars. [*Gives money*] Go to the station and see if there is any mail for me.

CON. Tin dollars fer going to the station? Yer paying mighty high fer a small service. [*Throws down money*] I won't go.

DEN. [*Angry*] Why not?

CON. I think you want to get rid of me, eh, me laddy buck?

DEN. You are a suspicious fool.

CON. Yes, that's the reason I'm going to keep me eyes on you. And ten thousand dollars wouldn't make me take them off.

DEN. [*Up stage*] Keep them on as much as you like, my meddling friend, but it won't save Billy or the Wright family.

COL. [*Inside*] Forward march! [*Enter from house Mose, Nellie and Colonel. Mose crosses and exits R.U.E. Nellie goes up L.*] Goodnight, Mr. Wright, we're off for home. You and the Mrs. be sure to come over next Sunday, good-night.

WRI. [*At door*] Wait a moment, Colonel. We'll see you off. Wife's in her room getting her hat or something.

COL. Don't bother, Wright. We know the way, good-night. [*Crosses and exits R.U.E.*]

WRI. Wait a minute, Colonel. [*Exit house, calling*] Mary, Mary!

NEL. Where can he be?

DEN. Looking for someone, Miss Bradley?

NEL. Yes, I was looking for Billy.

DEN. You are too pretty a girl to waste your time on a country lout.

NEL. Sir! I do not understand you.

DEN. A city man would be more to your liking, eh? [*Chucks her under the chin. She is astonished*]

NEL. Mr. Denver—!

DEN. There, there, don't be frightened. Give me a kiss before you go.

NEL. [*Slaps his face*] You cur! [*Crosses to R.U.E.*]

DEN. [*Hurriedly*] A thousand pardons. It was only a joke, I assure you.

NEL. We will see if the "country lout" looks at it in that light. [*Exits*]

DEN. The sting of that blow will cost you dearly, my lady. Damn their Southern pride, but I'll shrivel them all up before I'm through with them. [*Exits R.U.E. Enter Mary from the house, followed by Wright*]

WRI. Mary! For God's sake listen to me. You do not—you cannot mean that you are going to leave me forever.

MARY. Don't question me, I must.

WRI. Oh, I do not need an explanation. [*Bitterly*] Youth weds with old age. It could not last. I might have known it.

MARY. Stephen, it is not that. God knows I love you better than all the world. But I must leave you.

WRI. But why—why if you love me?

MARY. I cannot explain. It would kill me—it would kill us both.

WRI. You do not mean—disgrace?

MARY. Yes. [*Wright sinks on porch, overcome*] My heart is breaking. I must go. [*Staggers to C.*]

DEN. [*Enter R.U.E. not seeing Wright*] Yes, and you go alone.

MARY. I am going with my boy.

DEN. You can't. He's going to jail.

MARY. What do you mean?

DEN. That I acted on your suggestion, refrained from blows and struck at your heart. By this time your son is a criminal and answerable to the law.

MARY. [*Half screams*] What have you done?

DEN. Revenged myself—on your son.

MARY. And yours as well. Fool, could not your cold heart have prompted the truth? He was your own child. You have sent your own flesh and blood to destruction.

DEN. You lie.

MARY. I speak the truth.

WRI. [*Who has overheard. Rising*] What does this mean? [*Denver frightened*]

MARY. It means that there stands the man who blighted my past as· well as my present happiness. It means that he is Boyd Bradley, my husband, and the father of my boy.

WRI. Wait a bit, wait a bit. I can't seem to get these things straight somehow.

DEN. [*Drawing revolver*] Then get it through your head quickly. She is my wife and she is going with me.

WRI. [*Low and intense*] So—this is the man who caused my Mary's unhappiness—the man we thought dead. And now he returns to wreck afresh the life of the woman who trusted him. [*Slowly approaches Denver*]

DEN.   Be careful. Keep your distance. I am armed.

WRI.   And do you think I care for that? All the weapons this side of Hell couldn't keep my fingers from your throat. [*Wright grapples with Denver. They struggle. Mary screams, goes down R. Revolver explodes, killing Mary. They struggle toward the well. Denver gets his pistol hand free and shoots Wright. He falls half in well, head first. Denver stands frightened, looking around*]

DEN.   It was self-defense—he tried to murder me—he threatened to kill me—Mary heard him. [*Sees Mary*] Mary! Fainted! [*Goes to her*] Dead! God! I did not mean it. I did not mean it. [*Overcome, sinks on knees. Suddenly starts up*] They'll lynch me. [*Crying*] I am innocent. It was an accident and self-defense. They'll not believe it—they'll not believe it. [*In frenzy*] I must get rid of the bodies somehow. The old well—thirty feet deep and dark as a pocket. [*Throws Wright in*] My revolver, this must not be found. [*Drops it in well*] They will fill the well and all traces will be lost. His property will go to my wife—she is dead. But the boy—he stands between me and a fortune. Pshaw! He is an outlaw! I will put him where he will never trouble me again.

BILL.   [*Enters from house, black mask on*]   Here are the papers—why, what is the matter? [*Drops papers*] Mother! [*Runs to her*] Mother, Mother, speak to me! [*Looks up in agony, husky voice*] Mr. Denver—look at me—look me in the face. What has done this?

DEN.   I—I—don't—know.

BILL.   You are not speaking the truth. Where is my father?

DEN.   Your mother was going to leave him—they had a quarrel and—

BILL.   [*Half screams*]   Answer me. Did my father do this?

DEN.   Your father! Your father? [*Realizing that he is the boy's father*] Your—father—yes!

BILL.   [*Strong, but not loud*]   I do not believe it.

DEN.   As God is my judge, I speak the truth.

BILL.   My father shall be found. From his lips I will learn the truth.

DEN.   But you have no time for this. Do you realize that you are an outlaw? You have robbed your father's safe. Who will believe you did not kill your mother in an attempt to escape?

BILL.   You scoundrel!

DEN.   I know you are innocent, but will the law believe it, too? Make good your escape and leave me to find your father. I will take good charge of these. [*Stoops for papers Bill has dropped*]

BILL.   [*Takes pistol from table*]   Drop those papers. [*Denver does so*] My mind is dazed by this calamity. But one thing I know, the guilty shall be made to suffer. It shall be the one object of my life. [*Kneels before Mary*]

Mother, if you can hear me from above, record my oath of vengeance. And you—[*To Denver*] You who have plotted my destruction shall live to hear the outlaw you have created. Go, and leave me with my dead. [*Falls over body of Mary*] Mother! Mother! [*Denver slinks off L.U.E.*]

ACT II.

TIME: *Three years later.* SCENE: *Interior of the Broken Heart Saloon and dance hall. Low-roofed, rough interior. Bar R. Two tables and several chairs L. Entrance to dance hall in L. jog. Exterior door C. Small door behind bar. Door to dance hall is covered by long curtain. Oil lamp on bar; three more in bracket on the walls. All lighted. Reward notice pasted on R. of door.* DIS-COVERED: *Hank behind bar, cleaning glasses. Peanut leaning against bar. Bud at table with three rough-looking cowboys, playing cards. An old piano is heard in the dance hall, together with the shuffling of feet.*

BUD. Did I tell y'u about butting into Red Mike yest'day?

PEA. Some-a de boys tella me something about.

BUD. Mike used to be a bb-ba-ad man. But he got made a dep'ty sheriff and that spiled him. Got proud. Me an' him used ter sorter sidle sideways o' one another, both hearin' a bit that t'other was handy with his gun. But when he got made dep'ty his pride swallered his caution.

PEA. What was de trouble all about?

BUD. Just nuthin' at all. I went into Pete's place as meek as a kitten. Somebody says as how Red Mike had give it out that no one was to do any shooting in town but him. I allowed he couldn't make his bluff good. He happened to be there, so he pulled and I dropped him.

PEA. What-a de people do?

BUD. Offered me his job. [*All laugh*] Mike lost his nerve. It's all up wid a bad man when he once loses his nerve. Then a kid can make him take water.

PEA. And you never lost your nerve?

BUD. Not much. I ain't afraid of man, devil or the world to come, but 'spose my time will come with the rest. Until it does, I'm going to be a terror to these ba-a-ad men.

PEA. Why you no-a go after dis-a one? [*Points to reward circular*] Den dere be a five thousand dollars for you.

BUD. [*Turning*] Who's that? [*Peanut goes up. Con enters C., goes to bar*]

PEA. [*Reading*] Five t'ousand dollars reward for de capture, dead or alive, of one, William Wright, better known as Billy, the Kid. Age eighteen, height five feet t'ree inches, weight one hundred and twenty pounds—

BUD. Why, a baby.

PEA. —light hair, blue eyes, even features.

BUD. A baby *gal*.

PEA. Is the leader of the worst band of desperadoes the Territory has ever had to deal with.

BUD. Fairy tales.

PEA. De above reward will be paid for his capture, or for positive proof of his death. [*Con has been interested; Peanut turns to Bud*] Dere, what-a you tink of dat?

BUD. Nuthing.

PEA. Why you no getta him?

BUD. [*Rise*] Why, Peanut, I wouldn't waste no good powder on that youngster. If I had taken that job as dep'ty, I'd just land de kid an' give de coin ter charity. 'Cause it would be just like findin' it.

PEA. Dey say he vera badaman. Dey say he kill in fair fight, as many men as he has years on his shoulders.

BUD. De kid is a bluff, I tell you.

PEA. Man tole me yesterday de government he send from Washington a Secret Service man to capture Billy. Man go to Billy, say, "I a-want to joina-a your band." Bill he say, "Where you come from?" Man says, "Me work at Hick's ranch." Bill tell him to hole out his hands; man does. Dey are soft and white, not like a cowpuncher's. So Billy shoot him dead.

BUD. Peanut, if ever that kid comes in here while I'm here, I'll make a monkey out of him! *I'll* show you how bad he is.

CON. Sure, it's not fer me to be telling ye yer business; only this—when you come to mix it wid him, don't be sorry fer him on account of his youth!

PEA. Do you know-a him?

CON. Know him? I trotted him on me knee when he were a baby. I've watched him grow up into a fine, strapping boy, wid his head full o' nonsense about pirates and ransoms and things. Then I see him receive a shock that turned him into a man, fearless, reckless and brave.

BUD. And did he do all them things they tell about?

CON. Most o' them stories be lies.

BUD. That's what I thought. De kid is a bluff.

CON. Does that look like it? [*Points to circular*]

BUD. Well, just let me see him, that's all I ask. Just show him to me.

CON. Don't worry. You'll see him—some time; and it's meself that's thinking ye will take a fancy to the lad—[*Sotto voce*] if ye live. [*Bud goes to table*]

MOLLY. [*Enters from dance hall*] Who wants to dance? Well—don't all speak at once.

CON. Sure if we did, you'd have a picnic instead of a partner.

MOLLY. Well, speak for yourself, Irish.

CON. It's a bright girl ye are, to discover me ancestry. Well, I'll admit it, I am Irish—but I don't dance.

MOLLY. You can buy a drink, can't you?

CON. I have the power and I have the price but not the inclination.

MOLLY. You're a cheap skate.

CON. And while I'm about it, I may as well tell ye that I prefer to choose me own associates—present company not excepted.

BUD. D'ye mean that for an insult to me?

CON. No, sor, I don't. When I want to insult you I'll make it so plain ye won't have to ask who I mean. [*Turns to bar*]

BUD. [*Reaching for pistol*] *That's* an insult.

PEA. Hold on, Bud, dat only Irish wit.

BUD. Well, he don't want to get fresh around here. [*Con fills glass*]

DEN. [*Enters door in flat, hurriedly*] Hello, boys. [*Goes to bar, down stage*]

ALL. Hello boss, etc.

DEN. Whiskey. [*Hank sets bottle and glass before him, then goes to table to watch the game. Con is about to drink when Denver turns and sees him. Denver, in fright, stares at Con*]

CON. For the love of Heaven, turn your head. I never see a man so fond of watching me drink as you are.

DEN. You—here?

CON. Great guns! Can't you see I am? Sure, ye have eyes enough.

DEN. Where—is—the boy?

CON. None of yer dom business. Glad ye found out? [*Denver turns to bar and gulps down drink*] Now ye are getting sensible. Keep yer face at same angle 'til I get mine. [*Drinks*]

MOLLY. [*Comes down*] Hello, boss. Why what's the matter, you're white as a sheet?

DEN. Don't bother me. [*Crosses to C.*]

MOLLY. [*Laughing*] Hey, boys, the boss has seen a ghost.

DEN. [*Aside*] Yes, the ghost of my past misdeeds. The ghost of coming retribution. [*To table*] Peanut, do you know that man at the bar?

PEA. Yes, dat Con Hanley. He came here two—three times before.

Bud. If he makes a move at me—yes. [*Bud is seated behind table. Peanut at the R. Denver stands beside him. Jennie enters from dance hall, goes C. sullen and downcast*]

Molly. Gee, here's Miss Innocence. What are you doing in the barroom, going to come to the drink after all?

Pea. What you want here? Get back in the dance hall. [*Pause*] Well, do you hear!

Jen. Yes.

Pea. Why don't you obey den? Are you-a going?

Jen. No.

Pea. What! Why not?

Jen. Because I am sick of it—life, most of all.

Pea. [*Rise*] I'll take dat-a out of you.

Den. Hold on a minute, Peanut. [*To Jennie*] Now then, what's the matter with you? [*Pause, sneeringly*] Haven't you had all the place affords—and—money?

Jen. [*Passionately*] Money! Was it money that lured me to this dive? No, it was you. Did I pledge my honor for money? No, for you. Did you keep your promise to make me your wife? No. You liar and deceiver!

Den. You infernal cat. [*Slaps her in face, she reels. Con catches her*]

Con. [*In anger*] Strike a woman? [*Threatening*]

Den. Bud, drop him. [*Bud pulls pistol*]

Con. [*Holds out hand to Bud*] No need of that; I'm unarmed. Besides ye are six to one. I'll swallow me tongue and keep me own council. But, Mr. Denver, some day you and me will meet on an equal footing, then I'll kick the livin' daylights out of you. Come, me girl, brace up and forget it. Come into the hall wid me. [*Both cross*]

Jen. [*Crying*] If I could only die. [*Both exit to hall*]

Molly. For Heaven's sake, somebody let the girl die.

Den. [*Angry*] Why the devil didn't you drop him?

Bud. Why the poor fellow wasn't even armed.

Den. [*Crosses to bar*] What difference did that make? You are getting chicken-hearted.

Bud. Chicken-hearted? I'm in fer a scrap at all times—even or odd, but I gives every man a chance for his white alley. [*Rises*] Now if you think I'm chicken-hearted, I'll give you a chance to prove it.

Pea. [*Rises*] Hold on, Bud. [*Men rise*]

Den. [*Frightened*] I did not mean it, Bud. Truly I did not. I was angry at that Irish lunk-head and forgot myself. Come and have a drink. We won't quarrel.

PEA. He alla right, Bud. Put up-a de gun.

DEN. Come on, boys. Come, Moll—everybody take one on me. [*All go to bar. Denver down stage—Molly next, then Bud, Peanut and others at back*]

BUD. We'll let it go this time, Denver, but don't get flossy with me again.

MOLLY. Gee! I thought something was doing that time and it all petered out in talk.

DEN. Set out the good bottle. [*Hank sets out bottle and glasses. General conversation ad lib while they fill glasses*]

MOLLY [*To Denver*] Here's to the girl you would like to see most of all tonight.

DEN. I'll drink to that with a vengeance. [*All drink. Bud, Peanut and Denver go back to table*]

MOLLY. Gee whiz! You must love her.

DEN. I *hate* her.

MOLLY. Then what do you want to see her for?

DEN. To get even. I spoke to her one day, three years ago; she struck me in the face. Less than a year ago I met her while she was riding her pony. I apologized for my rudeness on the former occasion and she cut me with her riding whip. I carried the mark for many a day; and the longer it remained the stronger grew my hatred.

MOLLY. Gee, she must be a dandy. Wish we had a few spunky ones like that around here.

DEN. Well, this place would soon take the spunk out of them.

CON. [*Enters from hall, singing "Some day ye may be President or a gineral in th' army." Goes to bar, pushes Denver to one side*] Don't block up the bar when ye see a customer coming! [*Denver goes C. very angry, doubles fist as though about to strike Con. Con winks broadly at him and laughs*]

HANK. What'll ye have?

CON. A glass of water.

HANK. Water? What for?

CON. To drink. Did ye think I wanted to go in swimming? [*Hank gives him a glass of water. Con takes it and starts L.*]

DEN. I remember your insolence of three years ago—

CON. Well, forget it. [*Exits to hall*]

MOLLY. I believe that's the ghost you saw awhile ago, boss.

DEN. Have another drink?

MOLLY. To the same girl? [*Crosses to the bar*]

DEN. Yes. [*They fill glasses. Enter Mose, C., followed by Nell*]

MOSE. Halt. [*Salutes*] Who's in command here?

PEA. I run-a dis place.

Mose. Well, sir, we need assistance. The darkness overtaking us while in the hills, we lost our way. If you have a guide that can conduct us to Bradley's Place, he will be well paid. [*Denver turns at the mention of Bradley's and sees Nellie*]

Den. [*Aside*] God! It is she!

Pea. De night's very bad and de way is long and difficult. But maybe I find you a guide.

Den. By no means. These are friends of mine and I could not let them run the risk of getting lost. They shall remain here tonight.

Mose. Impossible. [*To Peanut*] Will you get us the guide?

Den. Never mind the guide, Peanut. They shall remain here tonight. I am sure it will be agreeable to *dear*—Nellie. [*Denver sneeringly takes off hat*]

Nel. At our last meeting I gave you a striking proof of my regard for you. Do not compel me to repeat that disgraceful scene.

Molly. Gee! Here's the girl that licked the boss.

Den. The scene, if repeated, will not be so onesided this time.

Pea. She very fin-a girl. Me like to have her here.

Nel. What a horrible place this is. Come, Mose, let us leave here at once. [*They turn*]

Den. Boys, guard the door. [*Two men spring to C. door*] Do not, I beg of you, leave us so suddenly. [*All laugh*] The dance, the wine, all the pleasure the establishment affords, are at your disposal.

Mose. You scoundrel. Open that door at once or I'll—[*Comes down, raises cane to strike Denver. Bud knocks him down*]

Nel. You scoundrel. To strike an old man! [*Kneels beside Mose*]

Bud. If he hadn't been an old man, I'd have put a bullet in him.

Nel. [*Rise*] You contemptible cur. A paid assassin for that coward. [*Points to Denver. Enter Jennie from hall*]

Bud. Wha-a-t? [*Raises fist to strike her. Jennie runs between them*]

Jen. Strike me, Bud, I'm more used to it than she.

Bud. Git out of the way. [*Throws Jennie violently against table; raises fist again*]

Den. [*Steps between them*] Hold on, Bud.

Bud. What the devil have *you* got to do with it?

Den. She's mine. Oh, she shall be humiliated. But let *me* do it.

Jen. [*Struggles to her feet*] You shall not do it, Boyd Denver. I've seen enough suffering here—I've suffered enough myself and I won't *let* you add another victim to your list.

Den. Indeed? And what can you do?

JEN. I will inform Con Hanley, he is in the dance hall. [*Starts; Peanut grabs her, places hand over her mouth, drags her across stage*]

DEN. Put her in the dark room, Peanut, until she gets some sense. Bud, watch the door, rope the Irishman if he attempts to enter. Hank, drag the old man behind the bar. [*They suit action to his words. Jennie is thrown in door behind bar. Bud goes L. Hank drags Mose behind bar. Men at door seize Nellie and drag her down stage and put her in chair*]

NEL. You shall pay for this outrage, with your miserable lives, every one.

PEA. If she-a going to squeal. [*He threatens her*]

DEN. [*Holds up hand*] Don't worry, Peanut. Now for the festivities first. A drink, to put the lady in good humor. Hank, bring me a cup of brandy. The lady may not like it; she may even refuse to drink with us. In that case, we will force it down her throat. [*Hank brings Denver tin cup*] Will you drink with us *willingly*, my dear? [*He is holding cup in right hand. Nellie, still held by the men, suddenly kicks cup, throwing the contents in Denver's face*]

NEL. That is my answer. [*All laugh*]

MOLLY. Gee! Can't she kick, though?

DEN. [*Very angry*] Laugh! That's right. The joke is on me this time, but the second portion of the entertainment cannot fail. Now, which of you gentlemen would like the first kiss from these fair lips?

ALL. Me—I would—*etc.*

DEN. One moment. As we seem unanimous on the subject, let us auction off the privilege. We will bid for the *first* kiss. Moll, you be auctioneer.

MOLLY. Here's a lark. [*Mounts chair*] Now then, gents, here's a prize. A kiss from pretty lips, unsullied by contact with coarse moustaches, such as yours. How much am I bid—

PEA. I bid ten cents. [*All laugh; Nellie hangs head in shame*]

MOLLY. Bid's too low; can't accept it. Come, come, gentlemen, bid up, bid up.

BUD. A dollar.

HANK. Two dollars.

MOLLY. Two dollars, two, do I hear any more. Who will make it three—anybody? Two, two—

DEN. Five dollars.

MOLLY. Now we are coming on. Five, five, who will make it ten? Going cheap, gentlemen. Five—five—do I hear any more? Five once—five twice—

JEN. [*Bursting through door R.*] I bid ten dollars.

DEN. You meddling brat. Get back in that room. [*He starts for her*]

JEN. [*Behind bar, picks up bottle*] Don't come near me, Boyd, or I'll brain you.

DEN. [*Turns to others*] My bid stands. She's not in this anyway.

MOLLY. Why not? She's got the money and her bid goes, eh, boys?

BOYS. Yes—certainly—*etc.*

MOLLY. The bid stands, according to the jury. Ten dollars, I'm bid. Ten dollars I'm bid—ten—ten—

DEN. Twenty-five. [*Jennie is about to bid when Peanut claps hand over her mouth and forces her under bar*]

MOLLY. Twenty-five—a good bid—any more? [*All shake heads*] Where's Jennie? Twenty-five—once—twice—three times and sold. The first kiss to Boyd Denver. [*Gets down*]

DEN. Here's your money. [*Gives Molly roll of bills*] Now for the reward! [*Bill enters door C.; all watching Denver, do not see him. Denver approaches Nellie with a laugh, as he stoops to kiss her, he glances up and sees Bill. Starts, recoils and begins to walk backward*]

MOLLY. Well, why don't you go ahead? You've paid enough for the privilege.

BILL. What's going on here? [*All turn. Men release Nellie who staggers up stage and sinks on chair R. Mose drags himself from behind bar and goes to her. Hank has released Jennie and both stand behind her looking at Bill*] Answer, some of you, what is the meaning of this?

PEA. A little sport. Just a little auction.

BILL. Well, stop it.

BUD. *What?*

BILL. Stop it.

BUD. Who says stop it?

BILL. I do.

BUD. And who are you?

BILL. Billy, the Kid. [*All these speeches are very quiet on Bill's part*]

BUD. Oh, you are, eh? Well, I've been looking for you.

BILL. That so?

BUD. Yes, it's so. You've heard about me, all right. I do nothin' but eat up ba-a-ad men—and bad kids, too. See that gun? Each of those notches stands for a bad man what ain't no more. That new one is for Red Mike planted yest'day. And there's room on there for a dandy, stuck up chap about your size. *I'm* Bud Monroe.

BILL. Never heard of you before. How are you? [*Takes Bud's hand. Bud astonished*]

BUD. How *am* I? How *am* I? Why, I'm in the pink of condition, I am. Ready to have it out with anybody.

BILL. [*Wiping his hand with his handkerchief*] Why don't you wash your hands? They are filthy.

BUD. *What!* Do you mean that fer an insult? [*Hand on gun*] If you do—

BILL. For Heaven's sake, don't talk so loud. I am not a thousand miles away. Lend me your hat a minute. [*Takes Bud's hat from his head*] The roads are very dusty. [*Dusts boots with hat*]

BUD. [*Astounded*] Here—you—[*Plucks at Bill's sleeve*]

BILL. Take your hand away. I told you they were filthy. Take—them away. [*Looks steadily at Bud. He removes hands, still astonished. Bill finishes dusting his boots; when through throws hat on floor*]

BUD. Draw—quick—[*Reaches for pistol. Bill's hand goes like lightning to Bud's side. Grabs his hand containing pistol as Bud draws it*]

BILL. What are you reaching so often for? [*Takes pistol from Bud*] Oh, a Colt. An old out-of-date pattern too. Ask Mr. Denver—he is a judge of firearms.

BUD. Gimme my gun. [*Plucks at Bill's sleeve*]

BILL. [*Whacks his fingers with pistol*] I told you to keep your hands off me. [*Goes to bar, tosses pistol on bar*] Here, bartender, give us a drink on the great Bud Monroe's shooting iron. [*During this scene everybody has remained motionless as though expecting something to happen. Now the strain is relaxed, all take in long breaths of surprise and saunter to the bar, except Bud who remains motionless and Denver who crosses to Bud*]

MOLLY. Gee! Ain't he the winner, though? [*General conversation as glasses are filled. Denver talks to Bud in dumb show, draws knife and offers it to Bud. The latter shakes his head. Denver in anger sneaks up behind Bill who is at bar with his back turned. When he is within striking distance, Denver raises knife. Bill wheels suddenly and faces him. Denver tries to conceal knife and gently drops his arm. Bill catches hand as it descends*]

BILL. Why, hello, Denver. Come up to shake hands, eh? [*Shaking*] I had no chance to do it before. What's that? A knife? Bad place to carry it, Denver, you might cut someone. [*Takes knife from him and tosses it across room*]

DEN. I—thought—you—might have trouble with Bud, so I slipped it up my sleeve to have it handy, in case I could be of service to you.

BILL. Very kind of you, I am sure. Come, get in line, there's a drink coming to you. [*Denver lines up to bar. Bill on the end, down stage. Bud has worked himself into a fury, crosses to Bill and slaps him on back*]

BUD. Look-a here, me young sport—

BILL. [*Wheels suddenly*] Well—what is it? [*Sharp*]

BUD. [*Wilts*] Why—why—don't I get no drink?

BILL. To be sure. Edge along, boys, and give the mighty Bud Monroe room. [*All drink and talk ad lib. Jennie leans over bar and whispers to Bill*]

JEN. For God's sake, get her away from here if you can. [*Bill nods*]

CON. [*Enters from hall*] Well, if there ain't Billy. The top of the evening to ye, Billy.

BILLY. Con, you are just in time. I want you to safely conduct Miss Bradley and Mose to their home.

CON. I'll do it wid pleasure.

PEA. [*Has crossed back to Bill; is on his L.*] Hold on. I have something to say to that.

BILL. [*Beside him*] Well? [*Hank sneaks up close to Bill's right*]

PEA. Dat-a a lady no-a leave here tonight.

BILL. She will leave this place in one minute.

PEA. I no permit it. [*Angry*]

BILL. How can you prevent it?

PEA. [*Draws knife*] I'll show you. *Strike*—Hank. [*Both spring at Bill at the same time. He knocks Hank down, grabs Peanut by hair with left hand, forces him over table and, with right, takes knife away, holding it at his— Peanut's—throat.* NOTE: *This action must be like lightning*]

BILL. I could kill you before you could raise an eyelash.

PEA. Mercy—mercy!

BILL. I am not in the habit of having my will disputed, don't *you* try it again. [*Throws Peanut to floor; tosses his knife after him*] Now, Con, we are ready. [*Con goes to C. door, Mose follows. Nellie starts, then turns*]

NEL. God bless you, Billy; you have saved me.

BILL. Thank Heaven I arrived—in time.

NEL. You will come with us?

BILL. No. I remain here.

NEL. But these men, they will kill you.

BILL. It is because I prefer death, I suppose, that my miserable life is spared.

NEL. Oh, Billy, is there no turning back?

BILL. None. Good-night. [*Takes her hand, kisses it. She exits C. followed by Mose and Con*] Could my life be rolled backward but three short years! [*Leans against door*] Could the weight of blood and crime be lifted from my guilty soul, what happiness might await me there. Oh, I must not think of her—not here—not *here*. [*With an effort he rouses himself*] Come, my girl. [*To Jennie*] We will dance; why it seems ages since I have had a dance. You shall be wined and dined to your heart's content tonight. Come! [*Takes Jen-*

nie's arm and they exit to hall. For a second after their exit no one moves. Bud and Denver are still at bar. Hank behind it, bathing his eye, Peanut is grovel-ling on the floor where he has fallen. Three men are at back R. talking]

DEN. [*Rousing himself and going to reward circular*] Well, are you all hypnotized? Or is money so plentiful that $5,000 grows on every bush? [*Taps circular. Peanut rises*]

BUD. I don't need the money. That fellow is a ba-a-ad man.

DEN. Are you all *afraid?*

PEA. [*Feels neck*] Well-a are you?

DEN. Of course not. But I have all the money I require. [*Peanut laughs*] Here, there are six of you. I'll give you two hundred dollars apiece if you will wipe him out. The reward you may divide to suit yourselves.

BUD. Now if I had only taken that dep'ty job—

DEN. [*Hurriedly*] He is now in the dance hall. There's a little door at the other end behind the piano. Go out this door. [*Indicates door C.*] Slip around and in the other. Get down behind the piano; when he passes, nail him. Don't be afraid of hurting Jen, she's outlived her usefulness, anyway. You can't fail. Surely there is one shot among you.

BUD. *One* shot? Give me my gun, Hank. [*Takes it*] What do ye say, boys?

ALL. We'll do it—yes—*etc.*

PEA. You come-a too, Boyd?

DEN. No-o, I'll watch the bar.

BUD. Ha-ha—chicken-heart. Come on, boys. [*They exit C.*]

DEN. [*Goes to door, looks after them*] They cannot fail. At last I shall be rid of him. How I fear him—how I fear him. My own son—son? Bah! I wish he had been throttled in infancy. [*Comes down*] There is the Wright place going to ruin—he cannot claim it, being an outlaw. I dare not claim it while he lives. What's that? The back door closing. They must be in position by this time. I must see the sport. From this doorway I shall see the end of Billy, the Kid. [*Goes L. to curtain, pulls it aside. Bill is standing in doorway. Denver starts back in terror. Bill enters*]

BILL. I thought I would find you alone. Kind of you to send the others away. Be seated. [*Denver drops in chair R. of table. He seems stunned. Bill sits L.*] I sought you out tonight, because you were a witness, three years ago of my oath to find my father.

DEN. [*In whisper*] Yes.

BILL. Well—I have found him.

DEN. [*Aside*] Caught. He knows me.

BILL. I had another object in wishing a private interview with you. To restore you a lost and valuable article. [*Throws pistol on table, Denver sees*] *it, shakes with terror and clutches the table*] A double-acting, shell-extracting, self-cocking revolver. We found it at the bottom of the old well. It is not in very good condition now, being rusted and choked with sand. Three loaded shells remain in the chambers, two have been fired. When you have a moment to spare, see how this bullet compares with the ones still remaining in your revolver. [*Throws bullet on table. Denver picks it up*] It was taken from my mother's breast. [*Denver drops it. Bill lights cigarette. Denver grabs pistol, points it at Bill and tries to pull trigger. It will not work. He drops it in despair. Bill does not move or show the least concern when Denver picks up pistol. Continues to light cigarette*]

DEN. [*As he drops pistol*]   The devil aids you.

BILL.   I told you it was out of order; a little oil will fix that, then you can try again.

DEN. [*In husky voice*]   What—what do you want me to do?

BILL.   Follow me until I am ready for the hour! Heaven has appointed me your executioner but the hour has not arrived. From now until your death you shall never leave my side.

DEN.   Give me a chance—only a chance to prove my innocence.

BILL.   You shall have sufficient opportunity. We will stand beside my mother's grave and you will tell me the truth. [*Rises*] We had best start before the others return. Bring that pretty revolver; I will need it. Come. [*Goes up to C. door. Denver takes revolver, struggles to his feet*]

DEN.   No—no—I cannot—will not go.

BILL.   *Will* not? You shall go with me though the whole world tried to stop you. [*Draws two pistols. Bud, followed by others, enters from hall. They scatter across stage during the following dialogue. Bud extreme R., Peanut next, three men C., Denver L., Hank R. of Denver*]

BUD.   He ain't there.

PEA.   Where he-a go?

DEN. [*Throwing table on end and getting behind it*]   There! There! At the door! Shoot! [*General fusillade of shots. Lights are shot out, leaving the stage in total darkness save the flashes from the pistols. Some twenty shots fired in all and from small caliber pistols so that the noise will not be startling. Suddenly firing ceases; silence and darkness for a second*]

DEN. [*In a shaky voice*]   Billy—Billy—are you there? [*Pause*] He is dead! Bud!

BUD.   Hello—is that you, Denver?

DEN.   Yes, strike a light—light up everything for Billy, the Kid, is dead. [*While speaking he arises from behind table. Bud has risen from behind table after lighting candle. As lights go up Peanut is discovered lying C., Hank L. Three men lying at the feet of Billy, who is standing C. a pistol in each hand]*

BILL. Come, Denver—you—go—with—me. [*Denver sneaks out of door C., Bill follows. Bud still standing behind bar holding candle as curtain falls*]

ACT III.

TIME: *One week later.* SCENE: *Colonel Bradley's dining room. Large window. Breakaway opening to floor C. Old flag draped L. of window. Closet door L.2., small table beside it. Exterior door L.U. Door R.3. Long table R.C. set for seven people. Tablecloth long enough to touch floor on sides, but short, so audience can see under in front. Small table L. of C. window. Chairs, etc. Canary in cage, up L.* DISCOVERED: *Nellie and Jennie putting table in order.*

JEN. [*Finishing story*] And then the lights were shot out. All was in darkness and the stillness of death prevailed. Suddenly somebody lighted a candle and there stood Billy, without so much as a scratch on him. Oh! It was wonderful.

NEL. Wonderful indeed!

JEN. That was my opportunity to escape. I couldn't stay there, miss, so I slipped away. Yours was the first kind, honest face I had seen in my two months' imprisonment in that awful den, and I wanted to come and tell you I had made up my mind to start all over again. I never expected you to offer me the place of maid, miss.

NEL. Let us say no more about it. Stick to your resolution to do right, and this funny old world, that trampled you under foot yesterday, will receive you with open arms today.

JEN. Do you think there is any hope for me? But, there, I don't need to ask that question. Your actions have shown that you do. [*With a desire to change conversation*] Was it not kind of your uncle to hold this little reception in honor of Billy's gallantry in saving you?

NEL. Not half what he deserves, Jennie. Oh, it was so noble of him!

JEN. You love him, miss?

NEL. Nonsense, Jennie, I only—

JEN. We, who have had our affections worn smooth by hard contact with the sharp edges of the world, have quick eyes for the flash of love, the ready blush, the catching of the breath at the sound of a name—things that we have forever lost.

NEL. You are mistaken, Jennie; at least in thinking that I care for him. It —it is impossible. He is an outlaw. Why, he and I could not be further apart if one of us were dead.

JEN. Perhaps he might reform.

NEL. It would make no difference. In this cold, hard world, when once one has fallen, all the angels in Heaven could not place him right again in the eyes of his fellow men.

JEN. [*Crying*] There is no hope, then, for me.

NEL. Forgive me, Jennie. It was thoughtless and cruel of me. [*Arms about her*] There, there, don't cry. We will make you the exception that proves the rule. [*They embrace*]

MOSE. [*Enter R.3.*] Attention! How dare you waste your time hugging one another? It's a waste of sweetness. You never saw two men hugging, did you? If you must hug somebody, hug me.

NEL. You old sinner! I have hugged you nearly to death on several occasions and you offered absolutely no resistance. In fact, I really believe you enjoyed it.

MOSE. Of course I did. A good soldier likes arms about him, don't he?

NEL. Well, as you are so fond of feminine arms, I wonder you never married.

MOSE. I did. That's why I became a soldier.

NEL. Oh, tell me about her. Black hair?

MOSE. Red.

NEL. Blue eyes?

MOSE. Yellow.

NEL. Nonsense. Why, that would be—

MOSE. A cat. Honest, that's what she was.

NEL. [*Laughs*] Then your matrimonial venture did not turn out well?

MOSE. Oh, yes, it did. Turned *me* out.

NEL. Honest, Mose?

MOSE. True as I'm standing here, and all because the dearest, sweetest little widow—

NEL. Bother. Served you right! What became of your wife, Mose?

MOSE. Dead. [*Feels in pocket*] Confound it! I always weep when I get to that point and I can't find my handkerchief.

NEL. [*Laughs*] You are an old fraud but the best old fraud that ever lived, so I'll give you a hug. [*Does so*]

MOSE. Bully.

NEL. —for the sake of your wife.

MOSE. [*Disgusted*] Don't. [*Nellie laughs; goes to table*]

COL. [*Enters R.3.*] Oh, there you are, eh? [*Mose stands at attention*] Gossiping like a schoolgirl, I'll bet.

MOSE. Superintending the spreading of the feast, sir.

COL. [*Surveying things*] Looks pretty well, eh?

MOSE. I am very well satisfied, sir.

COL. Oh *you* are, eh? Well, I'm glad it pleases you.

MOSE. [*Peevishly*] A body can't say a word but you must get sarcastic.

COL. [*Blustering*] What—what—sir—

NEL. There, there. We'll have no quarrel today. Haven't time for it. Postpone it until tomorrow.

MOSE. Now, Nellie, I'll leave it to you if I said anything—

NEL. But you are doing a lot of it now.

COL. Of course he is. If he couldn't keep that mouth of his going—

NEL. Uncle! Will you change the subject.

COL. [*Growling*] U-m-m!

MOSE. [*Growling*] U-m-m-m! [*They scowl at one another*]

NEL. Who have you invited, uncle?

COL. All of Billy's friends that want to come. Don't know how many he will bring but I guess seven plates will be enough. Nellie, Billy and myself are three. Then there will be four plates for friends. In case the places are not filled, Jennie, you and Mose shall be of the party.

JEN. Thank you, sir. [*Exits with dish, R.3.*]

MOSE. Well, I'll be one of the party anyway. Do you suppose I am going to give up my place to a lot of robbers?

COL. Attention! Billy is the son of my old friend, Steve Wright. Today he shall be treated as such. He and his friends are to be my guests and I don't need you or anybody else to tell me what is due a Southern gentleman's guest. Today I shall forget the lawless boy and remember only the wild harum-scarum youngster I used to love. Tomorrow, Billy the Kid may go his way. I never want to see him again.

NEL. Oh, uncle!

COL. My child, our roads lie apart. Today we will overlook that fact. [*Sighs; Nellie wipes her eyes*] Mose!

MOSE. Present.

COL. Set the wine near the head of the table. [*Mose does so*] And, Mose—

MOSE. Countersign is correct, sir.

COL. Remove that bird. Birdie won't need any chickweed today.

MOSE. Yes, sir. [*Takes cage and exits*]

NEL. What a tease you are.

COL. Well, I know Billy is overly fond of dicky birds and I want to put temptation out of his way.

NEL. Well, if you think an old excuse like that—

COL. There's one other thing, miss. Don't try to work off any extra champagne cork-popping. I've got the bottles counted. [*Mose enters with plate of cabbage salad*] And I know every pop. [*Nellie laughs*]

MOSE. It's a wise cork that knows its own pop.

COL. [*Laughs*] Very good, Mose. [*Nellie laughs and exits R.3.*]

MOSE. [*Tasting salad*] And it's a wise cow that knows its own fodder.

COL. [*Sharply*] Fingers out of the dish, Mose. You are not a cow.

MOSE. [*Indignant*] No, sir, I'm not. Do you know what I am?

COL. A—a—jackass?

MOSE. Yes, sir, I am. I mean, no, sir, I'm not. But I ought to be after associating half my life with a mule.

COL. What! Call me a mule?

MOSE. No, sir, I don't—you are a-a-a confounded old crank.

COL. Insubordination! You shall be courtmartialled.

MOSE. No, I won't. We are not on the battlefield now. I know my rights— I am a free-born citizen and have a vote.

COL. [*Snorts*] Vote! What good does that do you? You never voted.

MOSE. I never got my price.

COL. Nice citizen you. Talking about a price.

MOSE. I know my business. I've got a say in the management of this household and I'm going to have my rights.

COL. [*Furious*] Attention!

MOSE. We're not on the field now.

COL. No, confound you. If we were, I'd have you hamstrung.

MOSE. Sit down there and listen to me. [*Colonel sits, astonished*] To begin with, Nellie don't like the tactics, therefore, she must be relieved from all duty henceforth.

COL. You don't say so?

MOSE. Then—Nellie loves Billy, and you pretty near broke her heart when you told her she must never see him after today. That order must be revoked.

COL. Must, eh?

MOSE. Don't you call me musty. You're as old as I am.

COL. [*Rises*] Damn, this has gone far enough. I am commander of this post, and I won't have any rebellion. No opposing forces shall mar my peace. You get out of here as fast as you can go.

MOSE. [*A little frightened*] Get out!

Col. Bag and baggage. I won't put up with your interference another minute.

Mose. [*Blustering*] Hm! Hm! You can't discharge me. I'm your orderly.

Col. We're not on the battlefield now. You can go.

Mose. [*Voice trembles*] Go? Go where?

Col. To the devil for all I care. I've stood enough from you to try a saint. [*Sits*]

Mose. I ain't got no home but this, sir.

Col. Well, get another.

Mose. [*Whimpering*] I'm too old to start all over again.

Col. You're a free-born citizen—got a vote, you know.

Mose. Colonel, you ain't going to turn me out, are you?

Col. Yes, I am, confound you, and don't you go snivelling around Nellie to be taken back. I won't have it.

Mose. [*Firing*] You never heard me snivelling at Antietam, did you?.

Col. We're not on the battlefield now.

Mose. No. If we were, I'd tell you to take your horse and go to thunder. Oh, I'll go. [*Goes up*] It won't take me long to pack. I ain't not nothing but my bugle.

Col. Well, take it along. I'll be glad to get rid of it. You've nearly driven me crazy with your tooting, the last fifteen years.

Mose. I was going to give it to you, Colonel—but I'll not—trouble you any more. [*Wipes eyes on flag*] Why here's the old flag. I'd like to take that, Colonel.

Col. Well, take it along.

Mose. 'Member how at Antietam, the color-bearer was shot down and you grabbed up this same old flag?

Col. Certainly. No soldier would let the colors trail in the dust.

Mose. How the boys cheered you as you led 'em along. Why, it just put new life in 'em.

Col. Ah, they were a fine lot.

Mose. And then you were shot in the arm. I picked you and the flag up together and carried you back—out of the firing.

Col. That you did, Mose. A brave deed—bullets zipping all around us—men falling everywhere.

Mose. And then when the surgeon went to probe for the bullet—ha, ha—you said: "Drat your picture, stop it. It's the other arm—that's my vaccination"—[*Laughs*]

Col. [*Laughing heartily*] I remember, Mose, I remember. One on the doctor, eh?

234 WALTER WOODS

Mose. More like one on you. You got the worst of it.

Col. So I did. Ha, ha—glorious times, Mose.

Mose. All over now, Colonel. We're both old, and I'm turned—out. [*Wipes eyes*]

Col. [*Rises, goes to him*] Mose, dear old friend, forgive me. [*Holds out hand*] This tent is yours as long as you will share it with me. [*Mose shakes, still wiping eyes*]

Nel. [*Enters R.3.*] Well! Are you two quarrelling again? I declare, that selfsame quarrel and reconciliation has occurred at least once a year, as far back as I can remember.

Col. We need it, my dear, to strengthen old ties. And to serve as a reminder that we are still comrades. [*Pats Mose on back*] But I think Mose is an old friend. He gets these quarrels up on purpose, knowing discipline will be relaxed for a week or two, so he can run the place to suit himself.

Mose. Don't you believe it, Miss Nellie.

Nel. Of course I don't. Uncle is equally to blame. Well, everything is ready now. I hope they are on time. [*Horse effect outside*] There! Run and see who it is, Mose.

Mose. [*Saluting*] Once more the army is himself. [*Exit L.U.E. Sounds of several horses stopping. "Whoa," "Back Up," etc., outside*]

Col. Seems to be quite a lot of 'em.

Nel. [*Disappointed*] I was in hopes he would come alone.

Col. He knows his business best. Maybe it is not safe for him to travel alone.

Mose. [*Enters announcing*] Friends of Mr. Billy, the Kid. [*Enter Bud followed by three plainsmen. All have revolvers in belt at back. Blue shirts, broad hats, boots, etc. As Bud enters, Nellie starts back in alarm and watches them suspiciously*]

Col. Welcome, gentlemen, to this little feast given in honor of your noble comrade. [*Shakes with Bud*]

Bud. Thanks, Colonel, it's mighty kind of you all right—all right, but he's deserving of it. He's one of the gamest men in this section. And b-a-a-a-d? Well I guess. Me an' him used to be kinder on the outs, but he licked me an' a few more in a fair fight. So I struck me colors and joined his forces—an' I'm his'n for life. [*Nellie seems to accept his explanation*] This is Hank Burk, this is Bill Burnside and this is Bald Pete. Gentlemen, Colonel Bradley, one of the heroes of our last late war.

Col. And gentlemen—my niece, Miss Bradley. [*They bow awkwardly*] Now, sit down and have something while we are waiting for Billy. Mose, go out and keep watch for him.

MOSE. [*Aside, looking at Bud*] If that ain't the man that knocked me down a week ago, I'm a marine. [*Doubles up fists, looks at them and exits L.U.E.*]

COL. Nellie, see how the dinner is coming on. [*She exits R.3. Men in the meantime have seated themselves. Counting from downstage end of table Bud sits second chair R. Man third chair R. Man second chair L. The other third L. This leaves vacant, first chairs R. and L. and chair at head of table. Colonel sets two bottles of wine on table. General conversation while bottles are being opened*] Now, gentlemen, help yourselves and I'll give you a toast. Wait—I must get a julep for mine. Anybody else like one?

BUD. This'll do us, Colonel.

COL. Just excuse me for a second. [*Exits R.3. Bud jumps up and runs to window, opening it*]

BUD. Come in, Peanut. [*Peanut enters by window, head tied up where he has been wounded*] Quick, under the table. [*Peanut dives under the table, downstage, so audience can see him. He has two large revolvers in back of his belt*] If they see you they may get suspicious.

PEA. Yes. De girl she a know a me quick. Don't you tink Billy will tumble when he sees you?

BUD. Not a bit. I can square him all right—all right. Say, Peanut, how did you tumble to this banquet racket?

PEA. De fool boy dat a de Colonel send with de invitation to Billy come to my place. I read a de note and den sent it on to Bill.

BUD. Think he'll come all right?

PEA. Sure. He a sweet on the girl.

BUD. Wait a minute. [*Rises, goes up, gets bottle, places it on table by closet*] When the wine is about all gone, I'll call Billy's attention to this bottle. And ask him to get it. When he turns his back, that's the signal to jump on him. [*Resumes seat*] You understand?

MEN. Yes—we understand, *etc.*

BUD. Mind, we got the law on our side. I'm dep'ty now, so don't let the old Colonel bluff you.

PEA. What! You tink de Colonel could bluff—

BUD. Shut up, he's here. [*Kicks him*]

PEA. O-o-o, dat my shin.

BUD. Sh-h-h.

COL. [*Enters*] Ah ha! Here is the real article. A genuine Southern mint julep. [*He holds up glass*] All filled up, gentlemen?

PEA. All but a me. [*Bud kicks him*] Ouch!

COL. Eh? What's that?

BUD. I just bumped my foot, Colonel.

PEA. Well, don't bump it on a me.

COL. Now for the toast. Here's to comrade Bill Wright. [*All drink*] And death to his enemies. [*Colonel drinks. Bud chokes and spits out liquor*]

PEA. Good-a joke. [*Laughs. Bud kicks him*] Sacré-damn.

BUD. 'Scuse me for swearing, Colonel; it went down the wrong way.

COL. Never mind, fill up and have another.

BUD. Cut out the toast this time, Colonel. [*Glasses filled; horse effects outside*]

NEL. [*Enter R.3.*] They're coming, uncle. [*"Whoa," etc., outside*]

COL. Just hold the next round for a minute, gentlemen, and we'll have it together. [*Goes up*]

BUD. [*Low*] Keep up your nerve, boys, he don't know any of you.

PEA. Pass me a drink, to keep a up *my* a nerve.

BUD. [*Kicks him*] Shut up.

PEA. Wow! [*Loud*]

NEL. [*Turning*] Why, what was that?

BUD. My dog, miss, under the table. [*Low, to Peanut*] Growl, you Indian, growl. [*Peanut growls*] He's very cross, miss.

PEA. Cross? He's—a *mad*. You kicka me again and I'll—bite.

MOSE. [*Enter L.U.E., announcing*] Mr. Con Hanley, First Lieutenant to Captain Billy. [*Enter Con. Colonel shakes and motions him to seat. Con pauses at sight of the men*]

CON. My—my. But it's choice society the Colonel do be keeping. [*Sits first chair R.*]

MOSE. Mr. Boyd Denver. A—a—gentleman. [*Men all start and look up*]

COL. [*Astounded*] What!

NEL. That man—here? [*Enter Denver cowed and sneaking, slinks to table without raising hand or noticing anybody. Sinks in chair at head of table, head drops in hands*]

MOSE. Captain William Wright—Billy, the Kid. [*Enter Bill, stops at sight of men at table. Hand goes swiftly to pistol; glances sharply at Colonel*]

BILL. Quite a gathering, I see. [*Extends hand to Colonel*] Colonel.

COL. Sir, I did not think you would insult my little banquet, given in your honor, by inviting that man here. [*Pointing to Denver*] Still, I shall not refuse you my hand. [*Shakes*]

BILL. Colonel, some day I will explain. Now, I cannot. [*Crosses to Nellie*] Nellie—[*Holds out hand*]

NEL. [*Ignoring it*] Billy, how could you? [*Tosses her head, turns and goes to door R.3. Breaks down, cries and exits. Bill sighs and turns away, looks sharply at men again fingering pistol. Men are uneasy. Bill with sudden determination removes belt and pistol, handing them to Colonel*]

BILL.   Colonel, here are my only weapons. While your guest, I shall forget my hostility towards society.

COL. [*Takes belt*]   May you enjoy yourself, Billy. But I cannot—nor can I allow any of my household—to sit at the table with your *friend*. Come, Mose. [*Exit Colonel and Mose R.3.*]

BILL. [*Comes to first chair L.*]   Now, gentlemen, what's the game?

BUD.   Honest, Bill, there ain't none. The Colonel invited us to come. Asked me if I felt sore at you. I said "No, he licked me in a fair fight, and I takes me hat off to him." I'm square, Bill, and there's me hand on it. [*Holds out hand. Bill hesitates a moment, then takes hand*]

BILL.   If you are not square, Bud Monroe, the hand you are holding now will help you into eternity. [*Bud attempts to withdraw hand*] Don't take it away, Bud. I like to feel the pressure of an honest hand, even if it does tremble like a girl's and is cold and clammy. Bah! [*Throws hand away*] What poor liars some of us are!

BUD. [*To cover his confusion*]   Come on, boys. Fill up, fill up and we'll drink to Bill's health. [*All fill glasses but Denver*]

PEA. [*Glancing from under table*]   He no gotta de pistol now. Why dey no jump on him? [*Sees Con*] Oh! De Con man have dem.

BUD.   Now boys—[*All raise glasses*] Here's to the worthy Captain Bill. A b-a-a-d man. [*All raise glasses to lips*] And to the gentlemanly proprietor of the Broken Heart, Mr. Denver. [*All drink but Bill and Con. Denver raises head, looks hopefully at Bud*]

BILL. [*Aside*]   Drink to—him? No. [*Aloud*] I—ah—think there is a fly in my glass. [*Tosses contents under table; hits Peanut in face*]

CON.   Billy, I believe there is an elephant in mine. [*Dashes contents under table, hits Peanut. He sputters and turns around so his rear view is toward audience; his two pistols stick out in plain view*]

BUD.   Well, try some more. [*Fills Bill and Con's glass, then attends to other end of table*]

BILL. [*Looking at glass*]   This looks rather dark. [*Goes to toss it under table, sees Peanut, motions Con. Both reach down and each slips a pistol from Peanut's belt. Action is very quick*] Rather dark looking, eh, Con?

CON.   Looks kind o' black to me. [*Bill slips pistol in his boot*]

BUD.   Well, try some from this bottle. [*Goes to pour*] Why, it's empty. There's another bottle right behind you, Bill, will you get it? [*Nellie enters R.3.*]

BILL. Certainly. [*Bill rises, goes toward bottle on table L. Con has been eyeing the rear view of Peanut and contemplating his boot. As Bill's back is turned, all men rise slowly*]

BUD. Now, boys.

NEL. Look out, Bill. [*Bill without looking around, dashes in closet and closes door. Two men L. reach it almost at the same time. Con, without seeing the action of the others, has delivered an awful kick to Peanut, just as Bud speaks. Bud and man R. grab Con and bind him. Peanut is kicked from under table L. rushes to closet door, turns key which was in the lock and puts it in his pocket. Denver is standing and watches the scene in a dazed fashion*]

PEA. Gooda! We-a gota him!

CON. [*Who is bound*] Yes, and I gota one, too.

PEA. Sacré! [*Rubbing himself*] I have-a not forgotten.

CON. No? I think meself the sting of that kick will linger for some time on yer—memory.

PEA. Sacré! I geta even.

BUD. Where does that door lead to?

PEA. Nowhere. It is a blind closet. [*Shows key*] He-a is our prisoner.

DEN. [*Huskily*] Thank God, I am free. Give me some wine, I am choking. Oh, you shall be well paid for this. Shake. [*Shakes hands all around; drinks*]

NEL. [*At back*] I must warn uncle. [*Starts R.*]

PEA. Here, girl. [*She stops*] What a in data closet?

NEL. [*Comes down L. and speaks as Bill will hear*] Nothing—nothing but some dresses of my maid Polly. She will be here in a moment to serve you.

PEA. No-a weapons in-a dere?

NEL. None whatever. I will send my maid, Polly. [*Starts*]

PEA. Stop! You staya here. Let Polly come if she-a want to but I no-a have de house aroused by you.

BUD. I'll just lock these doors to keep anyone from butting in. [*Locks door R.3. and L.U.E. Goes back to table. The others have resumed places about table, all are drinking and laughing. Nellie stands L.C. watching them*]

PEA. Here-a girl. Give-a me dat bottle of wine. [*Points to bottle on table L.*]

NEL. Yes, sir. [*Gets bottle, comes to Peanut, pours him out drink with right hand, with left she steals key out of his pocket*]

PEA. Data a gooda girl. You learn to obey easily.

NEL. Yes, sir. [*She returns bottle to table, quickly slipping key in lock, unlocking door and taking key out again*]

PEA. Here, here! Bring back data bottle, I no-a tella you to take him away.

NEL. Yes, sir. [*She brings bottle, pours drink for Peanut and slips key back in his pocket, placing bottle on table.* NOTE: *Key business must be made very apparent to audience*]

CON. [*Who has been watching Nellie*] Nellie, fer the love of Heavin' give me a drink, before I choke wid laughter.

BUD. What you got to laugh about, cull? [*Nellie goes up to window*]

CON. It's too fine a joke to penetrate that thick skull of yours. But one thing I'd like to ask ye; what right have ye to bind me up this way?

BUD. I'm dep'ty sheriff, I am. [*Shows badge*]

CON. Oh, ho, ye are?

PEA. [*Mocking*] Ho, ho, yes he is.

CON. Go on, ye pizen-faced pup. I didn't ask you.

PEA. [*In rage*] I-a killa him.

BUD. Hold on, Peanut.

PEA. He-a kicka me.

CON. That seems to hurt your feelings, dago.

PEA. It-ah hurta my pride.

CON. Well, never carry your pride in your pistol pocket.

DEN. [*Getting drunk*] Kill him—kill them both. Oh, God! I could shout for joy at my deliverance. To be free again—free! Listen, men, for seven days I have been dragged in mortal terror, from place to place, by that fiend in yonder—tortured by the threat of approaching death, that increased my terror the longer it was delayed. I was given nothing but whiskey to drink in all that time—whiskey until I was driven mad. When I begged for water, he said: "you filled me with whiskey and then tempted me to my first crime. Your path to the grave shall be a river of it." [*Takes glass*] Come, fill up—fill up. This will be a glorious day. [*All crowd around table and fill up. Bill slips from closet disguised as maid. Goes to door L.U.E. tries to open it, finds it locked*]

NEL. Oh, here is Polly. [*All turn*]

PEA. How she-a get-a in?

NEL. Through the window.

BUD. I'll just lock that, too. [*Goes to window, locks it*]

NEL. Polly, will you serve the gentlemen?

BILL. Wiz pleasure. [*Goes to table; serves drinks. Mose appears outside window. Nellie up quick*]

NEL. [*Aside to Mose*] Mose, can you hear? [*Mose nods*] Quick! Stampede all the horses but Billy's, bring his to this window. You understand? [*Mose nods*] When it is done, give me some signal—sound your bugle. [*Mose nods and disappears*]

BUD. Here, you girl, don't try to get out that window.

NEL. I am not trying to. [*Bill has been busy filling glasses. All have seated themselves. Peanut first chair L. Bud R. Billy is beside Peanut*]

PEA. Oh, dat-a Polly—a very pretty girl. [*Pats Bill's cheek*]

BILL. Zank you, m'sieur, you are ver'—ver' 'andsome.

BUD. Ho—ho. She's stuck on the dago.

BILL. You 'ave such *beautiful whiscaires*. May I not 'ave a souvenier. [*Pulls hair out of his beard*]

PEA. Ouch! Sacré! What you-a do? Dat-a hurt like blazes. [*All laugh*]

BILL. I am ze sorry. [*Puts arm around him*]

PEA. [*Flattered*] Dat-a all right.

BILL. More wine, zentlemen? [*Goes to Bud. Takes pistol from his belt*] O-o-o! What a terr'ble big pistol. 'Ow do he work?

BUD. Well, pretty, I'll show yer. Pull the trigger an' somebody's dead, see?

BILL. Pull ze trigaire, an' somebody dead, oui? [*Points it at Peanut*] Bang.

PEA. Hold-a on. Don'-a you practise on me. [*Bill laughs*]

BUD. Pull the catch and out come the cartridges, see?

BILL. [*Empties cartridges*] Magnificent! Let me put zem back, eh?

BUD. Go ahead.

BILL. Zere is one—two—three—four—five, all in. [*Lets audience see he does not replace cartridges. Places revolver back in Bud's belt*] Zere! Now I have fixed you—plenty. [*Tosses shells away*]

NEL. [*At window*] Oh, why don't Mose blow the signal?

DEN. Here, girl, give me some wine—wine.

BILL. Ze zentleman want wine? 'E shall 'ave it. Plenty—plenty, rivers of it. [*Goes behind Denver's chair*]

DEN. [*Glancing up uneasily*] What did you say about rivers?

BILL. Ze river of wine, in which to drown your sorrow.

NEL. [*Down, aside to Bill*] When you hear a bugle call, be prepared to escape. [*Bill nods*]

DEN. Good girl! Glorious wine. Oh this is a happy day.

BILL. Be 'appy today, m'sieur, for tomorrow you *may* be dead.

DEN. What do you mean?

BILL. Zat is an old quotation from my country. Zat is all. [*Goes to man, L.*] Have wine? [*Steals his pistol, pulls up skirt and puts it in boot*]

NEL. [*At window*] No signal yet.

PEA. Come here, Polly.

BILL. O-o-o—I am forgetting my dear 'andsome man. [*Goes to him*] Such a *beautiful* beard. Can you not spare me one little— [*Pulls hair out of his beard*]

PEA. Oh! Hella! Diable! What you—a do? [*All laugh. All getting rather mellow*]

BILL. I 'ave ze two hair, soon I have 'nough for ze watch chain.

PEA. Not-a out of my—a whiskers. [*Nurses his face. Bill has gone to man R. steals his revolver and comes C. finds both boots full, at a loss what to do with it for a moment, then pulls dress up and puts it in pocket. Work this for comedy*]

NEL. Oh, why doesn't Mose sound the signal?

PEA. Here, Polly girl. How you-a like to come-a to my place? Wine, dancing, fine clothes, plenty de mon. Eh?

BILL. I love to go—if you give me just one mo—[*Pulls out whisker*]

PEA. Stop-a dat or I cut-a de neck. [*All laugh*]

DEN. Let's have him out, boys, and kill him.

PEA. I have-a de key. [*Rises, shows key, goes to door*]

NEL. Will Mose never come?

PEA. [*Pauses at door*] All get-a ready boys. Shoot as soon as he comes out it he no have his-a hands up. [*All rise. Bud has playfully chased Billy around table to C.*] Polly, go up-a by de window, so you not-a get hurt. [*Bill starts up*]

BUD. Wait a minute, Polly, I want to put my arms around you.

PEA. [*Impatiently*] We got-a no time.

BILL. [*Retreating*] Polly don't want your arms.

BUD. Polly has *got* to have some arms. [*Sharp bugle call. All turn. Nellie gives cry of joy. Bill grabs chair and dashes it through window. Mose appears behind broken window, bugle in one hand, leading horse with other. Bill reaches down, pulls up skirt and draws two pistols from boots*]

BILL. Gentlemen, Polly has all the arms she needs. [*All reach for pistols, find them gone. Except Bud who snaps his unloaded one. Peanut throws open closet door. Finds the closet empty*]

PICTURE

2ND PICTURE: *Colonel and Nellie R., Mose L., pointing pistols at men. Jennie down R., releasing Con. Bill astride horse, pulling Denver towards him by means of a lasso that is about Denver's body. Denver struggles but is slowly drawn up to window. Bud, Peanut and men down stage.*

ACT IV.

SCENE: *Same as Act I., except the whole act is moved nearer C. Return to house L.1. transparent when light is behind it, showing interior of room. Fireplace, at back; sofa and chairs. Windows on porch and windows in room boarded up. Porch, fence, etc., show signs of neglect and decay. Broken tree branches and leaves scattered about the yard. Pile of sand beside well, as though it had been dug out. Rope from porch to unseen flagstaff, supposed to be on top of house. Two long pieces of rope C. Con enters at rise, R.U.E. He is dirty and worn looking.*

CON. Sure, the place is just as we left it two weeks ago. [*Goes to porch; sits*] It's a foolish thing of Billy to come back here. They're sure to get him. An' think me own life ain't none too safe. They're hot on our trail. 'Tis a hard fight we had—and lost. The old gang do be broken up for good. What wasn't killed was captured—'cepting Billy and me. I wanted him to jump for the bad lands, but no—he must come here, back to his old home and—his mother's grave. Why, it's ten to one shot they'll watch this place. I made him stay in the little grove of trees back there a ways, 'til I had a look around. If it's all O.K. I run a little flag up to the top of the house. That's the signal for him to come. [*Rises*] Well, I guess it's all safe enough. [*Looks L.*] Hello! Who the devil do be this a coming. I don't know. [*Hides behind corner of house L.*] I'll make a quiet investigation. [*Peanut enters L.U.E.; glances around cautiously*]

PEA. He no-a here yet. But he-a come. He come because his mother buried out there. Dat-a good-a joke. We capture de kid through his-a dead mother. [*Laughs*] De boys wait back of de hill. When I-a sight him, I run-a dis flag up to de top of de house, den we-a have him. [*Crosses to R.*]

CON. Dago, if ye make another break like that, I'll blow the ends off yer whiskers.

PEA. Yes, you-a very funny man. But maybe you won't be so funny bye and bye.

CON. Well, mebby you will be and that will even things up a bit, fer ye look like a funeral just at present. [*They cross the stage eyeing each other suspiciously*]

PEA. [*Aside*] Billy must-a be near, I give-a de signal. [*Begins to unfasten rope on porch; takes out small Mexican flag*]

CON. What are ye going to do, dago?

PEA. Dis-a one Mexican holiday. I will-a celebrate by running up dis-a flag.

Con. [*Drawing pistol*] Do ye want a little fireworks, to help out the celebration?

Pea. [*Turns, throws up hands*] No-a shoot, Con, no-a shoot.

Con. Then drop that flag. [*Peanut drops it*] Now, we will celebrate in the decent way. [*Hands him small American flag*] Run *this* up to the top of the house. [*Peanut looks at it in disgust and hesitates*] Go ahead, or I'll start the fireworks.

Pea. Sacré! [*Picks up American flag and hoists it*] Sacré!

Con. Don't ye call me that again! Now elevate yer hands while I remove the arsenal. [*Peanut holds up his hands. Con takes the pistol*] Now, dago, I'm going to promote ye. You shall be my valet.

Pea. What-a dey?

Con. Why, me man, you must clean me boots.

Pea. I'll see you-a in Hell first.

Con. All right, ye can start now. [*Raises pistol*]

Pea. [*In fright*] Hold on. I shina de boots!

Con. And ye must keep me wardrobe nicely brushed and pressed.

Pea. All-a right. I press-a de ward.

Con. And trot around after me wherever I go.

Pea. Trot? You take-a me for a leetle dog?

Con. [*Raises pistol*] Good-bye, dago.

Pea. Hold on. I—I trot.

Con. [*Throws him key*] Here, open the front dure.

Pea. [*Taking key and going to door*] Dusta de clothes, blacka de boots, waga de tail, trot. Sacré! [*Opens door*]

Con. Now, me bucko, we will go around to the stable, and you shall have the honor of stabling me horse. Come—trot. [*Exit L.U.E.*]

Pea. Bud, he maka me bark like a dog, and now dis-a man, he mak-a me trot. Sacré! [*Trots off stage after Con. Enter R.1.E. Colonel, Nellie, Mose and Jennie, very unmilitary; Mose is carrying old flag and bugle. Colonel is carrying satchel. Nellie has bird cage and Jennie a large medicine case*]

Col. The army is demoralized.

Nel. Uncle, we can't stay here.

Col. Well, we can rest a minute, can't we? We've got to water our horses; besides, we want a look at Wright's old place before we leave the neighborhood forever. [*Wipes his eyes*]

Nel. [*Sees him*] Not forever, uncle. This will blow over.

Col. Blow over? How can it? To think of that measley—low—contemptible blackguard getting out warrants for our arrest, for "aiding, abetting and propensitating the escape of an outlaw."

Mose. And here *we* are, trying to aid and abet our own escape.

Jen. Oh, Colonel, it is a shame! [*She cries on his shoulder; Nellie cries on other*]

Col. Shame! Shame! It's a—Hold on, Mose, don't you *dare* to swear in the presence of ladies.

Mose. Why, I wasn't going to.

Col. Yes, you were. You were just watching for the chance. There, there, girls, don't cry! We'll pull through somehow, even with that profane Mose along.

Mose. *Me* profane? Huh? You're the champion cusser in this state—and proud of it, too.

Col. What, me? This to my face? You—old—sinner, look at these poor girls, crying their eyes out. All your fault. Why didn't you let 'em take Billy and be done with it?

Nel. [*Drawing away*] Oh, uncle!

Col. I mean it. [*Jennie draws away*] Then we wouldn't be in this fix. [*To Mose*] You brought his horse for him—and brought all this trouble to us, so I may as well tell you now, to get out.

Mose. I am out, Colonel, and so are you.

Col. That's so—both out—no home. Mose, old friend, put it there. We'll stick together through thick and thin. [*They shake*]

Nel. What a wreck the old place looks!

Col. Just as we left it three years ago, when Wright and his wife were killed. The lawyers locked up the place until they could find the heirs. Billy being outlawed, he didn't count. So far none have shown up.

Nel. [*Has crossed to porch*] Why, the door is open.

Col. Somebody must be here—sheriff, maybe.

Mose. Let's hide, quick.

Jen. What will *become of us?*

Col. Stand your ground like a soldier. If we must go to jail, let us go like gentlemen.

Mose. Women and all?

Col. Silence. [*Calls*] Hello there, anybody at home?

Con. [*Outside*] Hello—let go me arm.

Pea. [*Outside*] Hello—Sacré! You kick-a me!

Con. I know it. [*Outside*]

Mose. Had we better retreat in good order?

Col. A good plan, Mose. [*Colonel, Mose and Jennie turn R. and begin tiptoeing off*]

Nel. [*On porch*] Halt! [*They do*] Stand your ground.

Col. But my dear, a retreat in the face of overwhelming odds is always honorable.

Nel. Overwhelming odds? Fiddlesticks! There are but two men and I recognize the voice of one. It's Con Hanley. [*Con enters L.U.E., followed by Peanut*]

Con. Well, if it ain't the Colonel—and family. How are ye?

Col. Mighty glad to see *you*, Con. [*Shakes*]

Mose. Mighty glad you're not the sheriff.

Con. And there's Jennie. [*Raises hat*]

Pea. Jennie! [*Points at her*] She run away. She-a my girl. [*Jennie frightened*]

Con. [*Slapping Peanut's hand*] Put down your pointer, dago. What do ye want wid a girl anyhow? Ye've been married three times.

Pea. Well, dey all-a dead.

Con. Dead yer grandmother. Where do they be buried?

Pea. Dey no-a be buried. I have-a dem cremated.

Con. My! My! You've had wives to burn, haven't ye? And now ye want another. Bad cess to ye. I ought to give ye another kick.

Pea. No—no, no-a kick.

Col. Let him alone, Con. The poor devil is frightened to death already.

Con. Just as ye say, Colonel, but what are ye all doing here?

Mose. We're all outlaws now.

Col. You see, Con, warrants have been sworn out for our arrest because we helped Billy and you escape.

Con. The divil ye say? Well, one good turn deserves another. So Billy and me will help *you* all to escape. Just as soon as Billy takes a last look at the old place, we will all jump for the East.

Pea. [*Aside*] I knew Billy would come-a here.

Col. Don't believe I care to go that far, Con. Just over the border somewhere until this cursed thing blows over. Where would be a good place to stop?

Con. Right here.

All. Here? [*As Nellie speaks, Con turns and sees her for the first time*]

Con. [*Starts toward her, hand outstretched*] Hello, Nellie. [*Looks at Peanut*] Come on, valet, foller me up.

Pea. Bow wow! [*Trots over to Con who is shaking hands with Nellie*]

Con. Yes, sir, stay right here. Ye are over the border—just. No one ever comes this way and ye would be as safe as a bug in a rug as long as ye wanted to remain.

COL. By jove, you're right. We're over the line. I had forgotten that. Hurrah, we're safe. [*Hugs Mose, hugs Jennie, hugs Peanut. When he sees who it is throws him off in disgust*]

PEA. Dat-a worse dan being a dog.

NEL. Your hand is hot, Con, and you are shivering all over.

CON. It's them Texas mothers, miss.

NEL. Nothing of the kind. You are ill. [*Crosses down*] Uncle, Con has chills and fever, have you any medicine?

COL. Best in the world, quinine and whiskey. Brr-rr-rr, I feel a chill myself. [*Picks up satchel*]

JEN. Oh, I hope Con is not going to be ill.

CON. [*Coming down*] Divil a bit, Jennie; just the weather, that's all.

COL. Jennie, you and Mose move that table over here. [*They move table C.*] I'll soon have him all right. [*Puts satchel on table*]

MOSE. B-r-r, I feel a chill.

COL. Those chills that come just when the whiskey bottle is opened, don't go, Mose. [*Opens satchel*]

MOSE. Well you just had one.

COL. Mine were genuine. Why, I'd take the quinine if there wasn't any whiskey. [*Paws around in satchel*] Jennie, you and Nellie go in and start the fire. Brrr, I've got an *awful* chill!

NEL. Hurry, Jennie, or uncle will have a fit. [*Both exit in house laughing*]

COL. Hm! Don't see anything to laugh at. Made fuss enough when Con shivered.

MOSE. I *have* got a chill, Colonel. [*Shakes as hard as he can*]

COL. [*Still fussing in medicine case*] Won't work, Mose.

PEA. Brr. I got-a de chill—awful. [*Shakes*]

CON. Hold your whisht. Don't speak until I tell ye. Sit up on yer hind legs and beg.

COL. Come, what are you doing with that fellow in tow?

CON. Found him spying around here, so I captured him and made him me valet.

COL. Oh, where—the—devil—is—Mose, did you put that bottle of whiskey in the satchel or the medicine case?

MOSE. You wouldn't let me touch it. You said you would attend to it.

COL. What! [*Sinks in chair*] Alone—no friends—no home—and no whiskey.

MOSE. Never mind, Colonel, I didn't want it.

COL. *You* didn't want it—you—

MOSE. Hold on, Colonel, you never swear, you know.

Col. Oh no, *you* didn't want it. Well I'll have to give Con the quinine straight. [*Fumbles with boxes on table*]

Mose. You must take some quinine yourself, Colonel.

Col. What for?

Mose. Why, that awful chill of yours. You said you'd take it if there wasn't any whiskey. [*Colonel glares at him*]

Col. Give me the canteen, Mose.

Mose. [*Unslinging canteen from his shoulder*] If you don't take it, Colonel, I'll think you were faking.

Col. I wish you would mind your own business. Here, Con, take this. [*Gives him powder*] Wash it down with—water. [*Hands canteen. Con takes it*] Suppose I'll have to take one just to satisfy that old doubting Thomas, there. [*Takes powder*] Ugh, but this is awful. Anybody else? [*Mose and Peanut shake heads*] I knew it. Fakes, both of you.

Con. [*Sits on steps*] My, my! But that stuff was bitter.

Col. [*Sits*] Of all the lunk-heads—no whiskey—

Jen. [*At door*] Are you better, Con?

Con. I'm a dom sight worse.

Jen. I'm so sorry. [*Exits in house. Colonel and Mose ransack satchel and medicine case again*]

Con. Sure, it's a fine girl she is.

Col. I *must* have packed that bottle, Mose.

Mose. Hurry up and find it. Me mouth tastes like a glue factory smells.

Col. That quinine tastes like the—the very devil.

Mose. Say, Colonel, which box did you get those powders out of?

Col. This one, of course. [*Points to box*]

Mose. [*Astounded*] This one? [*Colonel nods*] Good-bye, Colonel, old comrade, good-bye, Con, old friend. [*Shakes with both*]

Col. Where are you going?

Mose. *I'm* not going. You are going. These powders are marked, morphine, poison. [*Colonel and Con clutch Mose by the arm*]

Con. Do ye mane it?

Mose. Read. [*Shows box; both read and stagger back*] Good-bye, friends.

Pea. Ha, ha! Dat-a good-a joke.

Con. Laugh—ye hyena. But before I die, I'm going to wind up your worldly career.

Col. [*Hoarsely*] Mose, old friend, don't let me go to sleep. *Don't let* me go to sleep. Walk me. That's my only chance. Keep me moving. [*They link arms and go out L.U.E. Con has been toying with his pistol, Peanut appealing to him in dumb show*] For Heaven's sake, Con, don't stand there. Walk, man, walk. Your life depends on keeping awake. Keep moving.

CON. Dago, keep me walking. Don't let me lie down. If I find meself getting sleepy, I'll put an end to ye're dialect.

PEA. I no let-a you sleep. [*Grabs him by arm*] Come, like one leetle dog—trot. [*Rushes Con off R.1.E.*]

NEL. [*Appears at door*] Come in, the fire is so cheerful. Why, where have they gone? [*Enter Colonel and Mose L.1.E. singing "While We Are Marching Through Georgia"; cross stage*]

NEL. Oh, uncle, the coffee is ready. Uncle!—*Mose!*

MOSE. [*Stops*] Eh? What?

COL. Don't stop, you idiot. Do you want me to die right here? Keep moving. [*Grabs Mose and both exit R.1.E. singing "While We Are Marching Through Georgia"*]

NEL. O-o-o-o, it's the medicine. I knew uncle couldn't stand the whiskey. [*Cries*] To think of it—and at such a time, too!

JEN. [*Enters*] What is the matter, dear?

NEL. The medicine—was too much—for uncle. [*Exits in house crying*]

JEN. Why, what can have happened?

JEN. [*Enter Con and Peanut R.U.E. Con is singing: "He Marched Thim Up the Hill, Me Boys, and He Marched Thim Down Again"*] Oh, Con, come and get some hot coffee. Con—Con!

CON. [*Stops*] Eh? What, me dear?

PEA. No-a stop. I want-a me dialect. [*Drags him along*]

CON. Farewell my dear, if I hadn't taken the stuff—

JEN. Was it the medicine, Con?

CON. I should say it was. Good-bye. Perhaps in another world—

PEA. No-a sleep—keep moving. [*Drags him off L.U.E. Con sings "He Marched Thim, etc.," in distance*]

JEN. Nellie! Nellie! Come here, quick. [*Nellie enters*] Something has happened to uncle. Con just went by, singing as though his heart would break.

NEL. So did uncle.

JEN. Con said it was the medicine.

NEL. Yes—whiskey.

JEN. O-o-oh! [*Enter Mose and Colonel, L.U.E., Colonel tired and frightened*]

COL. Mose, if I ever get out of this, you shall be promoted to Major. [*They come down C.*] Oh, what an end for a brave soldier! Mose, I'm tired.

NEL. You look tired, uncle. Sit down and rest.

Col. Rest? Girl do you want to be a murderess? Out of my way! Keep moving, Mose, keep moving. [*Exit L.1.E. singing "While We," etc.*]

Nel. They have gone crazy.

Jen. What can we do? [*Enter Con and Peanut L.U.E.*]

Con. Dago, if I ever walk this off you shall go free.

Pea. Good-a boy. [*They come down C.*]

Jen. Con, what *is* the matter.

Con. [*Stops*] Well ye see, me dear—

Pea. Don't-a stop. Keep moving. [*Drags him away*]

Con. [*Being dragged backwards by Peanut, talking to Jennie*] I hain't got the time ter explain now. Perhaps in another world.

Pea. Come-a on! [*Con turns, begins singing "He Marched," etc. Both exit R.1.E.*]

Nel. We must stop them.

Jen. How can we?

Nel. [*Determined*] We will lasso them.

Jen. But I can't lasso.

Nel. You can try. Here. [*Picks up piece of rope*] Make a noose in the end of that. I'll take this piece. Slip it over Con's head and I'll do the same to uncle. [*They fix ropes. Enter from R.1.E. Con and Peanut. Enter from L.1.E. Colonel and Mose. They stop near C. and glare at each other. Jennie slips behind Con and Nellie behind Colonel*]

Col. [*Glaring at Con*] There stands the cause of all this. If it hadn't been for that confounded chill—

Mose. Don't stop. Keep moving.

Con. [*Glaring at Colonel*] There stands me murderer.

Pea. Don't-a stop—Keep-a de move.

Con. I won't stir an inch further. I'm going to die before his very face.

Col. [*Folds arms*] So am I. [*Nellie slips noose over Colonel's head; Jennie same business with Con*]

Mose and Pea. Walk. [*Tries to pull them*]

Nel. and Jen. Stop! [*Both sides pulling*]

Col. Here! Stop it. Let go, some of you.

Con. What is this—a tug of war?

Nel. Now stand where you are and tell me what is the matter?

Pea. Tell her while-a walking.

Col. [*Desperately*] We've taken morphine for quinine. [*Groan. Nellie and Jennie scream; both run to table and examine boxes*]

Mose. Keep a-moving.

Col. Not another step. Let me die with my face to the foe.

NEL. There must be an antidote, somewhere.

CON. Dago, I'm getting sleepy.

PEA. [*In fright*] No-a sleep. Keep-a de move.

CON. It's no use. [*Sits on ground*] Dago, pull off me boots.

PEA. [*Pulling off boots*] Oh, I lose-a de dialect.

CON. I always swore I would never die wid me boots on.

MOSE. Want your boots off, Colonel?

COL. No, sir. This is the way a soldier should die.

CON. Shot in the stummick wid morphine powder. [*Mose shows Nellie box*]

NEL. Uncle, how many morphine powders did you have?

COL. [*Groans*] Just an even dozen.

NEL. Well, they're all here. Mose made a mistake in the boxes, that's all. [*They all look foolish*]

COL. [*Reproachfully*] Mose, how could you? This was all hatched in your infamous brain. Just to get me to promote you. [*Sadly goes to house, rope trailing behind*]

MOSE. On my word of honor, I did nothing of the kind. [*Following*]

COL. *Your* word of honor? Don't—don't add falsehood to your other crimes. [*Exits in house, followed by Mose, still arguing*]

NEL. How ridiculous it all was! [*Exits in house, laughing*]

CON. Dago, pull on me boots. [*Peanut does so*] Now, although I have lost me dignity [*Rises*], likewise me chance for a dacent burial, I'll keep me word with you. You can go.

PEA. Oh, tank-a you. [*Goes up L., aside*] Now to tell-a de gang. [*Exits L.U.E.*]

JEN. Come in to the house, Con, and get a cup of coffee. It will make you feel better.

CON. Sure I feel like a bird—cleaned and picked. I'm sorry to disappoint ye about the funeral.

JEN. Oh, Con, wouldn't it have been dreadful if you had taken morphine.

CON. Well, I dunno. Nobody would care a rap—except Billy.

JEN. Con, how can you say that. I would.

CON. [*Looks at her in surprise*] Jennie, me girl, if I thought ye would be glad to see me alive, I could die happy.

JEN. [*Laughs*] But I don't want you to die. [*Serious*] Ever since the night you tried to shield me from those wretches in the Broken Heart, I have felt for you as I never felt for another being except—my mother.

CON. [*Astonished*] Jennie! [*Holds out his arms*]

JEN. [*Drawing back*] No—no, not that.

Con. I thought the feeling was all on my side—

Jen. Don't say any more. I don't want pity—the old life is past.

Con. [*Thoughtfully*] Me work here is finished. In five minutes I leave this place forever. Me life is uncertain and me prospects more so. Jennie, will ye share me lot, whatever it may be? Will ye be my wife?

Jen. Your wife?—Oh, Con, I cannot. My life has not been—

Con. Neither has mine. The good book says; "Let him without sin cast the first brick." I'm not here to judge. I love ye. I offer ye an everlasting devotion and a strong arm, that will fight me way to the front when I get to New York. Will ye come?

Jen. [*Puts hands in his*] Yes—Con.

Con. Hurrah! I'm glad the dom stuff wasn't quinine. Jen, give me a hug. [*They embrace*] Now, let's not tell the folks anything about it. I'll leave a note for them explaining matters. My horse and the dago's is in the stable. We'll be married at the first station, then for New York.

Jen. What are you going to do in New York, Con?

Con. Why, be a policeman, of course. [*They exit L.1.E. Enter Denver and Bill R.1.E.*]

Bill. Have you lost your tongue? We stood beside my mother's grave and you shook like an aspen, but refused to speak. Why do you gaze at that well? You seem frightened.

Den. A grave—a grave—my grave. [*Sinks down*]

Bill. Very likely. You know why I brought you here.

Den. I am innocent. Don't kill me.

Bill. You killed my parents.

Den. You have no proof. You are trying to compel me to confess to something I did not do.

Bill. You killed them.

Den. I saw them die. Give me a chance and I will tell you how.

Bill. You killed them.

Den. As God is my judge.

Bill. You killed them.

Den. Yes—[*Head sinks in hands*]

Bill. Ah! [*More of a long drawn sigh than a word*]

Den. [*Shivers*] I am so cold.

Bill. You shall give me the details but we must be quick. As we came along I saw a number of horsemen circling about the hill yonder. In ten minutes this place will be surrounded. They are coming for me.

Den. With your own life in the balance, why can you not be merciful? Let me escape while there is yet time.

BILL.   No power on earth would make me release you. As for death, my work is nearly finished. I did not rush blindly into this trap. I knew the stakes and am prepared to pay the price. We shall die—almost—together—

DEN.   [*Shudders*]   I—am—so—cold.

BILL.   Go into the house. Con has a fire, I suppose. I will join you in time to hear your story, go!

DEN.   [*Sneaking to house*]   We—shall—die—almost—together. [*Exits in house. Bill sits at table. As Denver enters house the interior is lighted up, showing Colonel, Mose and Nellie seated. Denver goes to fire without noticing anybody and sinks down before it*]

NEL.   How comes that man here? [*Goes to exterior door*]

COL.   Come, Mose, we will go elsewhere. [*Exits with Mose door L. Lights go out in house. Nellie enters from house*]

NEL.   Billy! [*Runs to him*]

BILL.   [*Rises astonished*]   Nellie! What has happened? Why are you here?

NEL.   We are in hiding. The law is hounding us for aiding your escape.

BILL.   [*Bitterly*]   Noble law! To wage war on two women and two inoffensive old men.

NEL.   But I am glad it happened. We are all going East for a while. And Con said you were going too. So we shall all be united, where there is no trouble, sin or sorrow.

BILL.   Where there is no trouble—sin—or sorrow. Yes, that's where I am going. But I take a different road than you.

NEL.   Why can't we all go together?

BILL.   I cannot go your way. I would not have you go mine.

NEL.   Billy! You don't mean you are going to stick to this for life?

BILL.   God forbid. I am done with—everything. Our paths lie apart.

NEL.   Billy, have you forgotten the boy and girl vows we made? Our paths did not lie apart in them. Do you remember how we planned for a happy future—when you became a man? Our paths did not lie apart then. Billy, I have always loved you, for my sake will you not come with us and begin that other—better life?

BILL.   Don't! Don't! You torture me. Do you fancy I never think of those things? Out of the waste and desert of my life, with its memory of the fair prospects—the husk and the swine. I seem to be looking through a window at a peaceful life—as a hungry, lonely tramp may limp to a lamp lit window, and, peering in, see father, and mother, and round faced children, and the table spread whitely with the good sure food that to these people is a calm certainty, like breathing or sleeping—not a joyous accident, or one of the great things that man was taught to pray for. The tramp turns away with a curse or a groan, according to his nature—and goes on his way, cursing or groaning—or, if the pinch is too fierce, he tries the back door. With me the pinch is great and I feel like trying any door—not to beg for the broken meats of pity—but to enter as master of all the happiness that should be mine. But it is too late.

NEL.   It is never too late to mend. Oh say you will come with us.

BILL.   Nellie, I must tell you something. When I saw you just now, I almost cursed the fates that brought you, but now I am thankful I shall at least have about me, those I love, during my—last—moments.

NEL. [*Startled*]   Billy, what do you mean?

BILL.   This is the final chapter in my career. I am about to avenge the murder of my parents, but the effort will cost me my life.

NEL.   Billy!

BILL.   The house is already surrounded. I can never leave here. It is better so; otherwise I might be tempted to seek for happiness in that other life, with you. No, no. It is better as it is. Go—go in the house. I have but a short time to prepare for—[*He leads her to house; she is crying*]

NEL.   You must escape. Go now.

BILL.   I cannot. The effort would but hasten my end. Bear up, it is better so. [*Leads her in house; both exit. Enter Peanut followed by Bud, L.U.E. They crawl around to porch*]

PEA.   I tell-a you dat was-a him.

BUD.   Well, I wanted to be sure; that long coat fooled me.

PEA.   You got-a all de men stationed so he no get away?

BUD.   Bet your life I have. If he shows his nose at door or window he's a gonner.

PEA.   Shoot-a to kill. And mine, if dat-a Con man dere, I want-a him. He shin-a de shoes, he dust-a de ward, he wag-a de tail, he t-r-o-t!

BUD.   Get over there behind that wagon. Don't expose yourself and don't fall asleep. We'll have him, if it takes a week.

PEA. [*Going up L.*]   I get-a de Con man, don't forget. [*Exits L.U.E. Bud exits R.U.E. Lights go up in house; Bill and Denver discovered*]

BILL.   You say my mother's death was an accident and my father was killed in self-defense?

DEN. [*Wearily*]   I am speaking the truth.

BILL.   And the motive for this attack on you?

DEN.   He sought my life on learning my true identity.

BILL.   Which was—?

DEN.   My name is Boyd Bradley. Your mother was my wife.

BILL.   What!

DEN. When she married Stephen Wright, she thought me dead. I had been unkind to her—even deserted her. You see, I am not sparing myself; I am telling the truth.

BILL. You monster! And do you think the truth will save you after your cruelty to my mother?

DEN. I don't care for mercy. I am past that. I wanted you to know all before we—both—go—almost—together, for I am your father.

BILL. My father—you!

DEN. Had you a chance to live, you could easily prove my statement; your birth is duly recorded in New York. I took the trouble to look it up. You were a year old when your mother married Wright.

BILL. [Stunned] You—my—father.

DEN. I have told you all. Now kill me if you wish.

BILL. Oh, God, how little we know of Your greatness—Your power. This —is my revenge. My father—the father I should love and cherish—I have been hounding to his death, thinking I was carrying out Your divine will. I bow to Your mighty wisdom. I am justly punished. [Sinks on knees, overcome]

DEN. [Goes to him] My son—

BILL. [Rises] Don't touch me. Go—go, you are free. Go and let me have a minute alone—with my Maker.

DEN. There is no hope of your escape?

BILL. If there was, I wouldn't take it. Go! [Denver starts to door] Father! [He stops] Take my coat. You are thinly clad and deadly cold. My hat also; you are without one. [Denver puts them on] Here, father, is my revolver, I shall not need it—again. [Gives him pistol] Good-bye—father. [Holds out hand. Denver clasps it, then passes through door, leaving door open. Bill sinks on knees, Denver pauses outside, near well]

DEN. Free, free at last. He will be dead in ten minutes and then—a fortune for me. [Looks through door] There he is, praying. Pray, damn you. It won't do you any good. Suppose he should escape? He has done it before. I'll take no chances. [Raises revolver, aims at Bill through open door. Two gun shots heard from R.U.E. Denver throws up hands, screams and falls in well. At sound of shots, Bill springs to door and closes it. Enter Bud followed by two men, R.U.E. Enter Peanut followed by one man, L.U.E. All run to well]

BUD. [Listens for a second] Not a sound. Hurrah! Billy the Kid is dead! [Enter from door L. Nellie, Colonel and Mose]

NEL. [Half screams] Billy dead? [Sees him at door] Billy!

BILL. Sh-h-h!

PEA. Let's get-a him out.

BUD. Too much trouble. Why ye can't see the bottom. Let him stay down there. I'm off for the reward. If the authorities won't believe he's dead, let 'em come and dig him up. Eh, boys?

ALL. Yes. That's it, *etc.*

BUD. Come on boys, I want that dough in a hurry. [*All go up R.*]

PEA. [*Following*] I wanted de Con man [*Others exit R.U.E.*] to shine de shoes, to dust-a de ward—[*Exits R.U.E.*] To—[*Outside*] to—t-r-o-t!

BILL. To the law I am dead. Today my life begins anew. Come Nellie—we'll wander down life's pathway together, where the sun shines always—

NEL. Billy! [*Embraces*]

CURTAIN

America's Lost Plays

www.ingramcontent.com/pod-product-compliance
Lightning Source LLC
Chambersburg PA
CBHW030916090426

42737CB00007B/215